John McCormack

A voice to remember

GUS SMITH

MADISON PUBLISHERS LIMITED

Contents

A Madison Book

© Copyright Gus Smith, 1995

ISBN 1 870862 30 9

MADISON
PUBLISHERS LTD

Madison Publishers Limited
5 Lower Abbey Street
Dublin 1
Ireland

Author's Note

Acknowledgement by name of people who assisted me
with information and personal reminiscences about
Count John McCormack, and a list of my principal sources,
will be found at the end of this book. Suffice to state here
my grateful thanks to the McCormack family for their full
support and co-operation.

G.S.

This book is dedicated to Liam Breen,
Life President of the John McCormack
Society, who has done so much to
perpetuate the memory of Count
John McCormack by his talks, record
recitals and private McCormack museum.

THE JET-AGE SINGERS

Count John McCormack, at the peak of his remarkable career, sailed many thousands of miles for operatic and concert engagements. He sang to huge crowds in Australia, New Zealand, South Africa, America, China and Japan and on his own admission enjoyed himself enormously. And he thought nothing of singing around a piano at a ship's concert and maintained that the leisurely atmosphere allied to the bracing sea air was good for his vocal chords.

What a marked contrast today! In an exciting world singers must get there quicker – and away just as fast if they are to fulfil engagements elsewhere. Musically, and commercially, the JET-AGE – and Ryanair is now leading the way – is a marvellous advance since McCormack's time. Ryanair can now take on board a new generation of talented Irish singers. For this luxury no-one is more appreciative than the artists themselves.

Madison Publishers is proud to link up with Ryanair on the airline's 10th birthday, and to thank Dr Tony Ryan and his team for helping to make this book not only possible, but a fitting tribute to our greatest singer. McCormack was always happy to help young singers, so he would, one feels, be the first to congratulate an airline that can fly them at affordable fares.

The McCormack
Family Tree

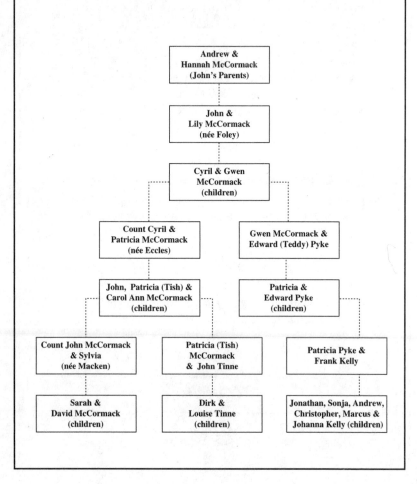

Andrew &
Hannah McCormack
(John's Parents)

John &
Lily McCormack
(née Foley)

Cyril & Gwen
McCormack
(children)

Count Cyril &
Patricia McCormack
(née Eccles)

Gwen McCormack &
Edward (Teddy) Pyke

John, Patricia (Tish) &
Carol Ann McCormack
(children)

Patricia &
Edward Pyke
(children)

Count John McCormack
& Sylvia
(née Macken)

Patricia (Tish)
McCormack
& John Tinne

Patricia Pyke &
Frank Kelly

Sarah &
David McCormack
(children)

Dirk &
Louise Tinne
(children)

Jonathan, Sonja, Andrew,
Christopher, Marcus &
Johanna Kelly (children)

INTRODUCTION

The McCormack Legacy

It's hard to believe that we are celebrating the 50th anniversary of Count John McCormack's death. Yet his golden tenor voice that thrilled countless concert goers and opera lovers is far from forgotten; indeed, scarcely a week goes by without the presenter of a classical or light classical music programme either here or in Britain playing such old McCormack favourites as "I Hear You Calling Me", "The Fairy Tree" and the incomparable "Il mio tesoro". And as in the case of Caruso, Bjorling, Gigli and Lanza, the McCormack recording legacy is considerable; in fact much bigger than in any of the celebrated tenors named. Furthermore, his name seems as durable as the Rock of Cashel.

So one can only imagine the profound impact the announcement of his passing must have made on the music world on that September morning in 1945. We are by now aware of the shock waves that reverberated around the world in September 1977 at the news of the untimely death in Paris of Maria Callas, truly a legend in her own time like McCormack. On that occasion opera lovers talked to me of the personal sense of loss they felt, as though it was a close relative who had died. One can only assume that McCormack's passing at the early age of sixty-one evoked the same emotional feelings, especially among his many admirers in America and Australia where his concerts invariably attracted huge audiences.

Fittingly, he died in his native land, for despite his universal fame and his popularity the tenor had never forgotten his roots. The year 1945 was in another way a fateful year: World War II had ended, even if the memory would long remain. Musically it saw the birth in Dublin of Our Lady's Choral Society, whose members marked this year's golden jubilee in style.

The scene, meanwhile, in the McCormack home "Glena" in Booterstown, Co. Dublin, was peaceful. Gathered around the bed was Lily McCormack and her son Cyril and together they watched in anxious silence as John drifted quietly into a coma and died shortly before midnight on that Sunday, 16 September. Lily had seen her husband in the preceding months and weeks grow physically more tired, though in spirit he surprised his doctor by his determination to keep on his feet. He had lost weight, his voice sounded croaky and emphysema had left him short of breath.

Yet, in the days before his death, he appeared in good spirits. Despite advice to the contrary, he had gone with friends to Croke Park early that month to see the All-Ireland Hurling Final; it was claimed later that he picked up a chill as he sat in the cold stand. Later in the week he was able to accompany his wife Lily to the Abbey Theatre but at the final curtain complained of fatigue, so decided not to go backstage afterwards as usual to greet the play's cast. At home in "Glena", he continued to entertain his friends, including the young Co. Limerick-born tenor Christopher Lynch whose voice had impressed him. After dinner, Lynch sang a number of songs which McCormack considered might be good for recording. Then he himself sang "The Fairy Tree" in a weak baritone voice, and immediately remarked good-humouredly, 'Ah, my top notes aren't so hot.'

In those final weeks of his life Lily McCormack had tried to pinpoint the exact time when her husband's health began to fail. She concluded it was during the series of wartime concerts he had given in British cities, some of them held outdoors in wet weather, others in draughty halls. 'Each time John came home from a tour he seemed more tired' she remembered. 'When I protested that he was going beyond his strength, he'd say, "This is the only thing I can do to help the British people. It's up to me to show them how much I appreciate what they have done for me."'

She was dismayed when he developed a cough that in her own words was 'as deep and spasmodic as whooping cough.' The family was shocked to see how thin he had got, and to make matters worse, he had had a return attack of streptococcal infection of the throat, from which he had nearly died twenty years previously; in fact, one New York newspaper had headlined the death of the Irish tenor. To Lily's relief, he had now given his last broadcast and would not perform in concert again.

The McCormacks sold their home in Ascot and returned to Dublin where for eighteen months they occupied a suite in the Shelbourne Hotel. On his doctor's advice the tenor later moved with Lily to "Glena" where, it was thought, the bracing sea air would be good for his emphysema. For a while he felt an improvement and enjoyed the company of his grandchildren. 'We had lots of fun in small ways,' mused Lily, 'and he was never more contented.' And in more private moments nothing pleased him more than to listen to his own records, and as he did so, his face would suddenly light up. 'How did I do it?' he would utter to himself with a chuckle.

Lily McCormack stood up courageously to his death. 'I could not write sadly about John's going,' she stated in her autobiography. 'Life rewarded him in good measure for the zest and kindliness and effort he gave to life. To his children, his grandchildren and to me he had left an inspiring heritage of love and faith and good works and only blessed memories.'

Monday had scarcely dawned when the first of hundreds of messages of sympathy began to arrive at "Glena", where the tenor lay in state in the colourful full-dress uniform of a Papal Count. On his chest were Papal decorations while his sword lay by his side on the bier. In 1928, he had been created a Papal Count in recognition of his artistic eminence and his services to the charitable work of the

Church, both in Europe and America. And he was on active duty in his resplendent uniform at the Vatican for one week in each year. It was said that on the first day the Holy Father noted with pleasure that McCormack's fluent Italian had a Milanese accent as pronounced as his own.

The first message addressed to Lily McCormack came from Dorothy Caruso in New Jersey, widow of the famed Italian tenor Enrico Caruso: 'No one in this world understands how you feel better than I do. I wish I could be with you. My heart yearns for you.' Dorothy's daughter Gloria cabled a personal message; she was a longtime friend of Gwen McCormack, the tenor's only daughter. During the day there were more cables, from Irish film actress Maureen O'Sullivan, pianists Teddy Schneider and Gerald Moore, and Alan Murray, the author of "I'll Walk Beside You", a favourite song of McCormack's.

Lily McCormack and her son Cyril opened the door of "Glena" to many callers, among them churchmen, diplomats, politicians, sportsmen and musicians. On radio the recorded voice of the tenor was heard in songs forever associated with him, "Kathleen Mavourneen", "Macushla" and "Somewhere a Voice is Calling". The nation mourned the passing of a great singer and a true ambassador of song; the newspapers of the day traced his long and distinguished career and carried columns of tributes from around the globe, confirming that truly he was a world figure.

It was appropriate that the first music tribute should come from Dr Vincent O'Brien, the tenor's first voice teacher and life-long friend. He was choirmaster at the Pro-Cathedral, Dublin, and had auditioned the young McCormack with a view to his joining the choir. 'It did not require knowledge to recognise that here was vocalism of an unusual order, and those privileged like myself to hear him on that occasion were at one in acclaiming the strength, beauty and sweetness of his voice,' recalled Dr O'Brien.

He was so struck by the difference between this young man's performance and that of the usual candidate for vocal distinction, that he invited him to a further meeting in the evening. He was even more impressed than before. 'John sang several songs with natural beauty of tone which left the sonorities of the Stradivarius or Steinway in the acoustic shadows and might be more accurately compared to the song of the thrush or nightingale.'

In today's more prosaic language Vincent O'Brien's tribute would be termed very colourful, but it was undoubtedly sincere. He revealed that the young Athlone tenor always had a firm belief in his personal abilities and gradually his self-confidence grew. And he possessed other qualities needed in the vocal field such as musicianship and an artist's temperament, and in time his exquisite tone was as much at home in Bach as in the more simple Thomas Moore melodies.

'McCormack would, when occasion demanded, discuss questions of rhythm or interpretation of the musical classics with the authority of a Toscanini, a Kreisler, or a Rachmaninov. Ireland today laments the departure of one of her most distinguished sons, one who sang the joys and sorrows and the hopes of the Motherland in the ear of a listening world. If the pulse of the patriot soldier or lover has throbbed at his lay, it will be their duty to remember John in the way he himself would have dearly wished – by a prayer to the Giver of all good gifts that he may find that Pax Dei which he himself so often brought to troubled hearts the world over with the gentle message of his song, "Go Sleep with the Sunshine of Fame on thy Slumber"'.

Dr O'Brien was asked by Radio Eireann to broadcast a special tribute and although he prepared one he was so overcome by emotion that he was unable himself to read it over the air. Inside three years he, too, would have departed the Dublin musical scene at the age of seventy-nine, having enjoyed a brilliant musical career.

Margaret Burke Sheridan's tribute hardly seemed adequate for the occasion. 'He sang Ireland's joys and sorrows as nobody ever did or probably ever will,' stated the former Irish prima donna, carefully adding that McCormack was regarded and rightly so, 'as the greatest Lieder singer in the world.'

While she never counted McCormack among her circle of friends, and for obscure reasons only known to herself disliked him, there were people in Dublin's music world who expected her to be more generous in her tribute to a great colleague; that she wasn't was a genuine disappointment.

As expected, Professor John F. Larchet was more generous and emphasised the musical gifts of McCormack. 'He was one of the greatest singers of all time. There were greater voices, but there was nobody in my view greater in interpretative powers. He was a master, too, of diction and his softest word could be heard in the largest hall quite plainly. No matter where he went he made a point of singing Irish songs and he made "Padraic the Fiddler" world famous.'

The *Irish Press*, a popular morning newspaper of the time, considered the occasion important enough to give it its main leader of the day. 'There is no music so appealing as that of the human voice,' the piece began, 'and none so transient. John McCormack possessed the most beautiful voice of his generation and few can have learned of his death without experiencing a sense of personal loss. To the younger generation he is known only by his gramophone records, and although in McCormack's case the lack is not so great as in those eminent artists who preceded him – Caruso and Melba, for example – of whose art none but imperfect recordings exist, yet even the most faithful reproductions cannot replace the sound of the living voice.'

The leader writer stressed that McCormack had achieved fame in all departments of his art, but it was as a singer of Irish songs that he became supreme; indeed, wherever he went in the English-speaking world he aroused the affection of Irish exiles for the homeland, and his career in the United States was an example of how they could feel proud. Ireland, the poorer for his passing, will cherish his memory.

Although the tribute was penned sometime later, I feel that McCormack's literary friend L.A.G. Strong struck an honest note when he declared: 'John McCormack was so vehement, so vigorously alive, that any written tribute to him must seem tame and colourless.'

In time, Strong would write a book about the tenor who in turn would good-humouredly call it 'anaemic'. The funny thing was that Strong agreed, and added: 'It certainly is: but I don't see how it could possibly have been otherwise. John, a Count of the Holy Roman Empire, was venerated by thousands and thousands of devout and simple people, who looked upon him as a musical saint. To record the pungency of his conversation and the gambols of his active intelligence would have distressed them, simply because they could not understand the world in which he lived.'

To Strong, McCormack could inhabit the artist's world and the cathedral with equal fitness and with no sense of disharmony. Yet he was not prepared to regard him as a saint; far from it. There is a suggestion that the tenor in the tough, bohemian world of singing was a man's man and could let fly a four-letter expletive as good as the next fellow; or when it came to that, be rude or blunt with a colleague who crossed him. And in his tribute Strong was to add: 'There are so many pictures of John, trying to get a rise out of the imperturbable Gerald Moore, imitating Richard Tauber, telling us how he was frightened to sing when Toscanini asked him, and of Toscanini's genuine astonishment on hearing this – "But I am the person the most gentle in all the world ". John crying like a child over a letter in which a young soldier made light of his wounds.

'He was a great man, a man on the grand scale, all superlatives, nothing ordinary or commonplace about him. He had no friends, only great friends, and he had far too much character to have enemies. In his prime he was the finest lyric tenor of his generation. On him the verdict of other great singers was all but unanimous. His immense hold on the public was due partly to this fact, but even more to the quality that brought his artistry within the reach of the common man and woman: his intense and lovable humanity.'

While dignitaries of Church and State joined in the funeral

obsequies on that soft September morning, there was also present a considerable number of the plain people of Dublin, and not all of them had come to look upon the famous. Many could claim to possess McCormack records, so they were there to pay their own homage to the man and his voice. It is doubtful whether the begrudgers turned up in any sizeable numbers; they never quite forgave McCormack for assuming the role of country squire, racehorse owner and Papal Count. He had in their eyes simply got above himself, in the same way that Joyce and Beckett and O'Casey had got above themselves and in their case deserted their native city. Singers like actors, they argued, should keep to themselves and not be aping the gentry. Furthermore, the fact that the famous tenor wasn't a Dublin man was enough reason in itself for their begrudgery.

There is still an element of begrudgery – admittedly small – whenever his name comes up in conversation, as though people refuse to acknowledge the singer's greatness and his singular achievements in a highly competitive profession. It is difficult to fathom. Perhaps it is an Irish phenomenon, or to be more precise, a flaw in the Irish character that makes people see their own as inferior to outsiders, this despite the fact that the world outside may have acclaimed the singer or actor or writer in question. For my own part, I find this attitude both exasperating and small-minded.

Like his friend George Bernard Shaw, McCormack believed it was a distinction to be Irish in the rest of the world and both men could be called patriotic Irishmen. Nonetheless, if Shaw was generous to Ireland, he was in no way sentimental. 'If you put an Irishman on a spit,' he said, 'you will always find an Irishman to baste him.' Shades of the begrudgery that McCormack and others encountered.

Despite the begrudgery, John McCormack was given a worthy send-off, as Brendan Behan might have said. Crowds lined the route from the Church of the Assumption, Booterstown to Deansgrange

Cemetery. Heads were bowed as the hearse drove slowly past, followed by a large cortege. The Requiem Mass had been an impressive ceremony with the McCormack family, headed by Countess McCormack, seated close to the alter. Special places in the church were reserved for President Sean T. O'Kelly and An Taoiseach Eamon de Valera. The music world was represented by Dr Vincent O'Brien, John Larchet, Professor of Music, Comdt. J.M. Doyle, Col. Bill O'Kelly (Chairman of Dublin Grand Opera Society), Michael O'Higgins, Royal Irish Academy of Music, tenor Christopher Lynch, as well as a large number of the singers and musicians of the day. Members of the judiciary, Dail Eireann, business people, clergy and sportsmen were there in force, a clear indication that the tenor's world transcended music.

The sombre music, meanwhile, of the Benedictus from the Office of the Dead later stilled the whispering tongues around the grave and sounded tremendously moving as the farewell ritual of the Church. It was sung by the Pro-Cathedral Palestrina Choir, which had numbered John McCormack among its earliest members. And close on the ground lay the profusion of red and white flowers which earlier had transformed a corner of the little Church of the Assumption into a dazzling garden. After the grave was eventually covered with the wreaths, Captain Cyril McCormack, in full Irish army uniform, saluted and remained at attention for a few seconds.

For a while people stood around in groups and chatted, for it is not uncommon in Ireland to find that some people only renew periodic acquaintance at wakes and funerals. Since McCormack in his retirement days had become a frequent visitor to the Abbey and Gate Theatres it was not surprising to find actors that September morning among the mourners. Cyril Cusack was there in the company of F.J. McCormick and his wife Eileen Crowe; the gangling figure of playwright Lennox Robinson stood out in the crowd, and not far away were Lord and Lady Longford of the Gate Theatre.

Lily McCormack bore herself with dignity through the morning ceremonies and later confided in friends that she was deeply moved by the warmth of the funeral tribute to 'my John', as she usually called her husband. A few days after his death, she found a few sentences scrawled on a memorandum book that lay on his desk. 'I live again the days and evenings of my long career,' he had written. 'I dream at night of operas and concerts in which I have had my share of success. Now like the old Irish minstrels, I have hung up my harp because my songs are all sung.'

A week later New York paid its own tribute. It was big, it was impressive, with nearly three thousand people taking part in St Patrick's Cathedral. Irish-American delegations and friends and admirers came from Boston, Philadelphia, Washington and even from as far away as Chicago. And the Requiem Mass was celebrated by Rev Timothy Shanley who had known McCormack for over forty years; they had first met when he was a student at Maynooth College and the young tenor had come to sing for the students.

As was the case in Dublin, the memorial service was attended by people from all walks of life, from Edward Johnson, manager of the Metropolitan Opera House to Judge Owen Bohan of General Sessions. Former Abbey actor Dudley Digges mingled with people like James J. Johnston, the boxing promoter, Edward Arnold, vice-president of the Friendly Sons of St. Patrick, Monsignor Fulton Sheen, Catholic University in Washington, and a Mrs James McGrath who once worked at the Athlone Mills where McCormack's father was employed.

'There were the musical dilettantes,' as the New York *World Telegram* reported, 'the Carnegie Hall habitues; there were professionals from opera and concert, some of whom decried the tenor's programmes as vulgar, while envying the satin purity of his tone in Mozart's "Il mio tesoro". And there were those – good, pleasant folk, humble in mien and purse – who recalled the lilt and the tears of his "Molly Brannigan" and "Mother Machree", a score of whom, with moist eyes, received communion at the side altars.'

The newspaper stated that the sorrow for McCormack was

sincere and genuine. 'For here were people of middle age and older to whom the span of life is measured only by memories. At the service today there was just the right amount of human reaction to foil the stately solemnity of the Church ritual.'

The tenor's brother James and his wife were in the congregation to hear the tributes and must also have been moved by the magnificent singing of the full cathedral choir. For all those present it was a worthy tribute to a singer who had afforded so much pleasure to Americans.

Until her death in April 1971, Lily McCormack had divided her time between Ireland and New York. Late in 1970 she had returned as usual to Dublin to stay with relatives but became ill and a few months later passed away in a Dublin nursing home at the age of eighty-four. She is buried beside Count John McCormack in Deansgrange Cemetery. Her funeral attracted little attention, presumably because of the copious amount of newspaper space taken up in the 1970s by the violent conflict in Northern Ireland, and also because in the twenty-six years since her husband's death a whole new generation of Irish had grown up and become in many cases more interested in pop than in Irish songs and ballads.

The McCormack legend, however, lives on and the tenor's superb vocal technique is often held up as an example to students in music colleges. His old records have been replaced by CDs and the quality of reproduction is uniformly good. The sales are consistent, so it looks like the McCormack voice will be heard for a long time to come. And the fairytale story of his success is surely worth retelling.

PART ONE

The Early Years

1

A Happy Childhood

Walking through the quaint streets of Athlone, you are soon made aware that it was in this town, uniquely divided by the River Shannon, that Count John McCormack was born on 14 June 1884. In a small side-street called the Bawn, stands the modest two-storey house which his parents rented for three shillings a week. And on the front is a faded bronze plaque with the words: *Birthplace of Count John McCormack, Worlds Famous Tenor*.

The missing apostrophe in 'Worlds' has unfortunately become the butt for jokes about the plaque and the people who put it there. Why it has remained uncorrected is to say the least puzzling. Beneath the plaque is a drawing that bears scant resemblance to the great tenor, and on another wall can be seen a full portrait of a portly figure one must presume is the singer, under the caption: *Song of My Heart*. For the sake of tourism in the town and the McCormack reputation, the Urban Council or the tourist authority for that matter, should ensure that this image is altered. The plaque was unveiled in the year 1938 during the tenor's lifetime.

It was not the only house with which the McCormack name was connected. As the family increased they moved from the Bawn to Convent Lane (now Friary Street), from there to Barnett Street on the Strand, on later to 5 Goldsmith Terrace, and ending up at 5 Auburn Terrace. On subsequent visits to the town McCormack liked to recall these different houses to friends, saying the house at Goldsmith Terrace was his favourite. He certainly had more vivid memories of it than any of the others.

Mary O'Rourke, deputy leader of Fianna Fail, thought that the McCormacks may have moved to Goldsmith Terrace because it was near the Mercy Convent which enjoyed a good reputation for teaching the piano and fostering the love of music generally. 'The nuns may have begun to take an interest in young John McCormack's singing voice and tried to help him along,' she said. 'Or there may be a different reason altogether for the move from Barnett Street.'

The house where he was born was converted in recent times to a restaurant. As I stood in the narrow street I wondered if a golden opportunity had been lost in not turning the house into a museum. Liam Breen, president of the Dublin-based John McCormack Society, believes this should have happened. The society, he said, would love to have bought the house but hadn't sufficient funds at the time to do so. He had been prepared to donate all his McCormack memorabilia if the museum had been set up. He expressed disappointment that the Athlone Urban Council hadn't bought the house. 'I've no doubt it could have raised the money. As a tourist project, it had outstanding potential, especially as a mecca for foreign visitors who were familiar with John McCormack's name.'

Mary O'Rourke, a native of the town, said the Urban Council had at one time considered the purchase of the house but was put off by the asking price. 'I remember there was also an effort made to attract a private buyer who would be interested in converting the house into a museum. Unfortunately, these efforts came to naught. I do agree, though, that an opportunity was lost, for with the change of emphasis in tourism the idea of a museum was, in hindsight, worth considering.'

A plaque, in my opinion, does not seem nearly enough by which to signpost the house where one of the world's finest singers was born and spent his early childhood. A museum, as envisaged by

4

Liam Breen, was undoubtedly the most appropriate project and it is regrettable that the chance was missed. In this respect, the saving of George Bernard Shaw's birthplace in Dublin's Upper Synge Street in the late 1980s set a glowing example. An energetic committee, led by Frances McCarthy and Nora Lever, toiled endlessly until the money was raised to buy the house, which was in poor condition, and subsequently converted it into a national Shaw museum. What a great pity, therefore, that Breen's efforts were not rewarded in Athlone.

I walked on until I came to the banks of the River Shannon where on the promenade stands an impressive nine feet high bronze bust of McCormack, executed by the Cork sculptor Seamus Murphy and carrying the inscription: *John Count McCormack, Born in Athlone 14 June 1884. Died in Dublin 16 September 1945. World famous tenor.*

The bust was unveiled by Count Cyril McCormack on a Sunday in June 1970, eighty-six years to the day of the tenor's birth. It was, Cyril told the large gathering, a proud day for the McCormack family, and his only regret was that his mother Countess Lily McCormack was too ill to be present. And he thanked Ms Mary C.P. Kilkelly, the local treasurer of the Friends of John McCormack, who had at last seen her ambition realised with the unveiling of the bust by the Shannon River where, he added, his father had spent so many happy school holidays fishing and boating.

It was a day of celebration in Athlone, with McCormack admirers coming from other parts of the country for the occasion. A dinner was held in the Shamrock Lodge and suggestions made for the inauguration of a 'Golden Voice Festival' in honour of the tenor. The show of enthusiasm seemed to answer those critics who contended that the people of Athlone were apathetic in their attitude to McCormack.

I found other reminders that the town had not forgotten the singer. They have called a row of houses after him – the McCormack Park – and in the oldest surviving building, Athlone Castle, which goes back to 1210, visitors can enjoy slides on his life. I walked on in search of his old primary school and came upon it adjacent to the towering St Mary's Church. It was here he began his schooling in July 1889. The school is now a centre for the local Knights of Columbanus. The inscription carved in stone reads: *St Mary's National School A.D. 1886.*

Any discussion on McCormack and Athlone inevitably raises the question of the circumstances of his family. 'We were genuinely poor,' McCormack would say later in America. 'But as a family we were happy.'

If they were poor, they were apparently seldom if ever hungry. The boy's parents saw to that. Hannah McCormack, his mother, was hard-working and ensured that no penny was wasted. A woman of reserve, she was of Scottish Presbyterian stock but became a Catholic on her marriage. Her husband Andrew earned about £2.10s a week as a foreman in the local Woollen Mills and on each pay day handed over to his wife more than £2 in cash, keeping a few shillings for drinks and cigarettes. He had come to Athlone from Galashiels in Scotland, though his paternal grandfather hailed from Sligo.

John Francis McCormack was the first son to be born to his parents and the fourth child of a family of eleven. Three died in infancy while two others died young. Child mortality was an all too common occurrence in the Ireland of the time. The boy remembered his father as strict though never cruel. 'Looking back, I realise now that my discipline was fairly rigid, yet there was nothing really harsh about it. Mother was a gentle woman and when there was trouble between family members she calmed matters without raising her voice unduly.'

The children had a normal upbringing and more than once young John McCormack indulged in fisticuffs with his pals in street fights. He was well able to take care of himself and was regarded as tough and manly and no easy target. In football he gave as good as he got and was reasonably talented. From an early age he could recall joining in sing-songs at home with his parents and before long he learned some Scottish songs from his father. Andrew McCormack was a member of the church choir and sometimes would join his army friends for drinks in the local military barracks where he matched the best of the vocal performers.

Young John was five when his father brought him along to the Marist Primary School for the first time. He was to prove an exceptionally bright and clever pupil and caused neither his parents nor his teachers any serious problems. A story goes that he began to arrive home late on some evenings from school and when questioned by his mother admitted that he stayed on in the park to listen to the military brass band. He begged his mother to say nothing to his father as he knew how he hated anyone breaking the 'house rules' and being late for meals.

'His mother gave him humour, gentleness and charm,' L.A.G. Strong wrote years later in his biography of the tenor. And he added: 'A look of half-bewildered melancholy, simple, almost childlike, which is visible in several of the early McCormack portraits and which still settles upon his face when he is tired, smoothing out the lines and making him seem young and vulnerable, is her legacy also. From her he inherited energy, drive and ambition. Andrew McCormack would declare, "If I had your education, son, I would be Prime Minister of England."'

It was McCormack who confirmed to Strong that musically he owed a great deal to his parents. He remembered being taught some lovely Irish songs by his mother who sang them slowly to him so that he could pick up every word. And she encouraged him to sing as often as he could. Strong observed: 'What part had inheritance played in equipping the singer is hard to determine. An exceptional gift has always something capricious about it: it lights as suddenly and irresponsibly as a butterfly, often on a place where there seems little to attract it. In John McCormack's case it chose soundly, and the physical endowment was bestowed in a place where there was much to help it. He himself feels that his love for the folk-music of

7

all peoples is as much from his Scottish blood as from his Irish. The same applies to his natural aptitude for phrasing these folk-songs. Yet there has never been an instant's doubt that he is Irish of the Irish.'

The McCormack legend is an integral part of Athlone, as I have discovered on visits to the town or talking to a native son like tenor Louis Browne. 'Yes, the legend is real,' Louis agrees. 'Put it this way: everybody's mother, father or grandfather either sat on the seat he used at school, or beside him. As Maureen Potter would say, "That desk must have been as big as Noah's Ark." It's true of course that we all grew up sharing that legend in one way or the other. Nearly every home in the town had McCormack records; in my own case I'd go down to my aunt's house and play some of her huge collection.'

In retrospect, he could not explain as to what exactly attracted him to the tenor's voice. Maybe it was the kind of songs he sang or the beguiling quality of his voice. 'Whatever it was, I loved listening to them. I think he recorded at his best between the years 1910 and 1920, and this is particularly true of his operatic recordings. Sadly, many of his later records do him little justice. I'm sure, though, that listening to his records as a boy inspired me to concentrate on singing and become a professional. It can be said that McCormack set an example for all tenors born in Ireland.'

Mary O'Rourke is also aware of the legend surrounding the tenor. 'As a child I became fascinated by the fact that John McCormack was born in our town and I wasn't contented until I sought out the different houses in which he lived. Some of the older generation spoke about his achievements with a mixture of pride and even awe, amazed that a local Marist schoolboy could rise to such dizzy heights as a singer. I feel, though, that the legend is perhaps stronger abroad than at home, particularly in America where they love success. One is prompted to ask whether his musical genius has been fully recognised in Ireland or whether we have paid him enough tribute.'

She recalled that the tenor had not forgotten his native town and in the year 1919 recorded a song about it entitled "That Tumble down Shack in Athlone". The song was, she thought, a romantic view of his native place and she suspected it was recorded in a sentimental moment. She was fond of singing its chorus as a party piece as she considered the lyrics appealing. As we talked, she hummed a few lines:

Oh, I want to go back to that tumble down shack
Where the wild roses bloom round the door
Just to pillow my head in that ould trundle bed
Just to see my ould mother once more.

There's a bright gleaming light guiding me home tonight
Down the long road of white cobble stones
Down the road that leads back
To that tumble down shack
To that tumble down shack in Athlone.

The song was also a party piece of the late Sean Fallon, a native of Athlone and chairman of the Seanad. The haunting melody was played on a violin at the requiem Mass at his funeral in July of this year. Sean sang the song with pride, said Mary O'Rourke, and in time it became identified with him. And the song can still be heard sung in pubs in Athlone, with its chorus evoking a good deal of nostalgia.

In her view it helped the town's image that the McCormack name was linked with it, and though he was no longer a daily topic of conversation, she felt the people were proud of the link. As an individual, she regarded the tenor as larger than life, a man with a strong personality. 'I find that very vibrant. I mean, he was such a vital person, it seems that you could never imagine him existing for a moment in an ivory tower. He wasn't liked by everybody, but then who is? I do believe that he was very fortunate in the woman he married, Lily Foley, for she obviously knew how to cope with his temperament, which mustn't have been all that easy in the hectic life he lived and the enormous amount of travel it entailed.'

Whenever McCormack was asked in America about Athlone it is interesting to note that he liked to describe it as 'a garrison town', though not in any derogatory sense. And he would add proudly, 'I would not change Athlone, if I could, nor would I ask to be born elsewhere. The town was kind to me and I can look back to a happy childhood there. Like all Irish towns, it had a certain culture, the people had simple tastes, and the Catholic religion was strong. I can still recall my mother singing "Believe me" in a very sweet voice. Education, however, was a priority with my parents and in the community as a whole the desire for knowledge was great.'

Despite the happiness that pervaded the McCormack home, the family also experienced anguish and tragedy. Mary Ann McCormack died as an infant, and another of John's brothers', Peter, passed away as a baby. A sister, Isabella, lived only to the age of sixteen, and another boy named Thomas died in infancy. John McCormack was a strong baby and healthy and there were no fears about his survival. The Marist Brothers later spoke highly of him as a potential scholarship winner. Michael Curley, a fellow pupil, was a few years older than young McCormack but they became boyhood friends. As a distinguished prelate years afterwards in America, Curley liked to recall those early school days, 'I remember John McCormack was a studious boy with an alert, enquiring mind. He was also good at sport and popular with the other boys.'

Whenever the tenor caught Archbishop Curley reminiscing about the past, he'd interrupt him with the words, 'Ah, there he goes now wanting to tell all my childhood secrets.'

There was joy in the McCormack home when John Francis announced to his parents that he had won a scholarship to Summerhill College in Sligo. The boy was twelve and ready for the biggest educational adventure of his young life.

2

College Days in Sligo

Students enrolling in Summerhill College in young McCormack's year, 1896, would be expected to consider in due course a vocation to the priesthood – and many of them I expect did so, said Canon Kevin Earley, who is today's President of the Sligo college. He discusses its history with evident pride and no little enthusiasm. Our records reveal, he added, that in those years there were regular vocations and no one was surprised.

John McCormack's sound faith was soon noted, though it was by no means exceptional. The tenor later admitted that the church had had an appeal for him but as time passed a degree of uncertainty grew in his mind. 'I could not shake off that vague questioning as to my fitness to be a servant.'

Archbishop Curley, a contemporary of his in Summerhill, was to say, 'There are some students for the priesthood whom it's better to persuade from that wish, and others who eliminate themselves in a perfectly normal way. John McCormack was of the latter kind.'

When he quickly realised he had no vocation, McCormack was philosophical about it. He laughed off the suggestion that his father was broken-hearted about his lack of interest in the priesthood, saying, 'I think it would have pleased him if I had a priestly vocation but I knew he had other ambitions for me, among them a career in medicine or in law. I don't think singing entered his mind.'

The college authorities never pressed him on the matter and the boy threw himself wholeheartedly into the academic and sporting activities. To the college president, Father Kielty, he was an intelligent and quick-witted student, up with the best, and with a gift for mimicry. Soon his singing voice began to be noticed and talked about in the college. His boy soprano voice was sweet and pure and very expressive. He was, however, shy to talk about it in that first year.

According to Canon Earley, Summerhill was small at the turn of the century and numbered only about one hundred pupils, and that included boarders. Today there were more than one thousand day pupils – the boarding school was closed in the early 1990s. But the college motto remains steadfastly the same, which translated from the Latin is: *Be doers of the word,'* with the rest of the line reading, *'and not hearers only.'*

Coming as he did from a big family, John McCormack experienced homesickness in the first few months, but at the age of twelve and considering it was his first time away from home, it was understandable. Soon the feeling left him as every minute of his time was occupied either with study or games; he also began to make new friends and this made him forget the pain of homesickness. The rules of the college were fairly strict, though not in his estimation harsh. It was early to rise and early to bed. Usually students were out of their beds at six in the morning, and with no heating in the dormitories, they didn't delay in dressing themselves, especially in winter time when the cold was severe.

Breakfast comprised plain, wholesome food, and there was no scarcity of it. Study took up most of the day. For recreation young McCormack played soccer and lots of handball, a game at which he soon excelled. At weekends he joined his classmates for walks to Rosses Point and other surrounding areas; if the weather was warm enough in May they swam in the sea. By now he had become a sturdy youth with strong shoulders and an athletic body.

The entry scholarship he had won was worth £30 and covered his tuition and residence fees; his parents were expected to pay for what were called 'extras'. Canon Earley at this point produced for me a leger from a drawer in the administration room dated 4 September 1896, containing the full cost of the 'extras'. For example, McCormack was charged £1 for his singing lessons, for his washing £1.10, stamps (2/9), dentistry (£1.7.6), books (£1.3.9) and glasses (5/6). He would say in later years that his father was put to the pin of his collar to find the money.

From all accounts, the boy took his singing lessons seriously, for soon he was promoted to sing solos in the college choir on feast days and at the concerts to celebrate the annual prize-giving. His debut as an actor was not altogether auspicious, though it gave obvious satisfaction to the audience. Cast as Lieutenant Molyneux in the popular Boucicault melodrama *Conn the Shaughraun*, he was struck by a fit of nerves so that his most dramatic line came out in a novel form.

'Stop!' cries the Lieutenant. 'If you put your head outside that door, I'll put a bullet in it!'

Cried McCormack, 'Stop! If you put your bullet outside that door, I'll put a head on it!'

The boy winced inwardly at the gaffe he had made and for years the echo of the laughter that followed haunted him. As a result he never trusted his memory on the concert platform, keeping always a little book with the words of the songs he sang. He was, nonetheless, enjoying his days in Summerhill and achieved excellent examination results. When he came home for holidays his parents showed a new pride in him and already regarded their son as the scholar in the family. For his brothers and sisters he retailed some amusing stories of the pranks he had played on fellow students, but was careful to add that they weren't wicked. He displayed his gift for mimicry as he took off his teachers and some of their odd mannerisms.

To his mother, he had improved in every way, yet he hadn't changed. He joined in the singing and his father noted that his son's voice was sweeter than before and stronger. It was easy to see also that any money spent on John Francis had not gone to waste. No

13

mention, however, was made of a priestly vocation and the subject wasn't brought up again. Even by the age of fourteen it was clear that young McCormack knew his own mind.

Back at Summerhill he was approached one day by Father John Hynes, the curate at Sligo Cathedral, who said he had the permission of the college president for him to sing on the following two nights at a concert in the Town Hall. Before he could say a word the priest asked him what he would sing. He would get five shillings for the two appearances. Young McCormack hardly knew what to say.

'For the rest of that day I scarcely heard a word that was said to me in class,' he recalled. 'All I knew is that I dreamt that night of ovations and applause until I was rudely awakened before six o'clock by the sudden sound of the bell ringing in my dormitory. The idea of singing before the local people made me feel nervous and I wondered if I'd forget the words of the songs.'

He didn't forget the words; in fact, he made a fine impression on the audience. Although he had felt nervous beforehand, he was delighted that it hadn't affected his performance. He was brought back to earth, however, next day when one of the college maids said to him, 'You sang grand last night, Mr John, but why did you sing in that foreign language we couldn't understand?'

He had sung all his songs in English and was happy to do so, but he appreciated what the girl had said. He made a vow also to improve his diction and to ensure that in future his words would be understood in every corner of a concert hall. That first public appearance stayed with him. 'Every fee I have ever received since then is simply an accumulation at compound interest of that original fee.'

With the money he got from Fr Hynes he bought a mouth-organ and in no time at all had mastered the instrument. 'John played it all over the college,' Archbishop Curley said long afterwards, 'and he acquired a good deal of technical facility in various styles of harmonic accompaniment and was able to play the tunes of the moment. I remember he invested in at least two more mouth-organs and his collection at one time included two instruments which bore on their sides "Key of C", and others similarly branded with "G and F."'

Despite the rigours of academic study and the abundance of homework, he never missed a music lesson. At this time Father Manley was in charge of the college choir as well as being organist at Sligo Cathedral. He made no secret of his admiration of young McCormack's sweet voice and he proceeded to teach him the tenor aria "In Native Worth" from Haydn's *The Creation*. Soon the boy became the star of the college concerts and counted among his favourite songs the Scottish air "Jessie, the Flower of Dunblane". When he pleaded with the president Fr Kielty to give him more time to study singing, he was disappointed that his request was refused. Apparently Kielty felt the boy's voice was not exceptional and that he was much better at academic subjects such as science and languages. Privately, he still hoped that John Francis, as he called him, would one day join the priesthood.

McCormack had by now won a scholarship in his junior certificate year and was considered one of the most intelligent students in the college. As he prepared for a second scholarship examination he feared he wouldn't be able to sit for it on that day due to a bad stye in one eye. The eye had closed and Fr Kielty advised him not to sit for it. Showing typical determination, the boy decided to go ahead. As he recalled, 'I felt I had a good chance of winning the sixty pounds and no one was going to stop me.'

To everyone's surprise, he was successful; indeed, he achieved record marks in Latin, English and Algebra. The scholarship successes secured his place free in the college for the next two years. He received £60 for his latest examination success and handed it over to his father with the proviso that he buy him a violin. After the holidays, he brought back the instrument with him to college and began to teach himself how to play it. One of his teachers took a dim view of what he described as 'this time wasting' and made young McCormack hand over the violin, saying, 'You are much too clever

15

at languages to be spending all your time fiddling.'

It was one of the few occasions that his anger surfaced. He could not understand why anyone should stop him playing a musical instrument that he so much enjoyed. But he continued to take singing lessons and make occasional appearances at concerts at the local Town Hall. And he remained popular with the other boys because of his pranks and expert mimicry and his involvement in games. He was by now the best handball player in the college and won prizes in competitions; he also kept goal in the soccer team, although his interest had waned.

By the time he graduated at the age of eighteen in 1902 John Francis McCormack had received a good education and was a well-rounded student, even if he had still no clear idea of what he wanted to do with his life. All he knew was that his parents wanted him to find a secure job, whatever that might be. He had come away from Summerhill aware also that he could sing better than the other boys and he remembered the encouragement he got to continue with his singing.

'Every chance I got I sang,' he later said. 'But a career as a singer never entered my head simply because I didn't know anything about it.'

Canon Earley is convinced that Summerhill played a paramount part in the educational and character development of young McCormack. Everything about the college seemed to suit his temperament and intelligence; he was meeting boys who were obviously intent on making the most of their education as well as the sports facilities available. And the atmosphere that encouraged a splendid *esprit de corps* among the boys must also have appealed to his friendly nature.

'I don't think he ever quite forgot Summerhill,' added Canon Earley. 'Seemingly on American tours later he met past-pupils of the college and liked to talk to them about the old days.'

In the middle of the 1930s, when he was already famous, the tenor returned to sing in Sligo's Town Hall and on the afternoon of that day popped into Summerhill to meet the president and the students. Michael Dunning was one the young college prefects chosen to welcome McCormack and remembers the air of expectancy around the place.

'We assembled in the study hall and applauded loudly at the entry of John McCormack,' recalled Dunning, who is now the parish priest in Cloverhill, Co. Roscommon. 'From the stage he waved his hand for silence and said good-humouredly to the gathering of pupils, "Much water has gone under the bridge since I was last here – and much ink, too!"'

Seemingly, his words produced a burst of laughter, followed by cries from the boys for a song. 'We were all disappointed when he nodded his head and asked to be excused because he was singing that night in the Town Hall. I suppose in a way we felt a bit cheated.'

To Fr Dunning, McCormack cut a striking figure and spoke in a strong, limpid voice that projected very well. That night, the tenor was accorded an enthusiastic reception by a capacity attendance in the Town Hall and among the songs he chose were "When Irish Eyes are Smiling" and "My Wild Irish Rose". As always, he was generous with encores and they included "That Tumble down Shack in Athlone" and "I Hear You Calling Me". And he told the audience that the best years of his life were spent in Summerhill College, cheerfully adding, 'I feel I'm back amongst home folk again.'

Meanwhile, Canon Earley has in his possession the tenor's most tangible link with Sligo. It is a gold chalice studded with eighteen tiny diamonds and bears the inscription: '*A token of deep appreciation from John McCormack. October 1910.*' It was designed by a friend of the singer's in Dublin and its present value could be in the region of £12,000. And how the chalice found a resting place in Summerhill College is intriguing in itself.

When McCormack was studying in Italy with Maestro Sabatini he ran out of money and on impulse decided to write to Bishop

17

Clancy of Elphin Diocese for £50. He later admitted that 'he was almost sorry when he let the letter drop from his fingers into the letterbox. What if the Bishop ignored his appeal?'

To his relief, a letter of reply arrived a few weeks later to his 'digs' in Milan. 'I'm glad John you asked the favour,' Bishop Clancy wrote, 'and I'm pleased to enclose for the moment £25. I will send you the remainder in three months.'

The prelate was true to his word and the extra £25 enabled young McCormack to continue with his vocal studies. A few years later as a token of his gratitude John presented Bishop Clancy with the gold chalice; in turn the Bishop inserted in his will that after his death it should pass on to the president of Summerhill College. To Canon Earley the singer's was a significant gesture. 'I think we were seeing for the first time John McCormack's sincerity as well as his generosity. We are very proud of the chalice here and I sometimes use it at special Masses.'

In 1992, when Summerhill was celebrating the centenary of its foundation the names of famous past pupils, including Count John McCormack, were recalled with pride. And Liam Breen, President of the McCormack Society, was asked if he would make available for exhibition in the college his historic private museum of McCormack memorabilia. He was delighted to oblige provided the college made arrangements to transport it *in toto* to Sligo.

Within a few days a large truck arrived at his suburban home in Sutton, Co. Dublin and item after item was packed carefully into the vehicle. So precious was the cargo to Liam Breen, that he took a seat beside the driver for the long road journey.

For the next week his museum was on display in a spacious room in the college and attracted thousands of visitors from Sligo and the adjacent counties. 'I was astonished by the interest in the singer's career,' Breen recalled. 'People of all ages came to view the medals, papal uniforms, operatic costumes, swords, music scores and old newspaper clippings. I must have been asked a hundred questions or

18

more about John's life, but I was ready for them as I had been giving talks about him for some years.'

It was, he admitted, a tiring week. He opened the museum around eleven o'clock in the morning and did not close it until midnight. He remembered it could be sometimes amusing when a bishop or parish priest came across a photograph they hadn't known existed. Once he heard a bishop exclaim aloud at the end of the room, 'Look! That's me as a prefect on the day John McCormack visited Summerhill.'

Liam Breen came away from Sligo convinced that interest in the McCormack legend would never fade.

Count John McCormack, I should add, is not the only distinguished Summerhill College past pupil. There are others, including Father Edward O'Flanagan of Boys Town fame in America, his namesake Fr Michael O'Flanagan who stood by the side of an t-Athair Tomas O'Ceallaigh, who had Irish on the Curriculum of the college long before the language was recognised, former Taoiseach Albert Reynolds who did so much for the peace process North and South of the Irish border, Ray MacSharry, the former European Commissioner for Agriculture and Rural Development and now a board member of Ryanair, Tommy Gorman, RTE correspondent in Brussels, *Irish Times* sports journalist Sean Kilfeather, Martin Howley, first Professor of Philosophy at University College, Galway, and Monsignor J. Hynes – a former President of U.C.G., once a curate in St. Mary's Sligo and founder of Conradh na Gaeilge in Sligo.

3

The Breakthrough

How persistent Andrew McCormack's attitude was against his son pursuing a career in singing is not altogether clear. By the age of eighteen it does seem that people in Athlone were aware of young McCormack's exceptional singing voice and believed he should have formal vocal training. Michael Kilkelly was the most prominent of them. A businessman and choirmaster in the old St Peter's Church (now the Dean Crowe Memorial Hall), he was determined to play a role in bringing the young tenor to public notice.

Gearoid O'Brien in his booklet *John McCormack and Athlone* tells how Kilkelly was once admonished by Andrew McCormack for interfering in his son's study. At the time John McCormack had begun to study for a Civil Service examination. Kilkelly replied that he had repeatedly heard artists sing who did not possess voices half as good or as pure as John's and they were paid as much per week and sometimes even more for one night's performance as John would receive in his first year.

Seemingly, Andrew McCormack laughed derisively and hurried away to his job at the local Woollen Mills. His attitude in a way was understandable. He was conservative and must have regarded a singing career as precarious and certainly not as secure as a Civil Service post. Since he sang for the fun of it himself, perhaps he thought that his son should treat singing in the same cavalier manner.

There is no evidence to show what his wife Hannah believed was right for her son, or whether she secretly wanted him to be a singer.

If, as Gearoid O'Brien states, young McCormack was already a regular contender at Feiseanna throughout the country, and that as a member of the Gaelic League movement he sang at concerts in Limerick and elsewhere, then one must assume that his parents knew that as a singer he was increasingly in demand. One wonders also whether he had to seek their permission to travel outside Athlone.

Furthermore, after his first public concert in the town in 1902 in aid of convent funds, his performance must have aroused some interest among the locals. It certainly was the case in January 1903 when he sang at a concert for the Athlone Technical School. The local critic in his newspaper review was high in his praise of his singing, describing it as 'magnificent,' and he added, 'John McCormack is endowed with an exceptionally pleasing tenor voice and already can be classed as a vocalist of a very high order. It is safe to say that if he went in for professional singing he would meet with much success. He was loudly applauded and had to come out a second time.'

Gearoid O'Brien says there is no indication as to who wrote the review of the concert but it is possible that it was a freelance piece submitted by Michael Kilkelly. We do not know whether the singer's parents attended any of these concerts; if they did so, then would not the audience enthusiasm for their son's singing convince them he was perhaps blessed with an unusually fine voice? I suspect that Michael Kilkelly chose his review words deliberately to impress on Andrew McCormack the urgency to have John trained with a view to becoming a professional singer.

By now the young singer had settled in Dublin. He sat for a science scholarship examination and was placed fourteenth in the results – the first thirteen places were granted scholarships. He took a job as a clerk to pay his way and on his father's advice began to study for the Civil Service examinations of 1903, but he never took them. He admitted later on that this was an uncertain period in his life and he was unsure as to what to do next. Athlone friends who had heard him sing had no doubt where his future lay. One of them, Frank Manning, who was a fine player of the mandolin, encouraged him to see vocal teacher Vincent O'Brien. 'I will go along with you,' he said. 'I think he can help you.'

Manning recalled that young McCormack was nervous as he introduced him to O'Brien but was soon put at his ease. A calm and affable individual, O'Brien had a growing reputation as a musician; he had received his first lessons from his father who was a distinguished organist. He was instantly impressed by McCormack's voice and invited him to join the Palestrina Choir at £1 a week.

The young tenor took immediately to Vincent O'Brien. 'After our first meeting, I felt deeply obligated to him. I regarded him as sincere and evidently a man of vision, who appeared intuitively to feel that all I needed was to study and get an opportunity to achieve my ambitions.'

He was also assisted by Dr Dudley Forde who urged him to enter for the Feis Ceoil, Dublin's biggest annual music event. He assured him he would. The test piece was "Tell Fair Irene" from Handel's *Atalanta*, regarded as a difficult aria requiring good vocal technique. He began to prepare it with Vincent O'Brien. 'I found him a very patient coach,' McCormack recalled. 'Over and over again he'd drill me in a phrase until I was able to approach the perfection he sought. I will not say that he was always satisfied but when the lesson was over he'd say to me, "Sing those songs as well at the Feis Ceoil as you have just sung them and you will win."'

The tenor section was by far the most popular competition in the Feis and it attracted a packed hall. There were fourteen tenors entered, with McCormack listed as fourteenth in line of appearance. Each was required to sing the test piece followed by a song of their own choosing. Early on he took his seat in the right hand corner of the hall, not far from the stage. For the next hour or more he listened attentively to each tenor and was not unduly impressed by any one of them. Three of the remaining five, however, did impress him, one in particular named William Rathborne who was clearly a favourite with the audience.

To young McCormack, he appeared to be a mature singer and sang both the test piece and his song convincingly, although he himself felt that some of his phrasing would not have got by Vincent O'Brien if he had been coaching him. Momentarily Rathborne stepped down from the platform and as he walked down the aisle towards the dressing room he clenched his hands and raised them, giving what McCormack interpreted as a victory sign.

How presumptuous of him, thought the tenor from Athlone. At that moment he forgot his nervous feeling and vowed in his heart to beat him if he could. Hamilton Harty was the piano accompanist and McCormack suspected that by now he must be feeling tired after playing for the thirteen previous competitors. Nonetheless, he gave the tenor a friendly smile and proceeded to play the opening bars of the test piece, "Tell Fair Irene". He began at a tempo twice as fast as Vincent O'Brien had taught him and at a pace that in his estimation would make skilful interpretation and good singing impossible.

'It's too fast,' he remarked aloud to Harty. 'I can't sing it at that pace.'

Harty tried to hide his surprise.

'Very well,' he said calmly. 'Show me how you like it.'

McCormack sang the aria as he had learned it, and followed it with the old Irish melody "The Snowy Breasted Pearl". As soon as he had finished there was a brief moment of silence, then the audience burst into spontaneous applause that to the tenor seemed to last a long time. The adjudicator Luigi Denza rose and waited for the applause to end before giving his verdict. Looking at the audience, he said with a smile, 'There's no need to tell you who the winner is, you have chosen him yourself. He is the young man whom you have just heard.'

It was an emotional moment for the young tenor as he received the coveted gold medal. Surely now his father would be convinced that he had a gifted son? Later, when he became famous he liked to recall the triumph and the first thing that came into his head. 'I thought of my parents, my schools, and all the people who had faith in my voice.'

For the first time his name got into the national newspapers. When he sang at a concert at Blackrock, Co. Dublin he got a fee of three guineas. After his name on the programme were the words 'Feis Ceoil Gold Medalist' and in subsequent concerts the promoters always used it, as though to remind audiences of his achievement.

He continued to have singing lessons with Vincent O'Brien. 'You have the voice, John,' O'Brien would say, 'now you must perfect your technique. We must be careful not to coarsen it in any way.'

In August 1905, he gave a complimentary concert in the Fr Mathew Hall, Athlone, following on the heels of some very successful concerts in Dublin. The local paper reported: 'It was a matter for surprise that the hall was not better filled. There was a nice crowd in every part of the hall but nothing as large as might be expected when John McCormack was going to sing.'

The paper told its readers that those who stayed away had missed a musical treat from a purely artistic point of view. 'The tenor was in magnificent voice.'

After his success at the Feis Ceoil it is hard to explain the apparent apathy of the Athlone people on this occasion; it seemed unfortunately to have had an adverse affect on young McCormack at the time, although I do not accept it was the beginning of 'a rift between him and the town.' Back in Dublin he was prepared to learn from more experienced singers such as baritones William Ludwig and J.C. Doyle and veteran tenor Barton McGuckin. He saved money in order to attend performances by English touring companies such as the Moody-Manners and the Carl Rosa. It was in fact a performance of *Tannhauser* in the Gaiety Theatre that first excited him about the possibilities of grand opera as a vehicle for his voice. And he was particularly thrilled by the performance of Limerick-born tenor Joseph O'Mara as Don José in *Carmen*. For a long time afterwards he talked about the dramatic impact O'Mara made and his

25

powerful portrayal, especially in the final act of the opera.

The writer L.A.G. Strong once observed: 'Irish voices are naturally sweet and sympathetic in quality, but the tenors tend to be nasal, high-pitched and thin on the top. Thus the singers from outside, particularly in opera, were an excellent corrective. No-one with John McCormack's instinct for singing could hear the open ringing tone of a good tenor without registering in his mind a quality at which to aim – a quality the native tenor often lacked.'

For the young tenor it continued to be a time of learning. After attending operas, he began to study the performances of the various tenors as interpretations of the part, rather than as a series of arias well or indifferently sung. Now that the Feis Ceoil had afforded him the musical breakthrough he needed, he wondered when he would ever get a chance to sing in opera. His income from concerts was meagre, the fees paid often ridiculously low. At times he was barely making ends meet. He was fortified, however, by the words of his friend and mentor Michael Kilkelly. 'I know that one day, John, you'll make your parents and Athlone proud of you. I have told your father Andrew the very same thing.'

4

The Young Lovers

The majority of young Irish classical singers tend today to put career before thoughts of marriage. It is understandable in a profession that offers scant security and is over-crowded. A few years ago in fact, eyebrows were raised when Veronica Dunne, that doyenne of vocal teachers, warned her more mature students against 'rushing into early marriage before their careers had been launched.' As an example, she cited the case of her own marriage in her mid-twenties and now confessed that the timing was a mistake.

'My international career was about to bloom,' she explained, 'and when I married Peter I soon had both a husband and young children to think about. It was a struggle as I commuted between Dublin and Covent Garden and put an extra strain on myself.'

Few voices were raised in disagreement with her words, not even when Ronnie, as she is affectionately called, added the bold rider, 'Girls...live with them but don't marry them!'

What we find now in the profession are short or extended courtships or trendy relationships with few teenage marriages. I'm not suggesting that romance is moribund; far from it. The truth is that it has been overtaken by a new sense of realism and responsibility that only young singers themselves will in time appreciate more fully as they struggle for recognition in what, to my mind, has become a network jungle.

It is against this rather cynical background that one must look back at John McCormack's budding romance and ask whether he was a naive boy from the country or simply blindly in love. Consider the facts: he is a young tenor earning less than £50 a year in Dublin and with no prospects of national success, let alone international discovery. He is not yet twenty and the girl he has fallen for, Lily Foley, is only seventeen years of age. In an old-fashioned way it is reminiscent of "Romeo and Juliet" as he quickly declares his love and his eagerness to marry Lily.

There is little evidence of soul-searching on his part or a willingness to accept the advice of his close friends to wait for a while longer. McCormack was of an impulsive nature and was not prepared, it seems, to postpone the day indefinitely. In their favour, though, the couple had much in common, even if Lily came from a better-off family. She was a talented singer and dancer, and was also taking singing lessons from Vincent O'Brien.

There is a charm and simplicity about the way she remembered her first sight of John McCormack that today's young generations will find hard to swallow. For as he was crossing O'Connell Street, Dublin, her sister Molly suddenly said to her, 'Do you know who that is? It's young McCormack. He's going to the Pro-Cathedral to sing at the six o'clock Mass.'

Lily turned swiftly around and was mortified to be caught looking in his direction. Much later he would remind her of the occasion and how he glimpsed her blushing. He had heard her sing at concerts and for some reason surmised that she was 'stuck up and reserved'. Lily Foley, for her part, was able to tell him proudly that she, too, had won a gold medal for a solo in Gaelic at the Feis Ceoil and was so pleased with herself that she didn't go to the tenor competition and so missed his triumph.

Slight, dark-haired and pretty, she did not want for friends and she made no secret of her intention to take up singing as a career. A few weeks after the Feis Ceoil Prizewinners' Concert she was engaged to sing at a concert in Athlone, with William Ludwig billed

28

as the star attraction. 'I was travelling down on the train with William and his two daughters,' she recalled, 'when, at the last minute, John McCormack arrived in a hurry at the Broadstone Station, looking pale and drawn. He told us that he had a bad cold and couldn't sing but that he'd come along to show that he was willing.'

Ludwig was inclined to pity the young tenor. 'What you need young man,' he said in a strong baritonal voice, 'is someone like Miss Foley here to look after you.' He then proceeded to introduce him to the young soprano. At that moment, both of them blushed, and during the journey the tenor scarcely spoke a word. Lily put it down to his feverish cold. Later, to their surprise, he did manage to sing and received an enthusiastic ovation. For the next week, though, he was confined to bed on doctor's orders.

With Lily in demand to sing at concerts, it was not surprising that she and John should sometimes meet and chat over the music scene in Dublin. When she was invited to perform at a meeting of the Celtic Literary Society in St. Stephen's Green, attended by Dr Douglas Hyde who would one day be President of Ireland, she met a Mr James Riordan, who was guest of honour. He had apparently been impressed by her singing and after the meeting invited her to perform at the World Fair in St Louis.

'I will have to get my parents' permission,' she told him. 'You see, I'm still going to school.'

Lily got their permission, provided her sister Molly was permitted to accompany her. The prospect of the long sea voyage and the knowledge that John McCormack was arriving a week later to sing at the Fair excited her no end. As she said, 'I was really on my way, I felt, to a career of my own which would lead me to musical comedy at least, if not Grand Opera.'

The most eventful aspect of McCormack's trip was that he experienced acute bouts of seasickness, so bad in fact that eventually he almost ignored the sight of the spectacular New York skyline. All he asked of the New World was 'solid ground'. Furthermore, two days and nights on the train from New York to Missouri did nothing to enhance his view of that vast country.

Meanwhile, to Lily Foley the St Louis World Fair was an awesome spectacle. 'We were swept off our feet by the imposing buildings with their fascinating exhibits, and by the gardens, a blaze of colour by day and a dream of beauty by night with their fountains and lights.'

Many Irish-Americans and others lingered over the displays at the Irish Pavilion that included Irish linen, Claddagh rings, Tara brooches, handmade lace and volumes of historic books. They listened to traditional Irish music or watched the green-costumed dancers performing jigs and reels, and there were scenes from the dramas of Synge and Yeats presented by Irish actors. Lily and Molly Foley were enjoying themselves as never before; soon they were joined by John McCormack and they immediately enquired about news from home.

It struck Lily that he was concerned about their welfare among the 'mixed races' at the Fair and volunteered his escort services. At first his persistence tended to annoy her. 'Several girls I'd met had attractive brothers,' she said, 'and it really made me cross that whenever one of them came around John was there, too. Sometimes I wouldn't speak to him for hours and then he'd come around looking dejected and ask me to have dinner with him before our concert at the Pavilion; and after that we'd ride in the mammoth ferris wheel, and then all would be forgiven.'

Soon she and Molly began to depend on him and had to admit they enjoyed his company. Although by now she realised he was quick-tempered and strong-willed, neither she nor her sister Molly were quite prepared for the kind of reaction he displayed when the management of the Irish Pavilion introduced a stage-Irish character on stage in a bid to get more laughs. The cast protested, with actor Dudley Digges as their spokesman. McCormack resigned on the spot and his resignation was accepted.

'I think the management found John a rather difficult young man

30

to handle', Lily recalled. 'Molly and I were upset because he had acted impulsively, especially since the stage-Irish character was quickly eliminated from our programme.'

Nonetheless, they were sorry to see him prepare to leave the World Fair. In a funny way his hasty behaviour had drawn them closer and Lily had to admit that by now they were almost inseparable. Yet she wasn't quite prepared for his next prank. He wanted her to surprise her sister Molly by telling her that they had just got engaged. Molly wasn't amused and turned on John. 'Don't talk nonsense at your age. You've got to think of your future first.'

It was too late. Lily had already pledged her love to him and in subsequent weeks he was seldom out of her thoughts. When he visited his family in Athlone he talked about the romance to his sisters and brother, Jim. They sensed it wasn't a fleeting affair, although Jim wondered whether his brother was too young to be thinking about marriage. He was more concerned about John's singing career in Dublin.

The tenor had some luck shortly afterwards when he was invited to sing with soprano Agnes Treacy at the house of a Mr Fair in Dublin's Pembroke Road. Fair, an amateur musician and avid music lover, was so taken by McCormack's voice that he suggested further training in Italy. 'I know just the teacher for you,' he said earnestly, 'it is Maestro Vincenzo Sabatini. He sang in opera himself for twenty-five years. What he doesn't know about teaching isn't worth knowing. I'll write to him at once.'

Years before, in 1762, Michael Kelly, a young Dublin tenor, had gone to Italy for voice training and in no time made his debut in a Piccini opera. And he would go on to become a friend of Mozart in Vienna and sing in the first performance of his *Le Nozze di Figaro*. Limerick tenor Joseph O'Mara had studied in Milan with Signor Moretti and later stated that he owed his success in the Italian repertoire to his two valuable years in Milan. Now McCormack came away, it is said, from Pembroke Road enthusiastic about Mr Fair's interest in him. Next day when he discussed the subject with Lily she shared his enthusiasm and hoped like himself that Sabatini would accept him. When the word came through from Mr Fair that Sabatini had actually agreed, plans were set in motion to raise some badly-needed funds for McCormack. Lily's father, along with Vincent O'Brien and other friends, booked a hall and among the performers was McCormack and Lily Foley, as she was named on the bill poster. 'All Athlone came to Dublin for that concert,' she wrote in her autobiography.

Michael Kilkelly and his friends, meanwhile, were organising their own concert for the tenor in Athlone. Local musicians and singers were engaged so as to keep the costs down. But it wasn't a success and only £30 was taken at the box office which meant that between the two concerts a sum of £200 was realised altogether. McCormack must have had some concert circulars printed for the Athlone concert, for in a letter to Michael Kilkelly he expressed surprise that some money was still owed to the printers.

He finished his letter on a bitter note. I quote from Gearoid O'Brien's *John McCormack and Athlone*:

> Now that all is over it is evident the concert was a dire failure and after expressing my deep gratitude to you and the committee I can only say what is my firm conviction, that some influence was at work against me and I have an idea of the quarter it came from and it is hard lines when in a strange city a man will be supported and in his very birthplace he will be injured by petty spites and jealousies.

In the circumstances such a letter was not surprising, as one could easily imagine today a young singer in any Irish town being disappointed if the locals failed to support a concert to raise funds to send him to Rome or Vienna, especially if his talent was being hailed as exceptional. What is surprising, however, is the inference by

32

McCormack of a jealous faction in the town. This is hard to believe, for if the figure of £30 is correct more than a few hundred music lovers must have stayed away from the concert at the Fr Mathew Hall. In retrospect, it seems a big faction for a small town of about 6,000 population. I prefer to believe that sheer apathy and not jealousy was the chief cause for such low box-office receipts. The episode does reveal that the young tenor was capable of strong emotions and was not one to pull his punches.

The episode would be soon forgotten, however, as he set out for his Italian adventure early in March 1905. He carried with him a letter of introduction from Mr Fair to Maestro Sabatini, and when eventually he arrived at his studio, No.4 Via Victor Hugo in Milan, he was welcomed at first by his wife Signora Sabatini. She was an English woman, so there was no language barrier which was a relief to young McCormack. Maestro Sabatini was seated in an armchair near the piano. He looked younger than his seventy-four years.

'I can see him now,' the young tenor wrote later, 'a wonderfully preserved man with white hair and a moustache, hair thinning at the top. There was a quality about him of old world courtliness which softened his piercing eyes. He listened as his wife read Mr Fair's letter and explained its contents in Italian. The old man spoke no English.'

The studio was small and apart from the piano and two chairs there was little else. Signora Sabatini asked McCormack about his training in Dublin and what he expected from singing. When he told her that he intended to learn the Italian language, she smiled and said that the Maestro would be happy to hear that. She asked him to come round to the studio on the following afternoon so that her husband could hear him sing. He had arranged to stay for the next three months with two old English ladies at their *pensione* in Via Brera.

It was a nervous young McCormack who called on the Sabatinis next day. How would the Maestro react to his singing? If he fell below his standards, would he send him home? But in such doubtful moments he tended to pluck up determination and recall what people like Michael Kilkelly and Vincent O'Brien had said to him about his ability. At least the Sabatinis were a friendly and understanding couple and that made him feel at home.

As Signora sat at the piano he put on the music stand the score of his chosen aria -"Ah non credevi tu" – from *Mignon* which he proceeded to sing in English. He could not tell how his voice sounded in the studio but he was careful not to force it. There was silence when he finished; then Signor Sabatini bent over and talked with his wife in Italian.

Signora smiled as she turned to the tenor and said, 'Signor Sabatini is pleased. He says he cannot place your voice, for God has placed it already.'

It was agreed that he would get a lesson a day every day, except Sunday for twenty dollars a month. Leaving the studio he felt happy and a little more confident. In racing parlance he knew he had jumped the first hurdle. His initial impulse was to write home to Lily and tell her the good news; it would be the first of many letters to her, all ending with the same words, 'My love, John.'

He was pleased with his lessons with the Sabatinis. 'I remember the Maestro was anxious that I acquire a good *mezza-voce* which I did not have by nature, and he also wanted me to achieve freedom in my high notes as well as to develop a better legato line. I was astonished by the way he detected flaws in my singing and the astuteness he displayed in applying corrective measures. Nor was I likely to forget the way he sang for me "Salve Dimora" from *Faust*, with an evenness of scale that was a revelation. Signora was a first-class accompanist and understood every direction of her husband. At the time they had a dozen students.'

Everything about Italy, its people and places, fascinated him. Like the other Sabatini students, he attended the opera at La Scala, and although he was in the cheap seats in the gallery, the performances of *Aida* and of *Il Barbiere di Siviglia* fired his musical imagination, particularly the singing of tenor Fernando de Lucia as Almaviva in the Rossini work. At weekends he visited the picture gallery of Brera and marvelled at the works of the great Italian masters as well as the gallery's countless volumes of books. It was the Brera Gallery, he would say later, that first inspired his interest in art. He never missed Mass on Sundays, his faith was as strong as ever, and as every week passed his knowledge of the language grew until he was soon able to converse freely with Maestro Sabatini. And back at the *pensione* the Misses Beethams fussed over his welfare and wanted to know more about his progress – and Ireland.

That summer on a visit home on holiday, he and Lily got engaged but with no money in his pocket to buy a ring, he gave her instead the ring he had got as a Christmas present from her father. 'I don't think father ever discovered what had happened,' recalled Lily. 'If he had he would have felt I was deliberately insubordinate.'

On his return to Milan, Maestro Sabatini told him that he could now study his first aria. It was from a long-forgotten opera and eventually when Signora Sabatini played it on the piano he was able to sing it with scarcely a fault. And there was even better news to come. The Maestro had arranged that he make his debut in Savona in Mascagni's *L'Amico Fritz*, a role ideally suited to a light lyric tenor. He would sing under the name of Giovanni Foli, a name Sabatini thought more suitable to his fellow Italians.

The opening night was scheduled for 13 January 1906. Savona was a small seaport town of some fifty thousand people picturesquely situated on the Gulf of Genoa; its opera house was regarded as one of the best acoustically in the country. McCormack was playing the role of Fritz, who is a middle aged and wealthy landowner. At the age of twenty-two young McCormack did not exactly look the part. He was also worried about his lack of experience as an actor. 'I knew I could cope vocally,' he recalled, 'but in those days I didn't appreciate what repose of one's body meant or the use of a gesture in a natural way to convey a point.'

He rehearsed with the rest of the cast for two weeks and felt he was ready for opening night at the Teatro Chiabrera, where the audience was reputed to be noisy and demanding. In spite of his initial nervousness, he sang competently and by the time the last act arrived was in better voice. Knowing, however, that he could not be easily heard over the full sweep of the orchestra, he did not attempt the high B flat in his big aria; instead, he opened his mouth and struck a typical tenor's pose. The audience, believing they heard a beautiful B flat, applauded wildly, and insisted on his repeating the aria.

In his heart he knew that his debut had been far from sensational, although one Italian critic referred to 'Giovanni Foli's beautiful mellow voice.' Back in Milan he recounted to Sabatini every detail of his Savona performances and confessed to his own disappointment. The Maestro was philosophical. 'You must build your career slowly, Giovanni. One day you shall be a big success.'

He was next engaged to sing ten performances of the title role in *Faust* at the Teatro Verdi in Santa Croce sul Arno, near Florence, with a cosmopolitan cast that included a Brazilian Margherita, a Greek Mephistopheles and a Russian-born Valentine; the mixed chorus was made up of local villagers. He would be paid a fee of twenty lire per performance, i.e. about sixteen shillings. He paid his own travelling expenses and lived frugally during the six weeks' rehearsals.

Except for a single setback, he enjoyed his Santa Croce experience. It was something, however, that he would never forget. He was singing the phrase after Margherita's exit in the second act, and came to the high B natural, when suddenly he broke on the top note. Feeling scared, he eased himself off the stage. The amateur chorus, mistaking their cue, walked off after him and the stage was left entirely empty during the playing of the waltz which ends the act. Luckily for McCormack, the fiery Neapolitan conductor was sympathetic to his plight and accepted his explanation, and instead turned his venom on the chorus.

'I felt I sang well as Faust,' remembered the tenor .'There was greater freedom in my upper register and my *mezza-voce* had improved. I was able to tell Maestro Sabatini that I was pleased with myself.'

He had by now picked up a lot of the language and was more at home in Milan and with the Sabatinis. He continued to write regularly to Lily about his progress. He was saddened to learn from her that her father, Patrick Foley, had died. He immediately thought of returning for the funeral but could not afford to do so. When he did go back two months later, in May 1906, he got Mrs Foley's permission to marry her daughter. He was determined not to return to Italy without her. And in the following week he and Lily travelled to Athlone to meet with his parents.

'I liked them and I felt they liked me,' she wrote later. 'Every evening John's parents and the rest of the family gathered round the fire for a sing-song, with John as conductor. Before our departure, he told his parents of our plans to marry.'

The marriage took place in the Pro-Cathedral early on the morning of 2 July 1906. As Lily and her family were still in mourning it was a small and quiet affair. Her wedding costume was a cream suit with a blouse of Irish lace. She recalled that when John arrived at the church, he looked 'pale and nervous, all dressed up in his frock coat and silk hat.'

After the wedding ceremony and breakfast, Lily changed into a brown travelling suit and John doffed his wedding finery for more casual wear as they set out to catch the mail boat for London. Whatever money they had they decided to spend on sight-seeing, opera-going and eating out. To Lily, London had never seemed more enchanting. The highlight for the young tenor was a performance of *La Traviata* with Melba as Violetta and Caruso as Alfredo. He admitted he was so overwhelmed that he was impelled during the interval to turn to Lily, 'That is where I'm going to be one day,' he said, his gaze returning to the stage. 'And let me tell you this, if I ever get my foot in there, they'll have a divil of a job to get me out.'

He returned to Milan with his young bride more hopeful than ever. When he introduced Lily to the Sabatinis, she got the impression they were anxious that John had taken on the responsibilities of married life before being established as a singer. And with so many young singers in the city seeking work, the tenor quickly realised, despite Sabatini's constant encouragement, that he was facing a struggle.

When subsequent auditions came to nothing, Sabatini still would reassure him. 'You are still young, Giovanni. Your voice is not yet mature. But you are on the right lines.'

His last real hope was the audition at La Scala where he would be heard by the powerful Gatti Casazza. Lily sensed that John was nervous and almost too anxious to do well. Later, when he came home, she read the truth in his face. 'I can't remember how I sang,' he said sullenly. 'I only know I flunked the top note. I've done it again. No job.' She felt sorry for him and tried to cheer him up by saying that it might be all for the best in the end.

His failures in Italy hurt him and dented his pride, making him wonder if his light voice would ever earn a living for him in opera, particularly in that country. After some months he and Lily made a decision to return to London where they hoped there would be more opportunities. How sharp and discouraging the struggle can be, he knew now. Yet he was heartened by his wife's optimism. After all, she told him, Vincent O'Brien cannot be that wrong, nor for that matter, Maestro Sabatini.

PART TWO

The London Scene

5

Sir John Murray Scott

A gifted Irish tenor today aged twenty-two years in search of fame and fortune would, I expect, arrive in London armed with a bursary or scholarship to study at an opera studio or to attend vocal lessons with a leading tutor. He may already have been successful at an audition for the Covent Garden chorus or the Glyndebourne Opera, or he may have made his mark at international vocal competitions such as the Belvedere in Vienna or the Cardiff Singer of the World. By now his course would be well chartered, and although this is no guarantee of ultimate success in his chosen profession, it is of significant advantage.

By comparison, John McCormack at the same age was arriving in London with no bursary or opera company to join. He had his own tough furrow to plough. Furthermore, unlike most modern young tenors, he was married and Lily was pregnant, so apart from finding work he had other responsibilities. Money was desperately scarce, his prospects uncertain and there was no powerful patron in sight he could turn to.

Lily McCormack was obviously aware of their poor circumstances, for she had urged her husband to travel third class on the trip back to London. 'I wanted to save as much money as possible, but at first John couldn't see it that way. Shortly afterwards, we found rooms to suit our purse in Torrington Square, where many stage people were living.'

The London music world was fairly close knit and before long the young tenor was introduced to managements and individuals who promised concert engagements. One such was Sam Geddes, manager of the Irish Club in Charing Cross Road, who offered him one Sunday night concert date. On another occasion, he sang for a fee of two guineas as 'assisting artist' at the Palace Pier, Brighton. He auditioned for Charles Manners of the Moody-Manners Opera Company and was invited to join the company for a salary of £8 per week. When he argued that he wanted ten pounds, Manners declared 'he would pay no more as he had no experience.' McCormack flared up. 'I'll allow no one to interfere with the training I've had from Maestro Sabatini.'

Singers need luck, and it came his way through a recording company – the Odeon – who had heard good reports about his singing. It is the kind of offer a modern tenor his age would hardly come by as only the stars or superstars are in demand in this sphere. The contract was for six years, the fee £150 a year, for which he was to make twelve double-sided records a year, mainly of Irish folk songs and drawing-room ballads. He was elated at the swift turn of events, although Lily was to say that even with the contract and money from various concerts it was still a difficult time for them.

They returned for a visit to Dublin where the tenor renewed his friendship with Vincent O'Brien. When he sang at a concert in the home of a wealthy Dublin resident, O'Brien was charmed by his improved artistry and vocal range. Lily stayed on with her mother to have her baby. Back in London her husband went in search of a house to rent as their 'digs' in Torrington Square would soon be too small for a family of three. He also managed to get an audition with Maestro Alberto Visetti, a well-known teacher of singing.

He sang for him and the Italian was impressed enough to give him letters of introduction, one to William Boosey of Chappell's, the other to Arthur Boosey & Co. The two were cousins and keen rivals in the entertainment business. When he called to the office of William Boosey he was told that Mr Boosey was very busy and if he

42

could possibly come back at another time. Exasperated, he went off to Arthur Boosey & Co. and this time was met by a well-dressed and polite young man. He handed him the letter but for some strange reason did not wait for a response; instead he hurried out of the premises. It seems that Boosey was intrigued by the Irishman's behaviour and next day got in touch with Maestro Visetti. An audition was arranged. McCormack sang "The Flower Song" from *Carmen* and the stirring ballad "Nirvana" by Stephen Adams. Boosey was highly impressed and suggested to the accompanist Samuel Liddle that perhaps he could sing "A Farewell", Liddle's latest song composition.

The tenor sang it from the music sheet and Boosey expressed his satisfaction. He engaged him on the spot for one of his Sunday night ballad concerts at the Queen's Hall, at a fee of three guineas. It was to prove a turning point in his career. For so successful was his first appearance that Boosey engaged him for the remaining concerts of the season.

In no time the critics began to take notice of his artistry. The critique in the *Musical Opinion and Music Review* must have particularly pleased McCormack. The writer 'W.B.' observed: 'Contrary to my own precept never to prophesy unless you know, I am about to be guilty of that rash proceeding. I believe that this unheralded singer will – at any rate on the concert platform – be one of the most popular and the most admired tenors of the day.'

Off-stage, it was noticeable around this time that the Irishman could be blunt and outspoken and flare up easily. Not a few people in the business mistook his attitude for arrogance. Arthur Boosey preferred to call it 'Irish enthusiasm.' Was there a danger that in time fame would go to his head? For when he read the rest of the newspaper the views expressed were almost all positive:

'McCormack possesses a singularly fine voice, and sang with great charm and expression,' stated the *Daily Telegraph*. And another critic remarked on 'his genuine tenor voice of particularly agreeable quality, range and power. He sang with wonderful smoothness and beauty of tone and notable feeling.'

In late March 1907, he became a father for the first time when his son Cyril was born in Dublin. Elated, the tenor hastened to be at Lily's bedside and stayed on for the next few days. Soon, however, he was back in London for more concert engagements, the most important of which was his first appearance as a soloist at a Henry Wood symphony concert. A celebrated conductor, Wood had inaugurated London's promenade concerts in 1895 and had also introduced many new works to audiences.

McCormack was eager to make an impression. The rehearsal went well, a fact that eased his nervousness. He was aware that Wood held rigid ideas musically, so he was more careful than usual. 'My object was to please sufficiently to justify being engaged to sing at one of his prestigious Friday night concerts.' He achieved that objective and the following Good Friday made a good impression on the large audience, among them some of the most important names in music in London. It now appeared more than ever that his concert future was assured; opera was another matter. He could see no early international breakthrough.

He was cheered, however, by an invitation from the Dublin Amateur Operatic Society to sing in *Faust* and *Cavalleria Rusticana* and returned not only to begin rehearsals but to rejoin Lily and the baby. He was able to tell her that he had found a suitable house to rent in London.

Barton McGuckin was directing both operatic productions, and though McCormack had already sung the role of Faust in Italian, he would sing it in Dublin in English; it was the same with the Mascagni opera. He was advertised as 'J.F. McCormack' and that he was making his first public appearance in Dublin since returning from Italy. He was joined by experienced singers such as Lillie Dempsey and J.C. Browner and felt more than confident.

Lily attended the first night of *Faust*, in fact it was her first time seeing him perform in opera. She almost forgot about Gounod's

44

music as she gazed on him on stage. 'I may have been prejudiced, but I thought no tenor could ever look as stunning as mine did in his costume of deep purple velvet and mauve satin trimmed with silver lace. I'm sure all our friends and relatives thought the same way. To me he was the sensation of the evening. He did not consider himself an actor, but I could not agree with him. Though he seemed a bit self-conscious when he was not singing, when he was he lost himself entirely in the joy of the music.'

The critics praised his performances as Faust and as Turiddu, especially his diction and expressiveness of tone; the majority of them were less enthusiastic about his 'stilted' acting. Success meant a lot to the young tenor, especially as he had been billed as the star attraction of the Spring Season so he felt he had a lot to prove. The first person to congratulate him was Vincent O'Brien who thought he sang Faust with the most beautiful of tones, in particular the Garden Scene where his voice blended naturally with Lillie Dempsey's Marguerite. The tenor vowed, though, to try to improve his acting as he had not given up hope of making the Covent Garden stage.

By the end of May, Lily and the baby, along with her own sister Peggy, travelled to London and were met by McCormack at Charing Cross station. A cab conveyed them to the house in Streatham Hill. To Lily's delight, her husband had everything ready down to the 'last stick of furniture', as he himself joked. Indeed, there was even a young maid in a cap to open the door. It was a small house but to Lily it was their first home.

When the tenor was invited to sing in the summer of 1907 at a party in the House of Commons for a group of Colonial prime ministers, he was heard by Winston Churchill, who was quick to note that it was the first time since the Act of Union that the Irish Nationalist members in the house had entertained a Minister of the Crown. On the occasion he sang "The Irish Emigrant" and one Colonial Premier said it was enough to bring tears from a stone. More important, however, was his meeting with the young Canadian

45

singer Eva Gauthier, who had been studying in Europe. Earlier she had heard him sing at the Sunday Night Ballad Concerts and wrote to ask him about his teacher. She was a friendly woman and a stylish singer and before he left the Commons she told him of a special reception that week at the home of Sir John Murray Scott and promised to ask Sir John to invite him along.

The Scotts, who lived in a baronial mansion in Connaught Place, were prominent in the music life of London; Sir John was responsible for giving the Wallace art collection to the nation. His sister Mary was a singer and another sister, Alicia, composed songs. They had already heard John McCormack sing and Mary Scott was 'terribly enthusiastic' about his sweet tenor voice, as she described it to Alicia. Sir John had been brought along to hear another singer on the programme, but when asked about his performance remarked, 'Well I don't know about So-and-So. All I know is that the other young man who sang "The Flower Song" – what's his name? – McCormack – he'll go far.'

Sir John was reckoned to be a very astute judge of voices; he was a regular opera-goer at Covent Garden and at the great Continental opera houses. His favourite tenor had been the Italian Giovanni Mario whom he had first heard in *Rigoletto* and *Martha* at Covent Garden. He argued with his friends that the tenor had no equal, so in this context his good impression of McCormack's voice was important for the young Athlone tenor, but he was not to know this at the time.

Sir John was a big man. He towered over first-nighters in the Covent Garden foyer and his booming voice commanded respect. A man of outstanding personality, he was an excellent musician, and was said to play the piano with the lightest touch possible. He used to claim that the true test of a pianist was his or her ability to play the slow movement of Beethoven's "Moonlight Sonata", just as the mark of a singer's skill rose or fell according to the *cantilena*, or the sustained flowing line displayed. Although he was an expert on pictures, on sculpture, and even furniture, his abiding passion was music.

He had a wide circle of friends, among them conductors, composers, politicians, business people, artists, and even members of the royal family. He was known to plough some of his wealth back into the arts, and not surprisingly headed charitable organisations of some influence and prestige. His receptions and dinner parties were renowned and people in the arts world vied for invitations. Already Lily McCormack felt she knew Sir John, for her husband talked a lot about his visit to the house and the people he had met there. 'I knew it meant a lot to John and I was very interested.'

Mary Scott, on that first visit, welcomed him at the door and said later that she was surprised by his appearance. 'His face was thin and drawn, his manner alternatively shy and friendly. In no way did he look the typically well-fed young tenor prone to weight problems.' As they talked, it struck her that while he seemed self-assured. regarding his talent, there was an air of desperation about his urge to get on.

When she reminded him that she had been impressed by his singing at the Queen's Hall, he nodded his head and said, 'It's not enough. I don't want you to think I'm ungrateful. But I've more in me than that. At least, I hope so.'

The young tenor was taken by Sir John's warm greeting and the way he introduced him to his powerful friends. Then he prevailed on him to sing for his guests and he was delighted to oblige; he was joined later in a duet by Mary Scott and, as they sang it together, the beauty of his voice sounded overwhelming in the room. To Mary Scott it was enchanting and before he left the house she begged him to come back again soon and with Lily.

Lily would say later that she found the atmosphere at the Scotts warm and friendly. Mary and Alicia were most cordial, she said, and before long they wanted to visit the McCormack home and to meet baby Cyril. 'I think that Mary Scott became a kind of guardian angel to John and myself.' There was another reason why she valued their friendship, and that was her acute awareness of the demands of

London society and the apprehension she felt confronting it. In this respect, she realised that Mary and Alicia Scott could play a part by smoothing the path.

For his part, John McCormack was flattered by the interest shown in his career by Sir John. The big man listened to what he had to say and what he wanted from life. One day, turning to the tenor, he asked earnestly, 'What do you want, John?'

McCormack, never the one to be circumventive, replied, 'I want to get to Covent Garden.'

CHAPTER

6

Covent Garden Debut

The popular Luciano Pavarotti likes to recall the story of how he arrived on the Covent Garden stage, via Dublin, early in the 1960s. The Dublin Grand Opera Society had engaged him to sing the Duke of Mantua in *Rigoletto*, and as regular opera-goers know, he was an immediate hit, displaying a honeyed lyrical voice and a silvery top register reminiscent of his fellow countryman Beniamino Gigli. One of the performances was attended by Joan Ingpen, the artistic administrator of the Royal Opera House, Covent Garden; she was looking for a young Italian tenor to cover the unpredictable Giuseppe di Stefano in forthcoming performances of *La Boheme*.

While in her estimation Pavarotti was only average as an actor, his voice more than compensated. She had no hesitation in booking him to sing the last performance of *La Boheme*. Subsequently, when di Stefano cancelled all but the premiere and first half of the second performance, the young Pavarotti stepped in and scored a sensational success.

The entry of Irish-born tenors to Covent Garden has not been quite so dramatic, though as success stories they are worth recalling. Joseph O'Mara in the early 1900s sang numerous performances there with the Moody-Manners Company and the Thomas Beecham Company in operas as varied as *Maritana* and *Il Trovatore*. It was around this time that he and McCormack became friendly, and

49

although O'Mara was twenty years his senior, it is said he spoke encouraging words to the young Athlone-born tenor, and they once sang together in a charity concert in Dublin.

Years later Belfast tenor James Johnston became a success at the 'Garden' in Verdi and Puccini operas. He had been invited to sing there after his great successes at Sadler's Wells, especially in Verdi roles. The young lyric tenor Dermot Troy joined Johnston in the late 1950s; he had done well at the Glyndebourne Opera Festival and was eager to sing at Covent Garden and eventually scored successes as Vasek in *The Bartered Bride* and David in *Die Meistersinger*. It was at Covent Garden, recalled James Johnston, that Troy's vocal gifts developed and his fine voice was heard at its best.

John McCormack was to arrive there as a virtual unknown, raw and inexperienced in grand opera, although beginning to make an impression by the middle of 1907 as a highly promising concert artist. True to his word, Sir John Murray Scott arranged for him to see the Covent Garden manager Harry Higgins. The latter wasn't enthusiastic, for as he pointed out to Sir John, 'I've a list as long as your arm, all wanting me to hear them.'

But the voice of Sir John carried weight and before he left the manager's office, he was told to bring along McCormack that week. Higgins was to agree that the tenor's was 'a lovely voice but too small and wouldn't be heard above the orchestra.' Sir John's reply was swift. 'Make your damned orchestra play softer, Harry!'

'The failure of the audition upset John terribly,' Lily McCormack said. 'I think he was reminded again of his La Scala audition and how it had ended his ambitions in Italy. For the first time I sensed a note of disillusionment, as if he began to despair of ever making the operatic stage. Unlike my response in Milan, I could not bring myself now to tell John that it was perhaps for the better. Frankly, I was worried for his sake.'

Sir John Murray Scott still believed in his voice and persuaded Harry Higgins to have the tenor auditioned by Covent Garden's musical director Percy Pitt. He was joined on this occasion by

Maestro Mugnone, from Naples. McCormack was nervous and felt he had not sung well, although the famous Italian conductor praised his Italian pronunciation. Pitt was non-committal.

The tenor found the wait almost unbearable. His operatic future, he knew, depended on the men's decision in the room. It was Pitt who spoke first. 'The management are pleased, and will be glad to engage you for the autumn season,' he said without emotion. 'Will you accept fifteen pounds a week?'

McCormack could scarcely conceal his joy. Turning to Pitt, he replied, 'I would accept anything to get into Covent Garden.'

Lily knew that her husband saw the signing that September of the Covent Garden contract as a cause for celebration. 'John liked to celebrate birthdays, anniversaries, jubilees and success generally, and invited my sister Peggy and me for a champagne dinner at the Carlton Hotel. After all the anxiety over failed auditions we celebrated in style, with John drinking more than his share of good champagne.'

The Scott sisters, Mary and Alicia, shared his joy and already were planning to attend his Covent Garden debut which was scheduled for Saturday, 15 October 1907 as Turiddu in *Cavalleria Rusticana*. While Lily McCormack would say that Sir John Murray Scott was having a big influence musically on her husband's career, Sir John remained cautious and impressed on the young tenor that he still had a great deal to learn. He had seen enough promising operatic careers flounder and young singers disappointed, so he was anxious that McCormack be thoroughly prepared. He thought that the role of Turiddu was a good choice for his Covent Garden debut.

The first rehearsal did not go auspiciously for the tenor. He had turned up in a silk hat and morning coat, and while his colleagues in the cast said little, conductor Ettore Panizza over-reacted and reported him to the management as 'no serious artist.' To its credit, the management listened to Panizza but did nothing. Once they got to know each other conductor and tenor got along fine. And

51

McCormack got along exceedingly well with the cast, especially the young Scandinavian Borghild Bryhn, whose agile voice and acting ability impressed him as Santuzza, and Italian baritone Scandiani, who was singing Alfio; they often conversed in Italian together and he imparted some useful hints to the tenor.

Lily McCormack, meanwhile, was feeling the pressure of the approaching first night. Members of her family making the journey from Dublin enquired about tickets and accommodation; they were naturally anxious to get good seats. She herself was worried lest baby Cyril get ill; she wondered also how her new gown was coming along; it would be of pale pink pleated chiffon and in her hair she'd wear a band of silver brocade. She had no jewels to wear with the gown.

On the day of his debut she hadn't seen much of her husband. That morning he left early to go over the role for the last time at Covent Garden, and after midday would visit the Scotts house in Connaught Place where Sir John had invited him to lunch. Mary Scott and her sister Alicia fussed over him, a fact that didn't altogether help his nervousness. Sir John was typically calm and told him that he had nothing to fear. Noting that the excitement of his impending debut was obviously getting to the young tenor, he suggested that he rest for a few hours in a room upstairs. Later he would call a carriage to take him to Covent Garden.

Before he left the Scotts' house early in the evening, the tenor telephoned Lily and she wished him good luck. The weather was fine and he felt better after the rest. As *Cavalleria Rusticana* preceded *I Pagliacci* on the double bill he went quickly to his dressing room and began to make up. Just as he was finishing, and getting ready to leave the room, Signor Bassi, the tenor who was singing Canio in *I Pagliacci* arrived and looked annoyed to find McCormack sharing the room with him; he scarcely uttered a word.

In the wings he encountered the other principals waiting for their turn to go on. He felt more nervous than ever and *Cavalleria* is not kind to a nervous beginner, for Turiddu has to open with the

"Siciliana" sung off-stage before the curtain rises, as a part of the overture. But he sang the aria confidently and took the top C effortlessly.

His wife Lily and her sister Peggy and the rest of the Foley family from Dublin sat in the fifth row of the stalls. That Lily was both self-conscious and pent-up is evident from her memory of the occasion. 'How well I remember wishing that I could get under the seat and listen from there, instead of having to sit in full view of the audience, wondering if I would faint when the curtain went up. I don't believe I have ever prayed harder than I did that night and I must say, my prayers were answered.'

As the youngest tenor ever to sing a major role at Covent Garden, McCormack had reason to feel proud. Six times he was called before the curtain. Shouts of 'McCormack, McCormack' echoed through the historic house, and though he was too shy to take a call alone, it was clear to all that the ovation was for him.

Undoubtedly, there were many Irish in the audience; at least two hundred and fifty had marched from the old Irish Club in Charing Cross Road to Covent Garden to form, as one loyal member put it, 'a powerful Hibernian claque.' The critic of the *Daily Telegraph* evidently believed that some of the loud applause and enthusiasm had come from the Irish contingent in the house, for he added: 'We need not stop to argue as to how much or how little of it was due to the love of the operas themselves. If it was in support of John McCormack, a young Irish singer of great promise, who as Turiddu took his first operatic plunge, who shall hold his hand against it?'

The tenor admitted to feeling 'tired and elated' after the performance and for a while sat in his dressing room accepting the congratulations of colleagues, including the general manager of the opera house, Neil Forsyth, who shook his hand and congratulated him warmly. 'McCormack, you have done splendidly,' Forsyth said, 'and what a wonderful reception you got.'

The McCormacks rose early next morning and Lily went out to

fetch the morning papers. The reviews were on the whole favourable, although a few critics found the tenor's acting below the normal standard expected at Covent Garden. As usual *The Times* was reserved and after criticising his portrayal of the boorish Turridu, described his singing in Act II as 'more at ease and he used his voice with admirable effect.'

The *Westminister Gazette* summed up: 'On the whole Mr McCormack's debut was successful. His voice is not, indeed, quite large enough for the vast spaces of Covent Garden, but it is certainly one of a very pure and agreeable quality, and he employs it with excellent judgment and taste. He has other qualifications for the operatic stage, too – for one thing, a slim and graceful figure, which attribute alone serves almost to place him in a class by himself among operatic tenors, while his acting, if less conventional at present, is easy and natural. No doubt in time, his voice too will gain in power without, it is hoped, losing any of its sweetness.'

Sir John Murray Scott decided to mark McCormack's Covent Garden debut with a luncheon at one of the city's plush restaurants. John and Lily were greeted on arrival by Sir John and his sisters Mary and Alicia and a host of musical friends. The atmosphere was convivial, the food opulent and the champagne flowed freely. The tenor was in great spirits, as though eager to thank his patron for his faith in him. After toasts were proposed to his success, someone suddenly proposed another to 'The Irish Caruso' and immediately Sir John was seen to frown. He hated comparisons being made between singers, most of all beginners. Lily McCormack recounted later that Sir John took her aside on the occasion and said to her, 'You mustn't let John attempt to copy Caruso. There is only one Caruso and there will be only one John McCormack. With his voice, he will make his own name; he doesn't have to copy anyone. You must see to that.'

And before the party broke up, Sir John had a quiet word with the tenor. 'There are bigger things ahead of you, my boy,' he said with typical sincerity. 'So neglect nothing. Prepare for them. So far you have rewarded my faith in you.'

McCormack, who already had met many young singers striving to build successful careers, realised he was fortunate to have found a patron like Sir John Murray Scott. How he must have been envied by his colleagues. He would be back in Covent Garden again that November to sing Don Ottavio in Mozart's Don Giovanni, an even more important date than his debut.

He worked almost every day with his Covent Garden repetiteur, a Cockney called Waddington, or for short, 'Waddy', who was revered by a generation of singers. To the tenor, he was amazing. '"Waddy" not only played the piano for us at rehearsals but was able to sing everybody's part in the opera, and he sang in any language required. I can say that in ten days "Waddy" made me letter perfect in the part of Don Ottavio.'

Although McCormack was single-minded and outspoken, he could also be a splendid team man. He got on well with the cast of Don Giovanni, particularly the Italian baritone Mario Sammarco, whose Rigoletto was regarded as an incomparable portrayal of the hunched jester. Critics agreed there was something hypnotic about both his acting and his singing, although for the part of the lecherous Don he appeared to lack suavity as well as stature. He was short and looked no romantic.

McCormack usually talked in Italian to the baritone, but Sammarco would good-humouredly say that he wanted to learn English and could he help him. 'As well as rehearsing Mozart's opera I found I had the job also of teaching the Don English,' the tenor used to joke later.

The Donna Anna was a Russian soprano, a woman of large proportions, and beside her the young tenor looked more like her son than her lover. If the critics had expressed reservations about his Turiddu, the opposite was the case as regards his Don Ottavio. 'A great success' was how The Times described his performance, and added, 'The arias were sung with fine taste and vocal finish, while the timbre of the voice is exactly what is wanted in the part.'

'McCormack's singing of "Dalla sua pace" was exquisite,'

commented the *Daily Telegraph*. 'It was an astonishing achievement for a twenty-three year old tenor singing his second role in a major opera.'

The *Daily News* stated that he sang 'with much beauty of voice and instinctive feeling for phrasing.'

Sir John Murray Scott thought his singing of "Il mio tesoro" superb, one of the finest renditions he had heard of the aria. It confirmed his view that the tenor was a natural Mozartian exponent and he looked forward to hearing his Tamino in "The Magic Flute".

Lily McCormack adored him in the part and was taken by his admirable costume. '*Don Giovanni* is not a tenor's opera,' she said, 'it is rather the Don's, but John I thought sang the music beautifully and told me that he loved every moment of the opera.'

'I loved to sing the part of Don Ottavio,' McCormack said, 'and I think I sang it well. I loved everyone else's part also. I used to stand all the time in the wings, so that I should not miss a note of that heaven-inspired music.'

He had proved an important point to the sophisticates of London's operatic world who had little time for ballad evenings or Mascagni's 'inferior music'; they now recognised in the Irish tenor someone who could sing Mozart's elegant music to perfection and that could not be said of many young singers. In their view Covent Garden had made a real discovery.

The Covent Garden management acknowledged the fact and engaged him to sing in the Grand Summer Season of 1908 when one of his partners would be the soprano Luisa Tetrazzini.

He could scarcely believe his luck.

7

Luisa Tetrazzini

McCormack was now in his twenty-fourth year and could be forgiven for regarding the world of the prima donna with a sense of awe. In time he would experience not only its glamorous side but its temperamental, even vindictive elements. Up to now he had performed with first-rate sopranos who could not, however, be classed as divas, so naturally he wondered about Luisa Tetrazzini.

Someone has defined the prima donna as 'a woman who wants her own way' and the description rings true if related, for instance, to the tempestuous Maria Callas. 'A woman who refused compromises' is also apt, if an over-simplification. It would be wrong, though, to confuse their celebrated whims with their innate vocal talent, for in the majority of cases prima donnas have proved themselves outstanding operatic artists worth every inflated fee demanded from managements.

It is said that McCormack was 'wildly excited' at the prospect of singing with Luisa Tetrazzini, who was already gaining a dazzling reputation. That he had been chosen to appear with her in *Rigoletto* was, he felt, clear confirmation of his growing status as a lyric tenor. He was convinced more than ever before that he owed a great deal to the coaching of Maestro Sabatini. 'The Maestro taught me the Italian style of singing,' he'd say with pride.

Covent Garden has often been a happy hunting ground for aspiring divas. In more modern times Joan Sutherland became an overnight star as Lucia, and in the early seventies Kiri Te Kanawa gave a sensational performance as the Countess in *La nozze di Figaro*, and also became an overnight sensation. Years before, Luisa Tetrazzini arrived there in peculiar circumstances. Born in Florence in 1871, she had little formal training as a singer, a fact she candidly admitted. She made her debut at the local opera house in 1890, then like most of the young Italian singers of the day embarked on the provincial opera circuit gaining valuable experience from some of her more experienced colleagues. She was already displaying distinct promise as a coloratura soprano and her voice was ideally suited to the works of Donizetti and Bellini. By the year 1892 she had decided to leave Italy and try her luck in Central and South America where soon her real gifts were discovered.

Although she became famous, her reputation in Europe remained virtually unknown except to a few opera house managements. Covent Garden manager Harry Higgins had booked her to sing in the autumn season of 1907 but fearing empty houses, tried to postpone her debut until the following summer. Tetrazzini was having none of it and threatened legal action. Higgins relented and put her name down to sing Violetta in *La Traviata* as previously arranged.

In her row with the manager it helped that her elder sister Eva – also a singer – was married to the distinguished Italian conductor Cleofonte Companini who had first come to Covent Garden as principal conductor of the Italian seasons in the house. It was said that he actually recommended Luisa Tetrazzini to the management. But the truth was that regular London opera-goers would treat Tetrazzini's debut as they would any other unknown French or Russian soprano.

Tetrazzini was no beauty. Small and plump, she was, apart from her brilliant black eyes, unlikely to attract shoppers in Oxford Street, and at thirty-seven was a comparative late-comer to the glittering operatic scene, so the odds looked decidedly against her. But she triumphed in the same way as Sutherland and Kiri Te Kanawa were to do.

She made her debut on 2 November 1907. Many of the expensive seats remained unbooked up to the morning of the performance, so the management invited friends to fill them. The members of the Italian community in London did, however, turn up in force and gave the house a well-filled appearance by the time the curtain rose. The soprano's impact was immediate and the story goes that at the first interval manager Harry Higgins rushed to telephone Fleet Street to send down some reporters to witness what was obviously going to be in his view no ordinary occasion.

'An unforgettable night,' was how critic Harold Rosenthal described it later, although he did point out that in Act I the audience was somewhat apathetic. The morning paper critics lavished praise on Tetrazzini's performance, with one describing her as 'the new Adelina Patti'.

For days afterwards a queue stretched right out of the Strand as opera-goers who had missed her debut tried to book for tickets. Many would have to wait until the summer season of 1908. In another way, Tetrazzini had achieved more than personal acclaim; she was about to break the dominance of Nellie Melba at Covent Garden where she had ruled for twenty years. Melba was on holidays in her native Australia when the papers headlined the arrival of what some of them described as 'Melba's rival.'

It can be only imagined what the young and raw John McCormack thought of these developments and the wave of publicity surrounding Tetrazzini's success. 'He talked of nothing else for weeks,' his wife Lily recalled. 'I feared that it might worsen his nerves as he approached the opening performance. I told him it was a great honour and that he had no need for anxiety. I think that helped, so did Sir John Murray Scott's words of calm encouragement. He was such a great help to John in this kind of situation.'

Meanwhile, as McCormack set out for the first rehearsal of

Rigoletto on that April morning in 1908, he had no idea of what to expect from Tetrazzini. He had heard stories of how prima donnas could be supercilious at rehearsals and impatient with little known colleagues. He was familiar with the old adage 'acting like a prima donna', so it wasn't far from his mind as he strode into the foyer of Covent Garden where he found most of the cast already assembled, with the Argentinian conductor Ettore Panizza seated at the piano in the corner, playing *arpeggios*. Mario Sammarco was in typical good humour and intent on trying out on the tenor some new English phrases he had picked up since they had sung together in *Don Giovanni*.

McCormack sensed a slight air of tension among the others, however, as they waited for Tetrazzini to arrive. Momentarily there was a babble of women's voices and in flounced the soprano with Edna Thornton, who was singing Maddalena in the opera. She looked relaxed and greeted them with a smile and said how delighted she was to be meeting them. She was anxious, it seemed, to get on with rehearsal. McCormack spoke to her at first in Italian, then slipped into an Irish brogue, a fact that amused her. From the outset, he liked the Italian's affable personality and lack of pretension. He was already looking forward to rehearsing with her.

After her resounding success as Violetta, there was an almost instant clamour by the public for tickets. She had already sung Gilda to acclaim in South America and opera buffs were eagerly awaiting her London debut. Her singing at rehearsals had greatly impressed McCormack; the voice was even and flexible and used with expressive fervour and there was something compelling about her scenes with Rigoletto. When Lily enquired how rehearsals were proceeding, he assured her that the soprano was kindness personified, a splendid colleague.

The excitement surrounding the first night of *Rigoletto* was remarkable even by Covent Garden's standards. The queues began early in the morning, and as the day advanced extra police had to be summoned to control the traffic. As he waited in his dressing room

McCormack was feeling nervous – he wondered would it ever be any other way. It was like no other night, and backstage he could detect the air of expectancy generated by the presence of Tetrazzini. As always, he was comforted by Sir John Murray Scott's words of advice, 'You can do it, John' he had said. 'You must not be afraid.'

For Luisa Tetrazzini it was another night of glorious triumph, though the papers insisted that both Sammarco's tragic jester and McCormack's Duke of Mantua had helped to greatly enhance the evening's performance. In fact, after his solo and duet with Gilda, just before the abduction scene, McCormack was recalled several times. A beaming Tetrazzini took his hand and together they bowed to the delighted audience. It was a moment he was not likely to forget.

While next morning's papers understandably concentrated on the soprano's beguiling Gilda, and to a lesser extent Sammarco, there was much favourable comment for McCormack. *The Times* stated that he 'made quite a furore by his beautiful singing of "La donna e mobile"'. The *Morning Post* pointed out that his voice was eminently suited to the music, and added: 'Mr McCormack sang the aria at the opening of the opera, "Questo o quella" with freedom and warmth, and gave "La donna e mobile" with good tone and delightful abandon.'

The paper, however, thought his Duke was 'not dashing enough and failed to suggest the licentious nature of the character.' For her part, Lily McCormack felt that Tetrazzini's and John's voices blended exceptionally well and although she still preferred his Don Ottavio and his Turiddu, there were moments of *Rigoletto* she enjoyed enormously. And she was already looking forward to his Edgardo in *Lucia di Lammermoor*, again opposite Tetrazzini.

Whenever the tenor recalled his early operatic days, he was always happy to include his performances as Edgardo in that summer of 1908. For in truth *bel canto* suited his agile lyrical tenor and long, expressive *legato* line and uniformity of vocal colour. *Bel canto* has in fact been called 'the best medicine for the voice' and McCormack would not, I believe, have disagreed. *The Times* review of that 1908 *Lucia* stated: 'It was well worth waiting until the final scene for Mr McCormack's admirable singing of the famous tenor aria.'

The fact that he was achieving stardom in opera did not mean that he was neglecting his concert work or recording for the Odeon Company. He had taken part in the whole of the 1907-8 Arthur Boosey ballad concerts and his Odeon recordings included eleven arias and a dozen ballads. Equally important, however, was his meeting with song-writer Charles Marshall, who one afternoon sat at the piano and played a song new to him. After he expressed a liking for it, Marshall said sadly, 'I like it very much, too, but none of the publishers will touch it.'

It was the famous song "I Hear You Calling Me". And when he sang it later at one of Boosey's Sunday Night concerts it was a tremendous success. Indeed, it has remained identified with McCormack's name from that day to this, and his record, first for the Odeon Company and later for Victor, has outsold all his other records.

It was proving an exciting year for the tenor. He was invited to sing in a Royal Command performance at Covent Garden, an Edwardian event that attracted wide attention musically and socially and was normally graced by a member of the royal family. He admitted he was more nervous than usual as he sang excerpts from Bizet's *I Pescatori di Perle* and Gounod's *Faust*. He shared the stage with Tetrazzini and Sammarco in the Bizet scenes and for the first time with Melba as they sang the Garden Scene from *Faust*. In the excitement surrounding the gala evening he scarcely met the diva though from what he could see she and Tetrazzini were entirely different singers.

Lily, who was expecting her second child, had attended the gala performance with her sister Peggy and recalled that the boxes were festooned with gorgeous red roses, and the gowns and jewels of the ladies in the audience were beyond description. Afterwards she was amused by John's wry comment of the scene. 'When I came on stage for the first time the blaze of fire from the breastplate of jewels worn by the Gaekwar of Baroda – who was sitting in a stage box – left me dazzled for a few seconds.'

She was not so amused when her husband confessed that their tickets had each cost ten guineas. 'I was shocked,' she said. Shortly afterwards she attended a charity concert at the Royal Albert Hall organised by Sir John Murray Scott, at which John sang "I Hear You Calling Me" and a few Italian songs. She admitted that she always felt more relaxed at concerts as John seemed less nervous beforehand than on operatic nights.

She returned to Dublin that July of 1909 to have her baby, leaving her husband behind to fulfil some concert engagements. To her surprise, he had decided to buy a house in Hampstead and furnish it with the proceeds of the sale of the furniture of their rented house in Streatham Hill. To Lily it smacked of extravagance, but she knew by now that when her husband made up his mind he would not change it for love or money. Two weeks after the birth of their daughter Gwen, she returned to London to be met by John who conveyed her to Rosaleen House, their new home. It was beautifully furnished and there was a gleaming new car parked in the driveway. She wondered where the money had come from for this 'display of luxury'.

When he confessed that he had borrowed some 'hard cash' from Sir John Murray Scott, she was naturally taken aback and was about to be angry with him when he remarked with a typical smile, 'Lily, you know as well as I do that nothing venture, nothing win, so let's not talk about it. I'll take care of it.'

She learned later that Sir John was appalled by her husband's request for money and immediately insisted that it be repaid on a specified date, which was agreed. But John did admit, 'I had the devil's own time doing it, even singing three performances a week at Covent Garden and accepting every concert that came my way.'

His action raises the question of the size of the fees he was getting at the time, and although they were presumably nowhere near those of Tetrazzini, Melba or Caruso, they cannot have been that small either, as he was singing principal roles.

It was plain that he would have to curb his extravagance if he hoped to remain solvent.

8

No Whiff of Scandal

Opera has never been without its backstage gossip and whiff of scandal. Covent Garden, I remember, a few years ago was agog about the passionate affair between a handsome Spanish tenor and an alluring Italian soprano; earlier, it was the case of the attractive English mezzo who walked out on her Welsh-born tenor husband for a lesser known colleague. Even Wexford Festival has not been immune from fun and gossip. I can well recall the story of the romantic young Irish politician who made unsubtle advances in a local hotel to a ravishing coloured soprano only to be rudely rejected.

It was no different in the Covent Garden of McCormack's time, when prima donnas occasionally provided backstage gossip; it was readily accepted in the social and operatic scene and one can imagine how spiteful ladies revelled in retailing the latest snippets of gossip that fell into their laps. When L.A.G. Strong was collaborating with McCormack on a book on his life for an English publisher in the early 1940s, I've no doubt they discussed the subject of scandal in and around Covent Garden, and although the tenor was understandably cautious, Strong concluded that young artists were vulnerable in such a liberal atmosphere. As he noted in his book:

> So John, thanks to his own good sense and to the good offices of Sir John Murray Scott and, more than anything, to the care which Lily took of him, avoided all

65

the snares that beset the young artist who has made a success. His head was not turned, either by the praise of critics or the adoration of that host of women with more money than sense, and more susceptibility than either, who besiege artists of all kinds. A good-looking boy with a tenor voice, and a great future before him for all to see – he was a marvellous bait. How hungrily would they have swallowed him, if they had the chance. But they did not get it. John was in good hands. And, for all his youth and lack of experience, he had strength and character.

If Lily McCormack was conscious of the pitfalls, as Strong put it, facing her husband in such a scene she made no reference to it in her autobiography, which suggests that she either ignored the possibility or her trust in him was so implicit that she had no fears. In a reference, though, to Luisa Tetrazzini, she did state: 'She was quite taken by my handsome young husband and never tried to hide it, even from me. John was tremendously flattered by the diva's attentions and their mutual regard worked out admirably for them both. They sang some of the most superb performances I have ever heard, breath for breath, note for note.'

McCormack, we are told, could be witty and a fine raconteur, so one can assume that if pressed hard enough his memories of those London days would be immensely entertaining. The trouble is that most of the books about him are dull and lack humour. The writers who knew him and talked with him were unable to inject enough life into their accounts. There are hints of his wit and humour in Lily McCormack's book and it is, on the whole, a valuable account of his exciting career and the people he encountered along the way.

There were occasions, though, when the tenor took himself too seriously. Looking back on his early Covent Garden days, he was quoted as saying, 'I was aware of my youth, and my sudden rise from obscurity into Covent Garden and concert popularity in a few months, were topics of conversation. There were pessimists, who hinted that I might not last, but their smallness did not affect me.'

With his talent had he, one is prompted to ask, any real need to worry about small-minded people? Was this attitude merely an Irish failing that is prevalent in our people to this day? At other times McCormack could be big, his personality more expansive, as for example when he chatted easily to operatic stars or mixed comfortably with foreign ambassadors, renowned authors and prominent politicians. If L.A.G. Strong considered him vulnerable, I doubt whether the tenor shared the same view. At the time he had scarcely time to think about the 'snares' as Strong put it, for in his case the work ethic was all important, or at least the equal of his home commitments. And he was ambitious to get on and proud of each of his successes.

He may well have discussed privately with Strong the pretty sopranos or mezzos he encountered and perhaps used his acerbic wit to describe them, but unfortunately he failed to tell his readers. So if one is looking for any whiff of scandal in the singer's career at this point, there is none to report. As far as one can gather, he was a faithful husband and a practising Catholic, and he had in his wife Lily an inspiring partner. L.A. G. Strong acknowledged this fact in his writings and left it at that.

The tenor was by now extending his repertoire to embrace oratorio. He sang a performance of *Elijah* at the Birmingham Festival as well as the Verdi *Requiem*. The latter, it seems, had gone badly for the singers and they did not disguise their disappointment. In the artists' room afterwards they were surprised by the arrival of a man in his fifties with a flowing moustache. He went straight up to the mezzo-soprano Muriel Foster and said bluntly, 'That's the worst performance of Verdi's *Requiem* I've ever heard.'

Perplexed, the singers looked at each other. McCormack, in characteristic fashion, flared up and said to baritone Clarence Whitehill, 'Who the blazes is that major-general and what does he mean by rushing in here and giving his opinion unasked?'

'Good heavens,' Whitehall replied, 'that's no general. That's Sir Edward Elgar.'

Elgar was by then famous. His *Enigma Variations* for orchestra, and his oratorio *The Dream of Gerontius* were being performed regularly. What irked McCormack was the fact that he knew soprano Madame Ackté was to blame for the failure of the *Requiem* as she had been 'all at sea' in the music. He now resented Elgar pointing the finger at all the cast.

'After all,' said Whitehill, 'Sir Edward Elgar ought to know something about music.'

'He may that,' McCormack replied, 'but thank God his music is better than his manners.'

It would be many years later before both men made it up; in fact not until he next met Elgar at the Royal Albert Hall and reminded him of the performance in Birmingham. By then the composer had completely forgotten the episode. After shaking hands, McCormack told him that he had always enjoyed singing *The Dream of Gerontius*; before long they were drinking champagne together.

Like most artists, he experienced highs and lows, but he tried hard to keep a balance. He agreed to sing a performance of Handel's *Samson* for the Welsh Choral Society in Liverpool and for some reason only known to himself, did not study the part. As he told his biographer L.A.G. Strong later, 'Disaster was averted only by the quick wit and the voice of the conductor Harry Evans.'

According to Strong's account, the tenor 'went to pieces' in his big duet with bass Herbert Brown. Evans suddenly came to his rescue and took up the cue. The line was "Go, baffled coward, go!" and McCormack felt that the conductor sang it with unusual emphasis and point. 'If I could have run from the platform I would have,' he later said. He vowed never again to tackle a new work without thorough preparation.

There were less stressful days ahead. Touring with Fritz Kreisler, he got to know the brilliant violinist well and their friendship endured. Although the concerts were a failure commercially, he said he had got excellent advice from the violinist about musicianship. And he counted himself privileged to tour with the Italian virtuoso pianist and composer Ferruccio Busoni. From the outset, they conversed in Italian and genuinely enjoyed each other's company. He came to admire Busoni's artistry and playing enormously. Finding him almost in tears one night after Chopin's C Minor Nocturne, the pianist said, 'Giovanni, come out front, and I will play an encore for yourself.'

He proceeded to play Liszt's arrangement of the *Rigoletto* quartet with 'thrilling fire and vehemence.' When, with the audience McCormack called 'Bravo!' he received a knowing wink. The pair had a champagne supper that lasted into the night.

For the most part he got on well with Italian singers and musicians. They shared his sense of humour and admired his fluency in the language. Mario Sammarco remained a firm friend and when rehearsing an opera they often dined together. One afternoon, he told the tenor that he had recommended him to the San Carlo Opera for the role of the Duke in *Rigoletto*.

'You sing it so well, Giovanni,' the baritone said. 'And that is what I told the management.'

Shortly afterwards the tenor was invited to Naples for his Italian debut in the opera. Lily decided to accompany him on the journey and en route they stopped off in Milan to visit their old friends, the Sabatinis. She remembered it as a warm and happy re-union. 'The Maestro insisted that John sing for him. As he said, "I will see Giovanni if you have formed any bad habits."'

'For the next half an hour,' admitted McCormack, 'the Maestro stripped my voice bare; then Signora Sabatini came into the studio and sat at the piano and began to play operatic arias her husband insisted he must hear me sing. He let me finish each one, then he would discuss the music and suggest changes which I instantly agreed would add to their interpretative value. I finished a wiser and better singer.'

Next day the McCormacks reached Naples in good time and proceeded without delay to the Excelsior Hotel. With time to spare before rehearsals at the San Carlo they took in some sight-seeing of the city and later visited the shops. Lily recalled that in a milliner's window they saw a huge Merry Widow hat of amethyst silk with five matching plumes and as she happened to be wearing a dress of the same shade her husband insisted she try on the creation. 'I could tell at a glance it was much too overpowering for me and it was evident from the expression on John's face when he asked the price that it was expensive, but nothing would do but that I must try it on and before I could say a word, he had bought it. I'm glad to say he thought it becoming, which was more than I did. If I had a dress or a hat he didn't like he'd say, "Please wear that when I'm not around." Then, naturally I never wanted to wear it at all.'

If the tenor was hoping for a repeat of his Covent Garden success in *Rigoletto*, he was to be disappointed. He admitted he got applause but no cries of 'Bravo!' or a standing ovation. 'I'm afraid I cannot put this engagement down as one of my major triumphs. Frankly it was not.'

Lily was to give her own version. 'The audience, though not roused to great acclaim, were at least complimentary in their applause. I think Italian audiences like a more robust voice than John's.'

It was during his visit to the city that he encountered for the first time a member of The Claque, or the mafioso of the opera world. The man called at his hotel and guaranteed him success at the San Carlo. As he unashamedly said, 'My men come to the opera every night and applaud the artists.'

The tenor had already heard of them and with typical bluntness told the man he couldn't afford to pay for applause, which was true as he had paid his own expenses from London to Naples. 'Then you will be a failure,' insisted the Italian. McCormack decided it was more discreet to pay up. But there was the question of the press notices – they, too, had to be paid for. Although he was flabbergasted, he agreed to do so for the sake of further argument. The funny thing was that he felt he was paying out his lira for nothing, as he did not believe The Claque could actually ensure a singer's success. And after the first night of *Rigoletto*, when neither they nor the 'paid' newspapers seemed to matter, he suspected he was right.

He was relieved to be back in London for the Grand Season at Covent Garden, where he was scheduled to sing principal roles in Lakmé and *The Daughter of the Regiment*, and he would be working also for the first time with the conductor Cleofonte Campanini, a musician he greatly respected. He had seen him conduct at La Scala, Milan, and since then he had worked with some of the greatest singers in the world. In spite of the fact that Luisa Tetrazzini was his partner in *The Daughter of the Regiment*, he was still feeling apprehensive about rehearsing with Campanini as he was reported to be particularly stern with tenors; his brother, Italo Campanini, had been one of the finest tenors in Italy.

He need not have worried, however. The conductor proved to be both understanding and sympathetic and McCormack could say that at rehearsals he had acquired new insights into the music of Donizetti. 'Campanini was the master of the *bel canto* style of singing and how it should be sung,' he later said. 'I enjoyed working with him, and so did Luisa Tetrazzini.'

Together they achieved a notable success in *The Daughter of the Regiment*, with the tenor delivering the ringing high Cs with confidence. Likewise, his performance as Gerald in *Lakmé* suggested that his voice was suited to the French repertoire and at least one influential critic hoped London would hear him soon in *Roméo et Juliette*. He was to describe the Grand Season of 1909 as the most momentous of his career, chiefly because of his success in operas he was singing for the first time, also due to his rapport with Campanini. And it was the conductor who one afternoon called him aside in the foyer of the opera house and said he must meet an American friend.

71

When the tenor turned his head he picked out a small, stoutish man with somewhat piercing eyes and a beard.

'Giovanni,' said Campanini, 'meet Mr Oscar Hammerstein.'

PART THREE

The Manhattan Opera

CHAPTER

9

Oscar Hammerstein

He had heard of the Manhattan Opera House but scarcely a word about Oscar Hammerstein, the man who had dared challenge the might of the Metropolitan, McCormack was now prepared, however, to listen to Hammerstein, who came quickly to the point. He said he had heard him sing in *The Daughter of the Regiment* and liked his performance. 'I can use your voice in my company,' said Hammerstein. 'Would you like to sing for me?'

'I'd be delighted to sing for you, Mr Hammerstein,' replied the tenor, trying to appear nonchalant.

At that moment the American impresario began to talk figures. 'In that case then Mr McCormack I'm prepared to give you a three year contract at seven hundred dollars a week for the first season, nine hundred for the second, and twelve hundred and fifty for the third. Signor Campanini, my general manager and principal conductor, will arrange all the details about your transportation and operatic repertoire. The best of luck.'

As they shook hands over the deal, McCormack was immediately struck by the impresario's quick business-like approach and he felt instinctively that they would get on. 'The man had an ingratiating personality,' he recalled, 'and a certain magnetism that was inescapable. And the offer he made me was simply too good to turn down. I wasn't getting anywhere near that kind of money at Covent

Garden.'

He was unaware at this time that it was Campanini and his sister-in-law Luisa Tetrazzini who had recommended him to Hammerstein, as they both believed he would be popular with American audiences. It is likely also that the tenor was unaware that it was Nellie Melba who had rescued the Manhattan Opera House after initial setbacks. Located on West 34th Street, New York, it had opened its doors on 3 December 1906 with a glittering first night, but in subsequent weeks the box-office receipts were poor and the future looked anything but rosy.

The astute, if somewhat desperate Hammerstein, decided he required a star to turn the box-office round. To the surprise of New York opera buffs, he plumped for Melba, a long-established favourite at the Metropolitan. It was hotly argued that she had turned her back on the Met for the $3,000-a-performance fee offered by Hammerstein; another reason put forward was that at the Manhattan she could pick and choose her operas.

The smiles quickly returned to Hammerstein's plump face, for within days of the announcement that the diva would sing Violetta in *La Traviata* on 2 January 1907 the house was sold out. And until her last appearance there on 25 March in the same year she drew the crowds. 'MELBA SAVES THE MANHATTAN' headlined one New York paper, and the assertion was correct, even if the paper overlooked some of the other outstanding stars who sang there.

The amazing Oscar Hammerstein continued to attract attention. His boast that in time the Manhattan would be a serious rival to the Met looked like coming true, though the cynics still expressed their doubts. Nearly every paper carried his profile, and it revealed an impressive record. He began his working life in a cigar factory spreading tobacco, but before long he invented a machine that could do the job more efficiently. His patents on this and other inventions made him a rich man, free to devote himself entirely to his passionate interest in the theatre. His great ambition was to produce opera in New York and it didn't seem to worry him that he had to

THE NEWLY-WEDS...
John and Lily
McCormack.

JOHN (with baby Cyril McCormack in his arms) and his wife Lily (right) on a visit to his parents Andrew and Hannah McCormack at their home, 5 Auburn Terrace, Athlone.

FASCINATING study of young Lily Foley.

THE TENOR... at the time of his Covent Garden debut in the year 1907.

PICTURED with his mother and father at their home in Greystones 1925.

LILY AND JOHN... at Leopardstown races with Golden Lullaby, one of their horses.

COUNT CYRIL McCORMACK... relaxing at his home
Courtfoyle, Co. Wicklow in 1984.

Resplendent in his papal uniform.

Wearing the tenor solo medal he won at the Dublin Feis Ceoil.

GWEN PYKE... the tenor's only daughter is back living in Ireland after sixty years.

CYRIL McCORMACK... taking the sun in the rose garden of Courtfoyle.

HAPPY FOURSOME... Liam Breen, Gwen Pyke,
Canon Sydney MacEwan and Count Cyril McCormack.

compete with the renowned Metropolitan Opera House.

As McCormack learned more about the impresario he felt his decision to go to New York was the right one. When he sought the opinion of Sir John Murray Scott, the big man agreed with him wholeheartedly, describing the offer as 'the chance of a lifetime.' Not surprisingly, he drew comparison between the London and New York artists' fees and argued that the Americans had more money to spend on singers. 'Have no fears,' added Sir John, 'you are doing the right thing.'

Secretly, the tenor had been apprehensive as he, too, had heard stories that the Manhattan would not survive. He was heartened, however, by Lily's optimistic view. From what her husband had told her she felt Hammerstein was no ordinary impresario; he was rich and trusted and apparently treated his singers well. She urged John to 'give it a try', that he had more to gain than lose.

As usual they celebrated in style, except for one snag. She had intended staying at home with her sister Peggy and the children in Hampstead but now her husband wouldn't hear of it. 'You can't do that, Lily,' John had complained. 'If you stay here to look after the children, who's going to look after me in America?'

Early in that October 1909 the McCormacks travelled to Dublin to say their farewells to Lily's family, with the tenor as usual spending a little time with Vincent O'Brien who had followed his career with the utmost interest. He showed no surprise when told of his Manhattan engagements, as though he had come to expect this and more from his old pupil. While Lily stayed for a day or two in Dublin, McCormack went to see his own parents in Athlone.

As he walked from the railway station to their home, he was stopped by local people who shook his hand warmly. 'Some of these people knew me as a boy playing in the streets and they now seemed happy to congratulate me on my successes,' he recalled. 'But as they wanted to hear more from me, I thought I'd never get to my parents' house.'

His mother Hannah was the first to greet him with a typical show of affection, then his father Andrew and after that his sisters and his brother Jim. He was in time to join them for lunch in the dining-room and tried to answer all their questions. He was a little amused that his mother was more interested in Lily and the children than in details of Covent Garden operas or the Hammerstein contract, but in lighter moments he used to joke that women usually got their priorities right. Nothing had changed, it was still the happy home he had left a few years before, and he could set out happily for America with his family's blessing.

A week later, on 15 October, he and Lily sailed from Queenstown on the liner *Kaiser Wilhelm II*. He had been moved by the emotional scenes on shore as relatives hugged and kissed their departing ones. At least, he knew his own stay in America wasn't permanent. That night he paced the deck for a time and watched the stars rise in the clear sky and a brisk wind make the atmosphere cool. In a more reflective moment he wondered what lay ahead of him. Could he repeat his London successes in New York, for instance? As he would be singing alongside Tetrazzini and Sammarco again, he felt he could. By the time he strode below deck he was filled with hope and a fresh optimism.

If he had hoped to rest his voice, he was in for a surprise. He was prevailed on to sing at the ship's concert, and was accompanied by a charming girl from Boston. As the ship was rolling, however, in the rough seas the concert was rather spoiled. The tenor was to remark, 'Between trying to keep myself on my feet while singing and keeping my accompanist on her feet while playing, I had a divil's own time.'

The voyage was proving uneventful, but then he always accepted there was a certain monotony about cruising at sea, such as the daily deck walks, the lolling in chairs, meals, a bit of gossip and sleep. At other times he studied new songs and operatic scores. Lily was engrossed in books she had purchased in Dublin and she also liked to chat about the children and their own American visit. After the busy operatic season in London, she welcomed the relaxed air of the sea cruise.

When he heard that Gustav Mahler was on board, McCormack expressed a wish to meet him but learned that the Austrian composer was seeing nobody. He was, it seems, returning to New York to take up a two-year contract to conduct the Philharmonic Orchestra. It was rumoured he was suffering from a heart complaint.

The tenor's arrival in New York was in stark contrast to five years previously, when he was feeling seasick after a rough voyage and had still to face the train journey to St. Louis for the World Fair. Awaiting him now was Hammerstein's special press agent, Billy Guard, and a photographer, and before he and Lily set out for their hotel on 8th Avenue, they were photographed together and he himself answered reporters' questions. Whether he liked it or not, he was being given celebrity status. It was the way Oscar Hammerstein organised things and ensured publicity for his star singers.

McCormack was scheduled to open the season in *La Traviata* on 10 November with Tetrazzini and Sammarco. Rehearsals, as expected, went exceedingly smoothly; the trio had after all sung together in numerous operas and were off-stage friends. A problem arose, however, for the tenor on the Sunday before the opening night when he went down with a sudden attack of flu and his doctor, Dr Alfred du Pont, expressed the view that he didn't think he would be well enough for the first night on the following Wednesday.

Knowing her husband's stubborn nature, Lily tried to calm him and pleaded with him to do as the doctor urged. 'I'll do anything to sing,' her husband replied, with a hint of panic. 'I'll take anything the doctor prescribes. I'm going to sing.'

Hammerstein was in constant touch with Lily. She admitted her husband was still feverish and that Dr du Pont felt he would be unable to go on. By Tuesday the impresario had arranged for an Italian tenor to stand by to take his place. When McCormack heard this, he panicked. 'I remember it sent him into such a fever,' recalled Lily, 'that the doctor decided to take a chance and let him sing.'

Looking back, she confessed it was a harrowing evening for her. John was literally going from his bed to the opera house and she wondered if he would have the stamina to carry the role of Alfredo. She was relieved that Dr du Pont would be standing in the wings ready for any emergency. She heaved a sign of relief, however, when the curtain finally came down. 'I don't think I ever sat through an opera so pent-up, though after the first act I sensed that John was determined to see it through. And, to my astonishment, his voice was clear as a bell and he received a special ovation, as an announcement had already been made that he might not be able to sing.'

The *New York Herald* summed up under the heading, 'PHYSICIAN ALWAYS NEAR': Despite his illness, McCormack made an excellent impression. Blessed with a robust frame and pleasant face, the audience liked him from the start.'

'The tenor is a decided acquisition to the company,' commented the *New York Evening Post*. 'He is a pure lyric tenor, with a carefully trained voice: pure, clear, even and flexible, and naturally placed. His tones are always true and sympathetic, and his *mezza voce* was most effective. At the outset, in addition to his apparent physical suffering, he was palpably nervous, but Madame Tetrazzini came to his rescue by crossing the stage and giving him a gentle pat of encouragement.'

He was back to his best voice a week later when he sang the role of Edgardo in *Lucia di Lammermoor*, with the critics unanimous in their praise of his expressive singing. He went on that season to sing Rodolfo, the Duke of Mantua, and Tonio in *The Daughter of the Regiment*, a part in which by now he was greatly admired. 'The tenor aria in the second part, "Pier viver vicini a Maria",' stated the *New York Herald* 'was so admirably sung as to win some of the most enthusiastic applause of the evening. He had to repeat it.'

Lily McCormack, meanwhile, was enjoying herself no end in New York. 'We had a wonderful winter,' she recalled. Invitations to homes and dinner parties flowed into their hotel, one in particular at the home of composer Victor Herbert being a memorable affair. They made new friends but because of his operatic and concert engagements McCormack had to curtail his party-going. Lily admitted she had fallen in love with the city and its people. 'I adored the way they regarded music and opera and how they rewarded their artists. Only the best was good enough for them and in that case they were prepared to pay for it.'

The city was enjoying a wonderful feast of opera, with the rivalry between the Metropolitan and Manhattan opera houses razor-keen. The brilliant team of Giulio Gatti-Casazzi and Arturo Toscanini had taken over at the Met and were determined to maintain the house's pre-eminence. They decided to stage Puccini's *La Boheme* with Enrico Caruso and Geraldine Farrar.

Oscar Hammerstein was tipped off about their plans and made arrangements to stage his own *Boheme* with John McCormack as Rodolfo and the beautiful Lina Cavalieri as Mimi. 'They may win the singing contest,' said the impresario, 'but we'll get the prize for good looks.'

The *Bohemes* caught the imagination of all New York opera lovers and were sold out within a few days. Lily McCormack was naturally at the Manhattan to see John sing Rodolfo, though on her own admission she wished she could be in the two opera houses at the same time. One of her friends, however, took seats for both performances and he and his daughters alternated, hearing half at each house.

When the opera was over at the Manhattan, Hammerstein's only comment was, 'Good work, Mike. And we rang down our curtain six minutes ahead of them.'

The ebullient impresario had always addressed McCormack as 'Mike' and the tenor had never bothered to correct him. He remembered *La Boheme* for another reason. Lina Cavalieri over-acted in the part of Mimi to the point where he was prompted to remark later, 'I tried in my quiet way to keep up with her in the first three acts, but in the last – well, she didn't act me off the stage, but she pretty nearly acted me off the bed on which she lay dying, and

81

she literally acted my wig off in the ecstasy of her love. I didn't tear my hair in paroxysms of grief at her death. She tore it for me. In fact, I had to buy a new wig for my next performance – and damned expensive it was too.'

There were other memories of his stage heroines that stayed with him long after the final curtains came down. He liked to recall the story of Tetrazzini in *La Traviata* when, as usual, she was tightly laced and corseted. One evening for some unknown reason she had left her corsets off. In the last act, as she lay dying, he rushed in and grabbed her in his arms and to his surprise he felt 'a huge bundle of fat, or what seemed like a couple of "Michelin Tyres"! She started to laugh, so did he, and he never quite knew how they managed to end the last act.

On another occasion, he was singing *Cavalleria Rusticana* with Carmen Melis, a fiery Chilean, when she protested at the dress rehearsal that he was too reserved and quiet as her Sicilian lover. She expected passion from her Turiddu. In one scene he is supposed to cast Santuzza from him in a fit of anger. The tenor was gentle about it, which made Melis mad. 'Do not be afraid, Use your strength when you throw me across the stage. I can take care of myself.'

He took her at her word the following evening, and hurled her from him with such vigour that she landed in the wings on the far side of the stage. He was terrified. Momentarily, she came on limping. The audience applauded, believing it was a bit of stage business. All he could do was to apologise profusely. He was certain she must be 'black and blue' from the fall.

There were twenty-one operas in his repertoire during these years of which his favourites were *La Boheme, Don Giovanni, The Daughter of the Regiment* and *La Traviata*. When the New York season closed, the Manhattan Opera went on tour. He treasured the memory of a later *Don Giovanni* in Boston, conducted by the great Felix Weingartner. When he finished the aria "Il mio tesoro", Weingartner laid down his baton in order to lead the applause himself.

When the company visited Washington they were honoured by the presence of President Taft at a performance. He invited the tenor to lunch with him next day at the White House. 'Before the luncheon John suffered a worse attack of nerves than before an opera,' recalled Lily. 'It was a men's luncheon and, being extremely shy, he couldn't see how he was going to face it without me. I went with him as far as the White House and we walked twice around it before he got up his courage to go in.'

If the story had come from anyone else, it would be hard to accept it, but Lily is consistent about her husband's faults as well as his virtues and I don't doubt it. It is, nevertheless, extraordinary in view of the fact that by this time he had faced audiences in London and New York and though invariably nervous, Lily had never to walk him twice around an opera house before he went to his dressing room. She did add, though, that he enjoyed himself at the President's 'stag party' and arrived back at their hotel later with a white cigar, but the fact remains that for him it was sometimes an ordeal facing famous people.

The company's visit to Philadelphia was to prove important for the tenor. Apart from singing at the new Oscar Hammerstein opera house in the city, which he considered an honour, he got the opportunity of meeting executives from the Victor Recording Company. They had come to hear him sing in *La Boheme* and next day met him at his hotel. It was agreed that he would visit the company's Camden studios, New Jersey, later in the month to record an operatic aria and an Irish song.

McCormack expressed satisfaction at the arrangement and eventually recorded the aria from the last act of *Lucia di Lammermoor*, "Tu che a Dio Spiegasti l'ali", and "Killarney". They were his first records to be released in America. On the strength of these, he was offered a contract. He had, however, two years more to sing for the Odeon Company in London. Victor cabled London and asked Odeon how much they would accept to release the singer. At the same time they cabled the Gramophone Company in London, urging them to pay half of this sum – they had a working agreement with the company about all their artists – the latter scoffed, however, at the idea. Only two years previously they had refused to engage the tenor at any price. The upshot was that Victor decided to pay the whole sum, and on 10 February 1910 they gave the tenor a contract which did not lapse until the 1930s. He was to receive ten thousand dollars in advance of royalties, and ten per cent of the listed price of each record.

By now the McCormacks had been nearly six months away from their children in Hampstead and were longing to get back to England. In April 1910 they bade their farewells to their many new friends and to Oscar Hammerstein and boarded a liner for home. After so much travel they agreed they needed some rest and relaxation. Everything had gone well for the tenor and he had earned more money than ever before. And with the new Victor recording contract under his belt, he could not ask for more.

10

The Melba Legend

'John told me he loved the Covent Garden audiences and found their sincerity and sympathy an inspiration to him to do better,' said Lily McCormack, no doubt remembering how generously they had applauded her husband in his first operas there. For his part, it was the glitter and glamour attached to the Grand Seasons in summer that captivated him as well as singing with the international stars of the day.

He was not back long from America when Covent Garden's manager Neil Forsythe informed him that Madame Melba had asked that he sing Rodolfo to her Mimi in that summer's Grand Season. He was agreeably surprised, but regarded the invitation as a great compliment. 'Please convey my thanks to Madame Melba,' he told Forsythe.

To the tenor she was already a legend on both sides of the Atlantic, and though he had heard stories about her temperamental behaviour and notorious dictatorial manner, he was inclined to reserve judgment until another day. Lily was thrilled with the news, so was Sir John Murray Scott who invited the couple around to his house to celebrate. Mary and Alicia Scott were there and the evening ended with McCormack and Mary Scott singing duets.

The Scotts were fans of Nellie Melba and had seen some of her most exciting performances. Yet the records show that the diva's start as an opera singer in London did not attract unusual attention. When she made her Covent Garden debut in *Lucia di Lammermoor* on 24 May 1888 the house was only half-full. In her autobiography, *Melodies and Memories* she recalled: 'There was a general air of apathy over the stalls and boxes. Even the orchestra, with whom I had had one hasty and slovenly rehearsal, seemed half asleep. It is true that those who were there were wildly enthusiastic, but they were so few they hardly seemed to count.'

Even the newspaper reviews were lack-lustre, save for *The Times* which predicted that 'Madame will in the end be successful there is little reason to doubt.'

A woman of less resilience than Melba would probably have quit the London scene altogether for the Continental opera houses – in fact a year later she was acclaimed as Gilda in Brussels – but she was a fighter. She was soon back at Covent Garden singing Gilda, but again with only moderate success. She had made a powerful friend, however, in Lady de Grey who lured the soprano back for a 'proper re-launch' as Juliette in Gounod's *Roméo et Juliette* with the redoubtable Jean de Reszke as her partner. She surpassed all expectations. *The Sunday Times* noted 'the extraordinary beauty of timbre and her brilliant vocalization.'

Newspaper profiles revealed that she was born Helen Porter Mitchell near Melbourne in 1861 and was well into her twenties before she began singing. By this time she had married and borne her husband a son, but by the time she arrived in Paris to study for an operatic career she had deserted him. Inside the next few years she fell for the twenty-two year old Duke of Orleans, Bourbon Pretender to the French throne, then exiled in England. After what was described 'as an intense and glamorous affair', which was much talked of in musical and social circles, it ended abruptly when the young Duke decided to go his own way.

With her career soaring at Covent Garden, Melba quickly absorbed herself in her singing. If John McCormack had discovered a generous patron in Sir John Murray Scott, then the Australian soprano had found a kindred spirit in Lady de Grey. She was a striking woman, six feet tall, and had a personality to match. Like Sir John, she was regarded as a good judge of a singer. Her husband Earl de Grey was a member of the committee which encouraged impresario Augustus Harris to stage opera at Covent Garden and ensured that the costs of each season were covered by advance subscription.

Throughout the Covent Garden Grand Season, Lady de Grey gave informal Sunday evening parties at her home, Coombe Court, at Kingston, to which leading singers were invited – Melba was a regular guest. On this occasion, it was the turn of McCormack and Maggie Teyte, a soprano he tremendously admired, notably for her exquisite singing of French songs. Among his songs the tenor sang "I Hear You Calling Me" and afterwards Lady de Grey told him that Queen Alexandra wished to speak to him.

During the evening, the Queen had sat beside Lady de Grey and listened with rapt attention to the music. Turning to McCormack, she asked him how he produced the soft A natural on the word 'calling'. He did his best to explain. She said she was a little hard of hearing and could scarcely hear a brass band in the Albert Hall. 'But I can hear that note with perfect distinctness.'

He had, like Melba, arrived at Covent Garden during the golden age of opera, and this would last up to 1914. It was a time, too, when great singers were said to exert real influence on management, most notably in the case of Nellie Melba. The fact that she nominated McCormack as her Rodolfo in her next performance of *La Boheme* was clear evidence of her power. Harold Rosenthal in his book *Opera At Covent Garden* raised the question and added that the extent of her influence would probably never be known.

Melba called such claims 'utterly fantastic', while Covent Garden director Harry Higgins denied that the management of the opera was ever influenced by the prima donna. Rosenthal argues, however, that the 'facts speak for themselves' and that Melba may well have been instrumental in keeping away from Covent Garden some leading singers, including Geraldine Farrar.

Whatever about the extent of her influence, the diva's singing continued to delight London's opera-goers. As a vocalist, she was likened to a bird rather than a human being. 'It is impossible to conceive anything more musical or more flexible than her marvellous voice, which is always as clear as a silver bell,' commented one London critic. Another, however, claimed she lacked charm and the true ring of pathos in her voice.

McCormack would soon be able to judge for himself, not only Melba's voice but her temperament. Together they undertook a short tour in England and before long he learned who was in command. Orders went forth that no one was to take an encore until she had sung one. The tenor regarded this as odd. Why should the great prima donna worry unduly if he was asked for an encore? He was prepared for the sake of peace on the tour to let the order go unchallenged.

Vocally, he had to admit, that she was exquisite. 'Her phrasing was often uninspired,' he recalled, 'yet she sang certain phrases in a way no other singer I had heard could even approach. I attribute it to her perfect technique. And her tone was beautiful, and beautifully placed.'

If his rehearsals with Tetrazzini had been harmonious, it was not always the case during *La Boheme*. At times Melba faulted his stage deportment and when she questioned his singing in the big love duet at the end of Act One he fairly flamed. He shot venomous glances in her direction, but she carried on as though nothing had happened. He began to suspect that she liked baiting her colleagues, as though to show that she was in total control. From time to time, it caused strained relations, although it did not affect musical standards. At rehearsals she strove for perfection and was often an inspiration to the cast around her.

To Melba, McCormack was a gifted but brash young man with much to learn; in his view, she was a domineering woman who supposed that the lightest remark should be listened to in awed silence. They were not long into rehearsals until he mentioned to Lily the problems, but she had by now heard enough stories about prima donnas not to take undue notice. In this respect, she was proving a sensible influence on his career, a fact that he would later acknowledge. And she thought their voices blended beautifully on the first night in *Boheme*. Lily knew that John loved the part of the poet Rodolfo, chiefly because he felt the character rang true and he could identify with it, and Puccini's music was a joy to sing. Despite her display of temperament on occasions, he was deeply grateful to Melba for choosing him to partner her in the opera. In time it would become his favourite operatic role.

Asked about her acting, he said, 'She was just as good or bad as I was. As the Dublin jarveys used to say, "I leave it to yourselves."' He preferred to emphasise her vocal genius. 'As Mimi she was superb. Whoever heard her in *Boheme* will never forget the finale in the third act, especially that phrase beginning "Vorrei che eterno durasse l'inverno"?' To me it was the perfection of the vocal art.'

He reckoned he had sung well in the opera and was thrilled by the warm response of the audience. Imagine his disappointment, therefore, when Puccini expressed scant enthusiasm for his Rodolfo. The renowned composer was on a visit to London and had attended the opera and afterwards they met on the stage. He asked the tenor with whom he had studied the part. He replied that he had learned it note for note from the score. Puccini shrugged his head, and told him there were certain spots *(certi punti)* on which he should consult an expert.

McCormack pressed him to explain the 'spots', but he declined to do so. Puccini is supposed to have replied, 'Oh, it does not matter. Good night, and bravo.'

A few weeks afterwards he was to meet Puccini again at one of Lady de Grey's Sunday night parties, and after dinner sang the duet from the first act of *Tosca* with Madame Edvina, a most expressive singer. After they had finished, the composer came up and thanked the soprano effusively. He had no word for the tenor. Naturally McCormack was puzzled, and thought: 'I couldn't have sung as badly as that. In fact, I know I didn't. Perhaps Puccini did not like Irishmen!'

Melba, on the otherhand, was in his view 'a mass of contradictions.' As he said, 'I have known her to do some of the kindest things, and some of the most cruel. In the matter of sharing applause, I can frankly say she was by far the most selfish singer I ever sang with. Applause was meat and drink to her.'

In musical circles she was accused of being a social climber. Rupert Christiansen, in *Prima Donna*, goes further: 'Melba revelled in money, chic, and titles, candidly announcing, "I'm a damned snob." Lady de Grey was her guide.'

During the Grand Season the diva's party was one of the highlights of the social scene and it was considered an honour to be invited to it, since Melba was known to be very sparing with her invitations to fellow artists. Lily and John McCormack were, therefore, surprised when they were included in her guest list, although the tenor was aware that off-stage she could be a different person.

Lily admitted she was looking forward to the occasion; indeed, she prepared for it diligently. On the recommendation of Mary and Alicia Scott she had her gown made by their own dressmaker; it was emerald green satin trimmed lavishly with Limerick lace. And the evening itself more than exceeded her expectations, as she was to recall in her autobiography.

'The party was a revelation to me – the ladies in their presentation gowns of wonderful brocades and rare laces and jewels beyond all description, and the men in court dress with decorations or vivid uniforms. Melba herself looked as if she had stepped out of the ballroom scene in *Traviata* in a robe of flesh-pink satin with flounces of priceless lace, a wonderful tiara, and all her famous jewels.'

Her own gown may have looked well but soon she found flaws. 'It was so tight that I could scarcely breathe, and looking back, I realise now that it was more for a woman of fifty than one in her early twenties.'

To Lily McCormack, the Australian prima donna was the perfect hostess, a woman capable of turning on the charm. She found it almost impossible to identify her with the singer her husband had said could be wicked and temperamental. She mixed easily with the guests who included singers and socialites, paying special attention it would appear to Lady de Grey and her husband. McCormack enjoyed the champagne and the conversation of ambassadors, impresarios, conductors and the wealthy. As the evening wore on he could be forgiven for forgetting that the hostess was his Mimi, a woman who must never be upstaged.

There was another surprise in store for him before the season was over. Melba invited him to join her touring company to Australia in the following year, 1911, and although this would mean applying to the Covent Garden management to reduce considerably his performances in the Grand Season, he was assured by the diva that this could be done. It was another supreme example of the power she exerted over the management. Since he would be the principal tenor on the tour, it was appealing to him and he had no hesitation in accepting the offer. As always, Lily was supportive and reckoned it would be good for his career prospects; Sir John Murray Scott, with whom he kept in close touch, was likewise in full agreement, although he regretted that the tenor had to cut short the Covent Garden Grand Season.

It wasn't all good news for McCormack. He bitterly regretted to hear that Hammerstein had been bought out by the board of the Metropolitan Opera, who straight away formed the Philadelphia Chicago Opera Company and took over its star performers. After a successful short season in Chicago, where McCormack was conducted by Campanini in Verdi and Puccini operas, the company moved on to Philadelphia for the world premiere of Victor Herbert's *Natoma*, with Mary Garden the dynamic Scots-born soprano, singing the title role of the Indian girl.

To McCormack, *Natoma* was more operetta than grand opera and he regarded his own role of Lieutenant Paul Merrill as fatuous. Joseph Redding's libretto was just as bad. In fact he appealed to Redding at one point as to how he was expected to phrase the sentence, 'Tell me, gentle maiden, have I seen you in my dreams, I wonder?'

The first night audience on 25 February 1911, however, gave an enthusiastic reception to the work, with Herbert taking a bow with the cast at the final curtain. Lily McCormack was already on her way back to England to try to find an urgent replacement for their children's nurse, so missed the prolonged applause. Seemingly, a few of her friends were surprised by her departure from Philadelphia.

'They asked me,' she revealed in her autobiography, 'if I wasn't foolish to put an ocean between me and such a handsome young husband. In those days, I knew very well that John, with his youth, good looks, and his voice, caused many a woman to resent his having a wife. This did not seem unnatural to me, although jealousy of this kind did not exist between John and me.'

That Lily thought fit to mention the matter in the first place was a clear indication that her friends – wise no doubt to the ways of pushy American women – had been advising her of what to expect in the musical world, without however quite realising the powerful bond that existed between the young couple.

By the time *Natoma* opened at the Metropolitan McCormack had more pressing things to think about, for the critics had expressed serious reservations about the new opera and it was already clear it wouldn't survive for long. At least one critic had criticised his poor acting and lack of dramatic impact in the part. But there was unanimous praise for his admirable singing. He couldn't complain. Earlier in the season he had made his Metropolitan debut in *La Traviata* opposite Melba and had been pleased with the reviews. Both the *New York Times* and the *Sun* commented on the tenderness he brought to the role of Alfredo.

He arrived back in England in ample time for the Grand Season, and took part in the gala performance given in honour of the Coronation of King George V. He sang in a scene from Rossini's *The Barber of Seville* with Tetrazzini and Sammarco, and gave fulsome praise to the soprano for her 'vocal fireworks' in the 'Carnival Scene'. The music, he later said, played second fiddle on the occasion to the 'colourful entry of the King and Queen and the roll of the drums before the orchestra broke into the National Anthem.'

Lily McCormack had been disappointed to miss the gala performance. She had decided to sail to Australia with her sister Peggy, children Cyril and Gwen and their new nurse. They would be joined in a few weeks by John. When he came to see them board the old *Themistocles*, he appeared to Lily 'quite forlorn.' She would say later that the voyage 'Down Under' wasn't eventful, except that her sister was paid 'quite a bit of attention from an unattached man.'

McCormack sailed two weeks before the Grand Season had finished, and crossed the Indian Ocean in comparatively calm weather. When he eventually arrived in Adelaide, he was instantly struck by the sheer beauty of the city, an impression that would long stay with him. The 800-mile rail journey to Sydney was none too comfortable as he had to change trains twice. By the time he met Lily and the others he was, in his words, tired and weary.

Melba's return to her native Australia had begun in 1902 with an ambitious tour; seven years later she was back again and set up house in the state of Victoria. It was said that she netted the large sum of £2,350 from one concert alone in 1902, but she was quick to make it known that she had ploughed a considerable amount back into local musical activities. She planned to open the season in Sydney with *La Traviata* and also to present *Rigoletto, Faust, La Boheme* and *Roméo et Juliette*. To McCormack, the Australian air appeared to work wonders with the soprano's temperament. Rehearsals were harmonious and the company responded positively to the more cheerful Melba.

The tenor must have passed on his good impressions to Lily, for she was to note in her autobiography: 'From the outset Melba was in the cheeriest of moods, seeming overjoyed to be back in her native land. No one could be more agreeable when it pleased her to be agreeable, and John was delighted by the friendly air that permeated the company.'

By now she had concluded that the diva and John got on better because she respected him when she found that he, too, had a will of his own and could not be bossed by her, even though she was the great Melba.

The opening night she remembered as 'a brilliant occasion, just like a first night at Covent Garden.' All Sydney it seemed turned out to honour the Australian diva. She gave an inspired performance as Violetta, a fact that McCormack – her Alfredo – was happy to acknowledge. Afterwards, she told the audience that she had realised her life's ambition. 'I have brought Covent Garden to Australia.'

To Lily McCormack it was a glittering night in the theatre, the attire of the men making a colourful background for the evening gowns and sparkling jewels worn by the ladies. It was one of those occasions that she felt relaxed and happy to survey the scene around her.

The papers devoted columns to the tour, stating that it was the most representative audience ever seen in Sydney, and more than one critic described the evening as 'a triumph for Melba and McCormack.' And within days the McCormacks felt the full impact of Australian hospitality as they were showered with invitations to parties and dinner-parties. The tenor had to exercise caution as he was singing in three of the operas.

He hired a car and drove Lily and the others on sight-seeing tours that included the lovely bathing beaches. They were warned, however, that sharks occasionally came in near the shore, and since none of them was able to swim, they had to forego the pleasure.

The beauty of Sydney harbour surpassed their expectations, with Lily finding it spellbinding. Although McCormack found the people insular, he was agreeably taken by their love of music, enthusiasm and appreciation of good singing. 'I will never forget their kindness to me in those days,' he recalled.

He continued to be on excellent terms with Melba and the spirit of the company was the best he had experienced. Once, he was unable to go on as Faust and was replaced by a tenor friend of his, Albert Quesnell. However, when the announcement was made from the stage, the gallery cried out in unison, 'We want John McCormack,' and the cries lasted until the orchestra began the overture. It was an indication of the tremendous impact he had made on local opera-goers.

He next got an opportunity to sing Roméo, a role he had wanted to do for a long time. According to Lily McCormack, he was by now able to afford his own costumes and had them made in London. And he had taken lessons in fencing in case, as he himself said, 'I try to use a sword like a shillelagh.'

He remembered the first night performance for other reasons. He was nearly overcome by the heat in the theatre and perspired freely. And afterwards Lily was to describe his wig as 'awful', something that irked him. She had attended the dress rehearsal and greatly admired the wig he was wearing on that occasion but on the following night he wore a different wig. Furthermore, she had wondered how a woman of Melba's age and weight – she was now over fifty – would look as Juliet, but she was able to say later, 'I think Melba looked and sang her best as Juliet, and on the first night she and John were both in splendid voice.'

After its success the company moved on to Melbourne where the tenor sang Faust and Rodolfo. Melba was baffled, however, that the enthusiasm of the audience in her native city did not compare with that of Sydney and in a fit of depression decided to cut the season short and return to Sydney. McCormack was annoyed and tried to talk the diva out of her decision but she remained unmoved. He had taken a house for the two weeks and Lily and the children were enjoying themselves as never before; now he had to pack up and leave.

Later he returned to the city for concerts, one in particular on New Year's Day 1912 being a huge success. It was during the Australian tour that he saw the true potential of concert work and planned to tackle this side of the business in earnest in future. From Australia he journeyed to New Zealand and was instantly struck by the beauty of the country but perhaps more important, he was overwhelmed by the enthusiasm of his concert audiences.

A few days later he and Lily sailed on the *S.S. Marama* for Vancouver. She noticed how relaxed her husband could be on sea voyages and how he enjoyed talking to fellow passengers. On reaching Honolulu he was prevailed on to give a concert which was nearly abandoned because of hailstones, but he did manage to sing "Mother Machree" and "I Hear You Calling Me".

For Lily it was a real adventure. She was seeing places whose names she had seen before only on maps. She was enchanted, for example, with her first glimpse of 'sleepy little Victoria and the boat trip to Seattle,' where they boarded a train for Portland. To their surprise, Charles Wagner was waiting for them in the lobby of the Multnomah Hotel.

11

Charles Wagner

I f McCormack hoped to pursue a successful concert career in America his first priority was a first-class agent or personal manager with both flair and honesty. When he first encountered Charles Wagner in New York, he was impressed by his professional approach, nerve, and evident knowledge of the entertainment business. The man simply talked in figures.

Wagner was an elegant dresser and certainly looked the part. Fresh-faced with small, shrewd eyes and greying hair, he was an associate director of the Johnston Agency in New York and by the time he met the tenor was already personal manager to two leading artists. He modelled himself on Charles A. Ellis, manager of the Boston Symphony Orchestra, who also handled Melba, Farrar, Kreisler and Rachmaninoff.

To Wagner, John McCormack's potential as a concert artist was immense, so he acted quickly in getting his name on a contract, beating off, as he said, tough competition in the process. And his terms were attractive. The Chicago-Philadelphia Opera Company was paying the tenor $1,200 a week, but he doubled the figure; not only that, he had begun offering him to local managers at $1,500 a concert performance. The contract would come into operation in September of 1912. Both John and Lily McCormack expressed satisfaction with the deal, not knowing then that it would last for the following thirteen years.

Charles Wagner had no doubt that up to this point McCormack had been badly managed by the Wolfsohn-Quinlan Agency. In one tour he was sent out with five other singers, all more or less known in grand opera and called the International Concert Company, and he was not properly exploited. 'I watched these errors of management with interest and was making notes,' recalled Wagner. 'I had other ideas about promoting him correctly.'

Emphasising the tenor's nationality was an unnecessary tactic, he thought, for he truly belonged to the entire musical world. During one particular tour McCormack had been announced as the 'Irish *ballad* singer' which was absurd since his classical song repertoire was extensive. Wagner made no secret of the fact that 'his own entire fortune', as he put it, was tied up in McCormack's future, so he explored every avenue to exploit his talent. He ensured that he was invited back to concert venues at least once or twice a year, something that had not previously occurred.

As time progressed Wagner and McCormack signed new contracts which were mutually beneficial, with the manager at one point sending $3,750 advance payment to London to secure one particular contract. The tenor's earnings began to grow considerably and it was soon obvious that he was on his way to becoming both rich and famous, while being kept busy on all vocal fronts. He sang his first *Don Giovanni* for the Boston Grand Opera Company in the 1912-1913 season, and in that year he gave sixty-seven concerts in America; in May 1913, Melba chose him as her Rodolfo in a gala performance of *La Boheme* at Covent Garden.

Luck continued to play a key part in his career. While in Chicago on a short concert visit he happened to hear the pianist Edwin Schneider accompany the American singer Clarence Whitehall in a hotel rehearsal for a recital that week. Schneider's playing appealed to him for he had what he liked to call, an instinctive touch on the piano. He decided to recommend him to Charles Wagner as someone he'd like to work with on concert tours.

Wagner found the pianist enthusiastic and before long a contract was signed making him McCormack's accompanist. 'I insisted that John sing more Handel, Bach and Mozart in his concert programmes,' Wagner said, 'and Teddy Schneider was happy to meet my wishes. We both knew that John was a splendid exponent of German Lieder, and while he could still include Irish songs, there was a place for Lieder too.'

By now Kerry-born Denis McSweeney had joined Wagner as an associate manager and was paid as his salary a share of the profits of all the artists employed by the agency. The amiable McSweeney was a loyal employee, intelligent and gaining quickly in experience. He had already introduced himself to John and Lily McCormack who at first found his over-enthusiasm off-putting in the extreme.

In his autobiography Charles Wagner put it more strongly. 'McSweeney's wild admiration was so extreme that it plainly annoyed John.' Nonetheless, the tenor would grow to like McSweeney and appreciate his good work. Lily would later say, 'Denis was my friend and advisor till the day he died.'

It is accepted that not a few Kerrymen are gifted poets and writers and in this respect Charles Wagner soon discovered that McSweeney was a prolific letter writer and on tour with an artist would write detailed accounts of places and individuals that never failed to astonish him. Soon Lily McCormack found also that McSweeney had a most efficient secretary. 'When John and Denis went on tour she ran the office expertly, so that they knew things would be running smoothly when they got back.'

Inevitably the question has been asked as to how McCormack achieved such great popularity as a concert artist, and for an answer one has got to look at the career of Luciano Pavarotti, who is undoubtedly the most popular concert artist of our generation. Harbert Breslin, his manager, tried to explain the phenomenon. 'When Luciano and I started out on all this, those years ago, I could see right away that making him widely famous was highly possible. First of all because of his voice and his artistry, but also because of his outgoing personality. It was just his openness and his ability to project himself, and what was being projected was so likeable and so worthwhile.'

That McCormack likewise was able to communicate easily with an audience, and create a unique mood, there is little doubt and as in the case of Pavarotti, he was always himself: friendly and amicable and eager to please. In Charles Wagner he had found a personal manager who could stimulate him to his full potential – in terms of artistry and in terms of audience. Later, Denis McSweeney would carry on the valuable work.

His next concert tour was scheduled for Australia and New Zealand. But before that he sang *The Barber of Seville* in Covent Garden's Grand Season and shared with Tetrazzini a remarkable success. He was particularly gratified because he had studied the role of Almaviva very hard and was delighted to find that one daily newspaper critic described his singing as 'Italianate in tone.' It was something he always wanted to achieve.

Nothing pleased him more, however, than a letter from Sir John Murray Scott praising his performance and recalling that he reminded him of Giovanni Mario in the same role. To McCormack it was an exceptional compliment. Soon afterwards Sir John fell ill and went down to his country house to recuperate. When he could, the tenor visited him and on a few occasions sang some well-known songs for him. As he said, 'I owed this to Sir John. He gave me my start in London and it was something I could never forget even if I wanted to. As long as he lived, he remained a true friend and patron.'

As soon as the Covent Garden season ended he began preparations for a concert tour. Since Teddy Schneider was unable to accompany him he decided to ask his old friend and voice tutor Vincent O'Brien, and went to Dublin with Lily for a few days. He found him as busy as ever, running choirs and teaching the piano, and with no ambition to see the rest of the world.

McCormack, however, could be persuasive and after some initial nodding of his head, O'Brien agreed to join him as accompanist, mainly it seemed because he wanted to get the tenor out of a dilemma. Lily was thrilled, for she felt that by John inviting him on tour was in a way repaying the debt he owed him for the help and encouragement he gave him when he most needed it.

McCormack did warn him, however, that it would be a gruelling trip that would take them 'literally round the world.' By now O'Brien's mind was made up and he was actually looking forward to going. 'I think he saw it as an adventure more than a musical exercise,' said Lily. 'And he was of course delighted to be asked.'

From the New York end, Charles Wagner had arranged that Denis McSweeney travel to Australia to supervise the tour. As he explained, 'Knowing that John was not overburdened with diplomatic qualities and realising he needed a kind of managerial valet and go-between, I thought that McSweeney's big handsome self and ready blarney would be invaluable.'

Wagner also knew that McSweeney would keep him fully informed about the tour with his lengthy letters of every detail. Meanwhile, Vincent O'Brien and the McCormacks were by now sailing on the high seas, with O'Brien exhilarated by the voyage. To keep fit, he and McCormack often indulged in sparring and once a powerful McCormack blow injured the other in the ribs. At other times, they went over the musical programmes or examined new songs that the tenor had been given by song-writers in London.

That the tour was eventually to prove a great success can be gauged from McSweeney's first letter to Wagner in which he stated that he and McCormack were getting along famously and the theatres were packed for each of the concerts. Later, the tenor told Wagner that it was the biggest concert tour ever undertaken by an artist in Australia. He had sung in sixteen concerts in Sydney in the first ten weeks, fifteen in Melbourne, and eight in Adelaide and that the girls 'were mad over his lovely Irish eyes and splendid complexion!'

Wagner met the party in San Francisco on their way back and was upset to find that one trunk containing McCormack's operatic and oratorio scores and many valuable early songs and manuscripts was missing. Despite a lengthy search it was never traced. Such was the success of the tour, however, that neither John nor Lily seemed too aggrieved. To Lily the Australian climate suited John's voice and she always felt he sang exceptionally well in opera or concerts there.

Surprisingly, he almost immediately undertook another concert tour in America in that October, 1913, and for the next five months sang in most of the principal cities, although he had yet to achieve success in St. Louis. Wagner and McSweeney worked strenuously on the publicity for the concert there on the night of 31 January and were amply rewarded with a packed house. McCormack was to say he put the city on the musical map.

Before they eventually left for England, he said something that made Lily ponder. 'I wonder if you feel like me,' he had said to her, 'that our home is really here in the United States.' She agreed that it was. She was even more surprised when he added, 'I know my future is here, and if you are sure it's all right with you, I'd like to become and American citizen.'

It was a decision that would have deep implications for him.

12

The Controversial Years

If we accept that an artist of brilliant talent is a free agent, performing where he is wanted, living where he chooses at a particular time, then McCormack had every right not only to leave Britain for America in 1914, but also to take out American citizenship. With the outbreak of war in that year, and in view of his successes in London as a singer in the previous seven years, his decision was bound nevertheless to appear puzzling to patriotic British people.

But neither patriotism nor sentiment was the real issue in this case; the fact remained that he was Irish, so he could not be accused of turning his back on the country at a time when it apparently needed his services most. Unfortunately, that was the way the press saw it: a singer letting down the people who made him famous. Because of his close association with Britain they mistakenly discounted the fact that he was an Irishman. It was an unhappy time for the McCormacks while the controversy lasted and they were the first to admit it. Furthermore, the tenor wasn't used to this kind of criticism – and it undoubtedly hurt.

Lily McCormack in her autobiography stated that 'John's position was rather awkward and altogether difficult.' Later when the papers had gone through and he became officially an American citizen the criticism increased and his enemies, she said, didn't spare him. She admitted that she and John had discussed the matter at length and agreed they could do nothing to stem the criticism.

When L.A.G. Strong came to write his biography of the singer he brought his own perception to one of the unhappiest periods in the tenor's life. The war years formed a chapter in John's life, he said, which he wished to cut short. Strong argued that his decision to leave for America was understandable, for all his prospects, all his future, lay there rather than in Britain. 'This was regarded by many people,' he added, 'as an act of desertion, and he heard himself denounced in Britain and in the Empire as a renegade, whose only motive had been to escape military service. But to a friendly nature like John's it was almost unbearable to feel that he was disliked.'

Before he left London in that year he sang the role of Faust in Boito's opera *Mefistofele* and his performance was critically acclaimed by the critics. He went on to record the arias "Dai campi" and "Giunto sul passo" and they have proved very popular with collectors. A month later in July, the tenor achieved another outstanding success, also at Covent Garden, in Tosca which was by now one of his favourite operas.

In October the McCormacks with their children Cyril and Gwen settled in New York, having found a comfortable apartment at 270 Park Avenue. The tenor began to sing in concerts for the Red Cross, which was raising funds for the war effort, and one of them at the Hippodrome, New York, raised $68,000; a week later the receipts in Chicago amounted to $75,000.

His popularity was undiminished. In his own concerts promoted by Charles Wagner and Denis McSweeney, he continued to fill halls and theatres across the country. At this time Wagner was quoted as saying: 'City after city was bidding for return dates for McCormack. His vogue with the public was soaring, his fees were rising, and the terms of our successive contracts reflected all this.'

It wasn't all work for the tenor. There were amusing episodes, and some not so amusing. Wagner said that McCormack usually took good care of himself on the road. 'John did love to hunt, however, and once, during several days' stay in Dallas, friends insisted he go hunting with them. I told him I thought it hazardous on the day before a concert and in the middle of a heavy concert season, but instead he bought a gun. A rainstorm came up and he returned about dinner time thoroughly drenched. Next day he was quite hoarse, but a doctor managed to get him through the concert. Two days later he was worse, but still able to sing.

'During all this time I hadn't uttered a word of censure. Suddenly John picked up the gun and said, "Here, Charlie you've been damn nice about that hunting trip. I want to give you this gun."'

He was a busy recording artist during this time. He recorded Braga's "Angel's Serenade" with violin obbligato by Fritz Kreisler, the first of many collaborations between the two. His operatic recordings included duets from *La Traviata* and *La Boheme* as well as the quartet from *Rigoletto* with Spanish soprano Lucrezia Bori.

Bori, whose voice blended beautifully with his own, was one of his favourite Mimis – the others being Claudia Muzio, Geraldine Farrar and Melba. During these years the McCormacks invited numerous artists to parties at their Park Avenue apartment, among them Bori, Farrar, Kreisler and Rachmaninoff, and it was here that their children Cyril and Gwen became friendly with the famous and began to take an interest in opera.

In fact, in March 1915 McCormack brought eight-year-old Cyril to a Victor recording studio to record the popular war song, "It's a long way to Tipperary". It is said that Cyril sang in piping tones with a clear Irish accent and his father joined in the refrain. He did the same thing two years later when his little daughter Gwen recorded "Poor Butterfly". And it was around this time that he recorded "Il mio tesoro", one of his most enduring records.

While his records were being snapped up all over America, producing royalties for the tenor in hundreds of thousands of dollars, it was on the concert circuit that he had become an institution. His popularity was comparable with that enjoyed today by Pavarotti and the attendances at his concerts was clear evidence of this. He repeatedly packed Carnegie Hall and the Hippodrome, which accommodated seven thousand people. And twice inside a month he attracted a capacity audience of five thousand to his Sunday night recitals at the Metropolitan Opera House. It was the same story from Boston to San Francisco. He had simply become a phenomenon of the concert circuit.

Lengthy travel meant disruption, however, to his domestic life, a fact that his wife Lily gave much thought to and finally concluded that it could have its positive side. 'We decided, John and I, that not being together all the time was a good way to keep two young people happy. We hated being parted even for a few weeks, but the parting was worthwhile in the joy of homecoming. We wired each other every day and I tried to have a letter waiting for him in each place where he sang; and I must say the children were quite good about writing to him, especially in French to show him how hard they were working. When he came back I would have some new gowns as a surprise and tickets for the latest Broadway plays.'

To get away from the stifling heat of New York in mid-summer, they rented "Pope House" in Darien, Connecticut, described by Lily as a 'charming grey-stone house on the edge of rocks overlooking the water.' Her husband bought a yacht which he named *Macushla* – he had recorded a song of the same name which was enjoying real success. Teddy Schneider holidayed in a cottage nearby and there were also poets and writers in the vicinity. As a hobby McCormack took up fishing and spent many happy hours relaxing with rod and line. For Lily and the children they were idyllic days and they came to hate the thought of returning to New York.

The Metropolitan Opera House loomed for the tenor. During the 1917-18 season he sang Rodolfo in *La Boheme* and as always received mostly favourable notices for his vocal style, although the critic of the *New York Times* thought his singing needed 'a livelier dramatic temperament than his, a potency of more passionate expression.'

The Sun critic did not agree. He stated that the tenor's singing 'excellently suited' the opera. He went on that season to sing Pinkerton in *Madama Butterfly* and Cavaradossi in *Tosca*, 'Dramatically, Mr McCormack is not an ideal Mario', commented the *New York Herald*, but the *New York Times* disagreed. 'Mr McCormack earned an ovation after Cavaradossi's aria in the final act, which he sang quietly seated at the prisoner's table,' the paper stated. 'The tenor has not been in better form in any opera, either during his occasional Metropolitan appearances this season, or years at the Manhattan.'

With the phenomenal sales of his records – not to mention his sell-out concert tours – he hardly needed opera, and since on his own admission he hated rehearsals, it seemed only a matter of time before he sang his last operatic performance. In 1918, for instance, his royalties from recordings alone amounted to $180,000 which was said to exceed those of Enrico Caruso. And his total income, it was claimed, was over $300,000 a year, if not more.

Inevitably his predilection for spending surfaced at this time and he indulged himself in the purchase of some notable paintings, including "Rembrandt's Sister" by the artist himself, "Nymphs Bathing" by Corot, followed by a Gainsborough, a Raeburn, a Romney and a Lawrence. When Lily occasionally complained of extravagance on his part, he laughed aloud and said they were both a pleasure and an investment.

'No matter how I felt about the money John was spending for these paintings,' she recalled, 'I shared his keen pleasure in them, loving to come home at tea time so that I could just sit quietly and enjoy them.'

His spending did not stop there; on the advice of friends he purchased Rocklea in Noroton, a spacious house with ample rooms for the children and their friends, and a music room which McCormack had built on where he and Teddy Schneider could work on rainy days. According to Lily McCormack, the two men were 'meticulous about giving attention to new songs submitted to them. They tried every one, making no quick judgments, always hoping for the best. The good ones were marked "G" and put on the piano; the ones for retrial were marked "R" and laid to one side, and the "N.G.s" were thrown into a large laundry basket to be taken away.'

Unfortunately, it was in Rocklea in November 1918 that McCormack was telephoned with the tragic news that Lily's brother Tom Foley and his wife Charlotte had been lost on the mail boat *Leinster* when it was torpedoed in Dublin Bay, on the way to Holyhead. They had left behind them ten children, five boys and five girls, all under the age of sixteen.

Displaying characteristic generosity, he set about ensuring that the orphans would be covered financially as regards their upbringing and education. Lily's mother and her sister in Dublin had taken in the children and later she made arrangements to adopt the youngest child Kevin and inside a few months he joined Cyril and Gwen to become part of the McCormack household.

Her husband's magnanimous gesture made Lily feel particularly proud, as she knew that he was already looking after his own parents' welfare and to take on the additional care of small children was a large commitment. 'I know one thing,' she recalled, 'both Cyril and Gwen were overjoyed with their new brother.'

As the autumn of 1920 approached the tenor was prepared for yet another tour of Australia and, as before, Denis McSweeney would join John and Lily there. As expected the tour began in a wave of enthusiasm with sell-out houses in Sydney and Melbourne for the first eighteen concerts, confirming McCormack's own view that the audience response in these cities was as warm as ever. It was a different matter in Adelaide, however, when unexpected trouble arose. Seemingly, when the British National Anthem wasn't played a section of the audience protested, and while the tenor was preparing to leave the stage later some of the crowd shouted "Sinn Fein", while others began to sing "God Save the Queen".

He was visibly upset by this unprecedented behaviour. He told McSweeney that he did not wish to sing in further concerts in the

COUNT JOHN McCORMACK... outside his restaurant in Dublin's Andrew Street.

LILY McCORMACK... greeted by Colum O'Brien of the John McCormack
Society as she arrives to talk about "her John" in the 1960's.

THE McCORMACKS... John and Lily, with Vincent O'Brien during the
Eucharistic Congress week in June 1932.

THE O'BRIENS... Oliver and his wife Elizabeth.

COUNT JOHN McCORMACK... and Liam Breen view the picture gallery at the formal re-opening of the refurbished McCormack Foyer in the National Concert Hall.

GRAMOPHONE RECITAL... in the QV.2 restaurant are (Left to Right) Joe Clarke (hon. treas. John McCormack Society,) Count John McCormack, Liam Breen (the society's president) and Donal McNally.

As Don Ottavio in 'Don Giovanni'.

As the Duke in 'Rigoletto'.

NELLIE MELBA... as (top) Rosina in 'The Barber of Seville' and Marguerite in 'Faust' (below).

LUISA TETRAZZINI...
as Oscar in 'A Masked Ball'.

AT THE KELLY HOME IN LISCLOGHER, CO. WESTMEATH... (seated 2nd from left): Mrs Patricia Kelly (daughter of Gwen Pyke, on right) with her daughter Sonja and son Jonathan.

city and that he was prepared to abandon the rest of the Australian tour. Within a few hours he carried out his threat. And in late September he wrote to Charles Wagner telling him of the circumstances surrounding the cancellation of what he called 'that damned tour', and added, 'I have never seen such splendid loyalty and friendship on the one side and on the other the most outrageous rudeness and boorishness and discourtesy.'

McSweeney as usual mailed one of his detailed letters to Wagner explaining the wisdom of the cancellation decision and pointed out that as other demonstrations were being planned against the singer and with the Irish organising counter-demonstrations, in his view the trouble could only worsen. Wagner appeared annoyed with McSweeney and believed he could have done something to 'lower the temperature' and that his 'confrontational approach' had not helped. Since Wagner was not on the spot it is hard to explain how he could blame his associate manager.

McCormack regarded the affair as an attack on his nationalism, a direct result no doubt of his earlier decision to renounce his allegiance to King George and declare his intention of becoming an American citizen. L.A.G. Strong must have discussed in depth this *cause célèbre* when he came to write his book on the tenor, for he speculated on the possible effect it had on him. For one thing, he felt the experiences hardened McCormack and drove him to rely more strongly on inner sanctions.

As he observed: 'But the John of 1918 was warier, coarser, more worldly-wise than the John of 1914. There was a new suspicion behind the eyes, the suspicion of a man who has been hurt and takes care not to uncover himself. Because such caution was foreign to him, for a while John suffered badly. He was able later to open up again and to be his old self, but the scars remained. Even today he is afraid of exposing himself and being misunderstood for his pains; and because he is irremediably open and direct, he is quick at self-mockery before the enemy can thrust at him.'

Strong argued that the tenor emerged from the ordeal of severe criticism a better artist. As he was to put it, 'His success came to the rescue. He leaned on it, and learned from it. It taught him to stand alone. And the moment he learned this, he was able to see how many others had learned it too, and to draw strength from them.'

Nor was it the criticism alone that was stressful. There were the tours themselves, with huge audiences roused to an enthusiasm which was almost frightening; and there were the personalities with which the tours brought him into contact. But he managed to cope as any celebrity like him must learn to cope.

Gordon T. Ledbetter in his biography of McCormack also touched on the stress factor, and stated: 'Even as performers go, McCormack was extremely highly strung. He found release from the strain of continual touring in high living. It did not combine well with a tendency towards obesity. At an early age he presented a rotund figure and one who was in less than a state of prime physical fitness.'

Luciano Pavarotti, who operates of course in the modern jet-age, has acknowledged that vocally concert work is more demanding than singing in opera. For the singer has no rest periods when others carry the evening, no-one to console the audience if you are not in top form, no other element like sets, costumes, dancers and other singers. 'It is the ultimate test for the singer – a *mano* of the vocal world.'

As in the case of a modern-day Pavarotti or Domingo, McCormack was often so busy between recording sessions, recitals and operatic work that he hadn't time to ponder for too long about the disadvantages of his profession, in particular his absences from home. However, April 1922 found him back in New York preparing for a sell-out concert at the Hippodrome. According to Lily's version, he put in a leisurely morning and for a time preoccupied himself with reading the newspapers. Early in the afternoon he strolled in Central Park and seemed his effervescent self. Before lunch he rested for some hours and was already looking forward to the concert. It was during dinner that he complained of a sharp pain in his throat and asked his wife Lily to look at it.

'To my dismay I saw an angry red patch on one side,' she remembered. 'I sent for his throat specialist and he came immediately. He ruled out any concert appearance that evening. I called Denis McSweeney and told him to notify the Hippodrome and to contact the press about the cancellation.'

By morning a severe streptococcal infection of both tonsils had developed and inside the next twenty-four hours his condition had worsened. Soon the newspapers took up the story and before long prayers were being recited in churches for his recovery. It was Holy Week and by Thursday night he was in Lily's words, 'sinking rapidly.' On the following morning, to her surprise, Archbishop Hayes of New York arrived at the house and after imparting his blessing to the tenor placed a relic in his hand. It was his own relic of the True Cross.

Within two days her husband had improved and was out of danger. Lily was convinced that it was the Archbishop's prayers and the relic that saved his life. It was a time of great faith and there were many who accepted her word. It was, though, the closest her husband had come to death. When he eventually recovered, she called the recovery a miracle. And she and John were sure it was when later he visited a renowned Harley Street throat specialist in London and showed him the medical report.

'All I can say is that you have experienced a miracle,' he said to McCormack. 'I can't see how you got through this.'

13

Acclaim in Monte Carlo

H e was in his 39th year when he decided to make his last appearance in grand opera. The decision came as a surprise to his admirers who could be excused for regarding it as premature; in today's context it certainly appears that way. Take the case, for instance, of three of the world's leading tenors who in spite of their ages are still achieving notable successes and have not hinted at retirement from the operatic stage.

Spanish tenor Alfredo Kraus is sixty-eight and delighting audiences as Faust, Werther and Edgardo; he attributes his longevity to his 'clear-sighted, realistic assessment of his voice.' At sixty, Pavarotti is as good as ever in roles such as Riccardo in Verdi's *Un ballo in maschera*, Cavaradossi in *Tosca* and Rodolfo in *Boheme*. Domingo, for his part, is extending his repertoire to embrace Wagnerian roles and though in his mid-fifties, his Otello is as riveting as ever it was.

Admittedly, McCormack intimated that he intended to give up the operatic stage before he was forty, yet few believed he actually would. His decision, one suspects, was precipitated by factors that included a weight problem, pressure of concert work, recording, and perhaps the most obvious reason of all – his financial independence. He often admitted he found rehearsing boring, so it made good sense to concentrate on the concert and recital work that he clearly loved.

When I discussed the question with Count Cyril McCormack in

the nineteen eighties, he said his father had given up singing opera to preserve his voice for years ahead. 'He achieved this by switching entirely from operatic to concert performances; he also reached out to wider audiences. He was a shrewd man and knew the direction he was going and how to achieve vocal longevity.'

At least he bowed out at the zenith of his powers. The Monte Carlo Opera had a unique glamour that made it the mecca for many of the finest singers of the day. McCormack arrived there in February 1922 and was described as a singer who 'enjoys an extraordinary celebrity in America,' so opera-lovers were looking forward to his Cavaradossi, Almaviva and most of all, to his Tamino in Mozart's *The Magic Flute* which was being performed for the first time at the Monte Carlo Opera.

From all accounts, they were not disappointed. Dr Tom Walsh in his history of the Monte Carlo Opera, says the tenor 'caused a real stir' and he was much talked of. One French critic thought his light tenor voice was extraordinarily well placed and used to perfection as Cavaradossi. 'There is not the slightest blemish of bad taste. And the manner in which he sang the last act of Tosca was a real feast of delicacy.'

His 'impeccable artistry' was noted by other French critics in his singing of Tamino's music, though the production itself was described as undistinguished. After his performance as Almaviva in *The Barber of Seville* the great Jean de Reszke, then living and teaching in Nice, told McCormack, 'You are the true redeemer of *bel canto*. My congratulations.'

The tenor was invited back again for the 1923 season and sang Pinkerton in *Madama Butterfly*, Cavaradossi, Almaviva, Lionel in Martha and created the role of Gritzko in *La Foire de Sorotchintzi* by Mussorgsky. The critic Andre Corneau stated that in the latter opera McCormack had found his best role of the season and stated: 'He sang divinely with a sigh of exquisite melancholy, tinged with tenderness, quivering with nostalgic Slavonic charm.'

And though the opera provoked an enormous response and

McCormack took countless bows, the acclaim did not change his mind. He had made his final operatic appearance. One can only assume that his mind was made up long before he arrived in Monte Carlo and that he was fulfilling a promise to himself. Strangely, Lily made no mention in her autobiography of his decision to retire from opera, so presumably it was very much his own. It is likely, though, that he did tell some of his colleagues and friends, for a report appeared in a London newspaper that 'at the height of his talent John McCormack was quitting the concert stage in order to leave his reputation intact.' Apparently someone had got the 'rumour' the wrong way round.

He had enjoyed himself tremendously in Europe. His concerts in Paris, Berlin and Prague were eminently successful; and from Prague he wrote to Lily: 'I could feel that I had the audience in my hand and lost all my nervousness. At the end of the evening people rushed down to the platform and I had to sing three encores. It was funny to hear the people applauding the opening bars of "The Last Rose of Summer".'

In early September he was back in London and as usual Mary and Alicia Scott extended a typically warm welcome; Sir John Murray Scott had passed away after a short illness. Little else had changed in the six years he had been away from the operatic and concert stage, but secretly he wanted again to sing in the city that had made him. Before he left on a short visit to Dublin plans were finalised for his 'comeback' concert on Sunday 6 October at the Queen's Hall.

It was no ordinary visit to Ireland's capital city. The tenor was about to receive a singular honour – the freedom of the city, and there to confer it on him was Lord Mayor Alfie Byrne, a man much revered by the citizens. In his introduction, he stated, 'This is the first time within living memory that this honour was been unanimously accorded to anyone.'

Lily McCormack recalled that she could scarcely hear a word of the speeches, but for her it was sufficient to see the glow of pride on her husband's face as he affixed his signature to the illustrious roll of honour.

It wasn't the tenor's only honour. Papal decorations had already come his way for faithful services to the Church. In 1913, he was made a Commander of the Holy Sepulchre; four years later he received an honorary doctorate of literature from Holy Cross College, Massachusetts, and in 1921 Knight Commander of St Gregory. In 1923 he became Knight Commander of St Silvester. Despite these decorations it could be said that he never wore his religion as a badge; he remained a man's man, at once exuberant and robust of spirit, receptive to witty or ribald stories. The clergy always knew where they stood with the singer.

With the Dublin celebrations behind him, he got down to rehearsals for his Queen's Hall recital. He did not try to disguise the fact that he was anxious. Would the 1914 'scandal' arising out of his departure to America come back to haunt him? 'After a lapse of six years since the war, there was still a considerable amount of feeling against him,' L.A.G. Strong recalled.

Lily McCormack admitted they had received a few menacing letters warning her husband that he would not be welcome in London. They could only assume that the cause of the animosity was the fact that he had become an American citizen. To her relief, John seemed in no way intimidated by the threats and begged her not to worry.

The Queen's Hall was sold out for the recital. 'I could sense it was a special occasion,' she recalled, 'and I could feel the air of expectancy round me and, I suppose, a certain tension too.'

After a guest pianist had opened the programme, the tenor accompanied by Teddy Schneider walked on stage to loud applause. McCormack looked pale, though outwardly composed, and as usual he held in his hand the little note-book in case he forgot the words of his songs. His hands, said one observer, were 'visibly trembling.' As the applause died down, a voice from the gallery cried, 'God bless you.' The tenor was seen to bow once more and the applause rose again.

The recital went with extraordinary enthusiasm. Members of the audience called for their own favourite McCormack songs, and as he obliged with encores, it was clear that the tenor was back to his old self. The critics next day paid tribute to his performance, remarking that his personality had not changed even if his voice had lost a little of its ring at the top, and something of its volume, but they were unanimous in noting the greater intelligence and sensitivity of his singing.

Since he was now about to devote himself almost entirely to concert and recital work, it is appropriate to examine his approach. L.A.G. Strong had attended many of his recitals and his observations carry authority.

'Usually, particularly in the later years,' stated Strong, 'John would come on first for a short classical group. On several occasions when I heard him, he began with an exquisite old German *Minnelied*, which not only perfectly suited his voice and manner, but was excellent for "singing in" – the compass not too great, the top notes touched lightly. Then he would follow with something by Handel. For an encore the song chosen would be in keeping with what had gone before.

'The second group of songs would have wider range, but would still be of musical value. A typical group here would contain songs by Schubert, Quilter, Elgar and Bantock. The third group would be Irish, including one of Moore's Melodies, two or three of Herbert Hughes's Country Songs and something else thrown in for good measure. He liked to include "The Meeting of the Waters", "Believe Me" and "The Garden where the Praties Grow".

'The last group was a sort of free-for-all. It contained the things which a large part of the audience had come to hear, and the encores would go on until John was so tired that he would shut the lid of the piano.'

How times have changed in this respect. It is not uncommon in

117

Dublin's National Concert Hall to find international singers begin their programme at 8pm, break for an interval of twenty minutes, and return to the stage and finish by ten o'clock. He or she may, if the applause is enthusiastic enough, give an encore of one or two songs, seldom if ever any more. Compared with McCormack's exhausting programme, contemporary singers certainly seem to earn their money easily. Strangely, Irish audiences have become accustomed to this policy and apparently don't feel cheated or short-changed. They are easily pleased, or so it seems.

What of McCormack's platform mannerisms? L.A.G. Strong remembers they were few. 'He walked on with a kind of broad dignity difficult to describe. Just as there was about Fritz Kreisler a leonine dignity, courteous but aloof, so John at his first appearance was withdrawn and grave, no matter how impassioned his welcome. He sang with one hand clasping the little note-book, and the other held loosely beneath it, moving occasionally in a half-gesture to supplement the expressive movements of the head. The emotion of the song, tragic, contemplative or humorous, was strongly expressed upon his features; he sang usually with closed eyes, except in the lighter songs.

'In a word, he was himself on the concert platform, not the studied, conventionized exhibit which many singers put in place of the self.'

Although by now in his fortieth year, McCormack was as energetic as ever, evidently unprepared to reduce his heavy work schedule. During the week of the revival of the Tailtean Games in Ireland in 1924, he gave a recital in the 4000-seater Theatre Royal in Dublin to raise funds for the Games. It was a sell-out recital; indeed, it was reported that more than sixty people were content to sit in the orchestra pit. Once again he came off the stage perspiring and exhausted after singing up to a dozen encores.

A few months later, on 1 January 1925, McCormack was back in New York where he sang in the first celebrity radio broadcast with the soprano Lucrezia Bori. According to Lily McCormack, 'it came over the air perfectly and caused quite a sensation.' And in April of the same year he was in Camden Studios, New Jersey, making the first electrically recorded disc, a pleasant little song, "When You and I Were Seventeen". It was said that the early electrical recording process added a slight edge and trace of nasality to the reproduction of his voice. He went on to make many radio broadcasts, one in particular with Bing Crosby proving a big hit with Americans.

On the recommendation of his friend Fritz Kreisler, he decided to undertake an extensive concert tour of Japan and China and Lily planned to bring their daughter Gwen with them. The social side was to prove in her view as fascinating as the musical side and there was seldom a dull moment. As she recalled, Japanese audiences were warm and appreciative. 'It was enlightening to us to find that with the wide gulf between their conception of melody and ours, they wanted so many classical selections. This was gratifying to John and Teddy Schneider.'

The tenor and his accompanist quickly became a popular duo, with one Tokyo newspaper commenting, 'We cannot forget that there exists the accompanist Mr Schneider behind the success of Mr McCormack.'

Likewise, Chinese audiences appeared to prefer classical songs to Irish ballads or Neopolitan love songs. To Lily McCormack they were, however, less effusive than their Japanese counterparts, being sometimes reserved in their response. Looking back, she described the tour of these countries as 'incredibly impressive.'

On their return to America they made arrangements to sell Rocklea, their spacious house in Noroton. With two of their three children, Cyril and Gwen, attending school in England, they decided in that year 1927 to have a house in Ireland. They took out a fifteen-year lease on historic Moore Abbey owned by Lord Drogheda and situated about twenty-eight miles from Dublin in Country Kildare. The mansion stood on 300 acres of land and skirted the River

119

Barrow. It was clear that McCormack had entered a new and more extravagant phase in his life, for the upkeep of the place would require substantial outlay.

To the villagers in adjacent Monasterevin the coming of the famous tenor to live in their midst caused a stir and one old wag soon labelled him 'Squire' McCormack. He had two hard tennis courts constructed as well as a swimming pool. And after a visit to Kildangan, the home of the More-O'Farralls a few miles away, he got interested in owning racehorses. The More-O'Farrall sons ran racing stables and one day as the tenor was being shown around them Lily anticipated the worst.

'I wasn't in the least surprised coming home when John casually mentioned what a grand interest it would be for us to have just a couple of racehorses. With Roderick More-O'Farrall to train them and Kildangan being so near, we could run over every morning to see them exercising.'

Usually they closed Moore Abbey in the late autumn and spent the next few months in New York, returning for the summer months to the green Kildare pastures to entertain friends from many parts. Lily thought the leisurely life suited her husband and he did regular walks to try to control his weight. It wasn't an easy task, however, as he continued to enjoy dinner-parties and convivial evenings of song, with which he loved to regale his guests as he drank champagne and smoked large cigars.

He found the time in August 1928 to go to Athlone and make his last public appearance in St. Mary's Cathedral. People paid £1 each for tickets to attend the solemn Gregorian Mass, and the sermon was preached by his old school friend Archbishop Michael Curley. Lucretia Bori, who was a guest of the McCormacks at Moore Abbey, came with them to Athlone and sang in the choir, as did young Cyril McCormack.

'I remember my father talking about the occasion,' said Louis Browne, 'and he actually gave me part of the green-coloured ticket which he had purchased for the Mass. He told me the McCormack party spent some hours that afternoon in my aunt Molly Curley's place where he and Archbishop Curley recalled the old days.'

In that same year, 1928, McCormack received his highest honour when he was elevated to the Papal Peerage, with the title and dignity of a Count. It was conferred in recognition of his eminent position in the world of music, together with his lifelong devotion to his faith and to the Holy See, and for his generosity to Catholic causes.'

His wife Lily was to remark, 'From the beginning of his success John could never say no to a request to sing in aid of a hospital, church or school. He was quite a trial to his managers at the time. I'm quite sure no artist ever gave his services more generously than he did, and all artists are generous in this way. He gave little thought of how much he did in this respect, and he was informed by Cardinal Hayes that he had been created a Papal Count in recognition of his services to Catholic charities.'

The tenor's next destination was Hollywood where he had been signed up by Fox Pictures for five hundred thousand dollars – with an option on a second movie – to star in the new movie, *Song of My Heart*, in which he would sing no fewer than eleven songs, including such firm favourites as "Just for Today", "The Rose of Tralee" and "I Hear You Calling Me". Scripted by Kansas City dramatist Tom Barry, and directed by Frank Borzage, it was one of the first major talkies featuring a star singer. Up to that time only short items had been screened in which stars of the Metropolitan, like tenor Giovanni Martinelli, sang "Vesti la gubba" from *I Pagliacci* to the incredulous ears of cinema audiences. Hollywood producers believed the musical could be profitable if the star was popular enough with the public. McCormack fitted this category ideally.

Fox Pictures chose a simple, if sentimental story primarily aimed at showing off the tenor's voice. Since he stubbornly refused to play love scenes, there was no current romantic interest to whom he sang; because he has remained ever faithful to the lost love of his youth, she is the one he is in reality singing to. He finds true happiness at the end of the film by uniting two young lovers who would never have made it without his help. I doubt very much if the script would get past a first reading in today's sophisticated Hollywood.

Few complained about its naivety in those days. Wasn't it the age of true romance? Frank Borzage, who had directed Janet Gaynor in *Seventh Heaven*, came to Ireland to try to find a girl to play the romantic lead. According to Lily McCormack, the director spotted a pretty girl called Maureen O'Sullivan at a party in Dublin and next day signed her up. Soon she would be accompanied to Hollywood by her mother. While in Ireland Frank Borzage visited Moore Abbey and was so struck by the magnificent scenery that he arranged for a scene in *Song of My Heart* to be shot there. He had a small cabin built at the edge of the river and McCormack, with a group of children gathered round him, sang "A Fairy Story by the Fire".

In that year, 1929, the McCormacks rented a house in Hollywood and Cyril and Gwen came to join them there. Lily's only worry was John's weight and she tried to persuade him to lose a stone or two. 'He was supposed to be playing a dashing Irishman, and I didn't think he was looking the part! Gradually as the shooting proceeded he did shed more than a few pounds and looked all the better for it.'

There followed an amusing episode when the tenor decided to have his hair cut, and obviously forgetting he was now a film star, had his own ideas about it and ignored Borzage's orders as to how much was to be taken off. On his return to the set the director was not amused and was obliged to dismiss the cast for the day. It would be two weeks while McCormack's hair grew, before the scene could be continued.

Asked later if he missed an audience while making the talkie, he replied that he always had one. 'For me it consisted of seventy or eighty hard-boiled electricians and other studio workers. If an actor can move them then he is a success. They are the world's toughest audience.'

Nor was it all work in sunny California. The tenor played tennis regularly with friends, swam a good deal, and accepted invitations to dinner-parties where the guests included legendary names, Ronald Colman, Basil Rathbone, Wallace and Michael Beery and Charlie Chaplin. 'Our life there was happy and busy and gay in the nicest sense of the word,' summed up Lily McCormack.

There was a glittering first showing of the movie in New York in March 1930 that attracted the cream of the city's political and artistic life. McCormack, accompanied by Lily and a party of friends, was among the crowded cinema audience and as he left later he was warmly applauded. It was generally felt his voice was reproduced beautifully and that he showed himself an excellent natural actor. The film must have done him a lot of good, as it brought his voice to a public who had not yet heard it.

Apart from some snide remarks by the more sophisticated press critics, the reviews were mostly favourable, with special mention of Maureen O'Sullivan's performance, which was said to reveal charm, personality and an innate ability to act before the cameras. She would go on to become a screen star in her own right. Abbey actor J.N. Kerrigan, as the old cab driver, brought to the movie a welcome professionalism. It was noticeable that on its first showing in Britain a few of the press critics revealed a begrudgery that seemed to be more personal than cinematic where McCormack was concerned. 'I am sorry I cannot join in the fuss made by some people over the film,' remarked the *Sunday Express* reviewer. The *Daily Telegraph* contented itself by stating that the film reproduced the personality of one who was a world figure, and that it gave some 'great singing.'

The Dublin premiere of *Song of My Heart* was marked by scenes of great enthusiasm in the Metropole Cinema in O'Connell Street. After the screening, President Cosgrave left his seat to shake McCormack's hand and thank him for some lovely singing. The tenor was seated in the front row of the dress circle with Lily and their daughter Gwen. It was one of the most distinguished audiences to gather in an Irish cinema and at the end of the evening presentations were made to Lily McCormack and to President Cosgrave. His was a bound volume of the songs sung in the film.

In making the presentation to the President, McCormack admitted he was more nervous than at any of his concerts, for at least in them he was on the other side of the footlights.

Watching a video screening of the movie one day this year in Liam Breen's house in Sutton, Co. Dublin, I found it revealing on two counts: firstly, because it shows McCormack singing in the concert hall, with his upright stance at the piano and his easy rapport with the audience; secondly, since Teddy Schneider plays his accompanist there is ample evidence of their harmonious relationship and of the art that conceals art. Once more the tenor comes on stage gripping in one hand his little 'prompt' book. For those, like myself, who never had the pleasure of seeing this supreme concert artist in the concert hall, the screening of *Song of My Heart* served a useful purpose.

During the shooting of the movie the tenor admitted he had fallen for the Californian climate and wanted a foot in the place. This he achieved by buying the Runyan property of about 160 acres. Before long he tore down the old cottage and built in its place a moderate sized house with a large music room, acoustically perfect. 'San Patrizio' would become his periodic home for the next seven years when he wasn't staying in New York or Moore Abbey. For some months each year he rented the house to screen stars including Charles Bowyer. 'Someone always wanted to rent it when we were staying elsewhere,' recalled Lily McCormack.

Because the sunshine of California suited her husband's health, Lily said that they had intended to make 'San Patrizio' their retirement home for the rest of their lives, with yearly trips to Ireland, but subsequently when their grandchildren began to come along nothing would keep the singer there so they reluctantly decided to sell the house in the late 1930s.

They left a lot of furniture and personal things in storage in Hollywood, expecting to return one day, but it remained a dream. Lily had private regrets at the outset but when she witnessed the joy that the arrival of their first grandchild brought to John these quickly vanished.

CHAPTER

14

Farewell Appearances

How will the great Luciano Pavarotti choose to mark – dare I use the word "celebrate" – his retirement? Can we expect the customary round of farewell concerts and operatic performances at the world's greatest musical venues? Or will the big man summon his colleagues Placido and José to join with him in one mammoth television spectacular so that his countless fans can see him bow out in typical bravura style?

Maybe we are wrong in our assumptions. Maybe Italy's most flamboyant tenor will simply do it his own way. I quote from the last paragraph of his book *My Own Story* published in 1981:

> As for retirement, I used to tell myself that when I no longer sang my best, when I heard deterioration in my voice, I would stop singing for good. I have changed my mind. This kind of talk is ego. I am very competitive and a little bit of a perfectionist. To feel that I'm singing in an exceptional way is very gratifying to me. My satisfaction does not come from believing that each time I open my mouth I am beating out a number of other tenors. Singing by itself gives me enormous joy. So does the feeling that I am making music. But the greatest satisfaction comes from knowing that my singing makes many people happy. As long as I feel that

is true, even if to a lesser degree than today, then they will not be able to stop me.

Bravo Luciano! Who knows, he may keep his promise and defy age – and the critics. His father is after all over seventy and still has a good tenor voice. In this demanding jet-age, however, it is hard to see how he can go on into his middle sixties singing in grand opera.

McCormack, on the other hand, entertained no such wish to prolong his career indefinitely, even though he shared a Pavarotti-like passion for singing. Perhaps he thought he had already gained immortality as a singer, and who can claim he hadn't?

Although he would sing at wartime concerts in Britain in the early 1940s, McCormack made his official farewells as a singer, beginning in the spring of 1937 at a concert in the huge Consistory Auditorium in Buffalo, and carried on into the following year in Britain. With Teddy Schneider ill and unable to travel, he chose the brilliant English accompanist Gerald Moore to replace him. Moore later recalled their first meeting at the home of Lady Ravensdale: 'Though I had never met John before there was no mistaking him. The thousand pictures I had seen of him with his black hair, twinkling eyes, fine head, all came to life in that imposing personage whose presence filled the room.

'Momentarily he clapped me on the back and said, "Let me turn over the music for you, Gerald." And that was that! Whenever I met him after that there was always friendliness, that calling me by my Christian name (it was as much as to say "I know all about you, my boy, and your work") which brought unction to the soul of a young musician.'

They met again in the summer of 1938 when he and McCormack set out on tour with a programme that consisted of twenty songs, some in Italian and German and a selection of English and Irish ballads. At the first rehearsal, when he had been seated at the piano only for a few minutes, McCormack suddenly remarked, 'What the hell are we rehearsing for? It isn't necessary with us.'

To Moore, the singer was a splendid musician. In his view, most violinists and pianists were fine musicians but sometimes one came across a singer who had a wonderful voice but who was not musically educated. 'John was not like that. He could read a piece of music at sight wonderfully.'

The mood of the English provincial tour was set in Manchester when the pianist tapped on the door of McCormack's hotel room, and when he opened it, said, 'Count McCormack, I've come to let you know I'm here.' Whispering as usual before a concert, the tenor replied, 'John, not Count.'

Moore was to learn a lot about the singer as they played to packed houses in Liverpool, Glasgow, Edinburgh, Leeds and elsewhere. For instance, he carried his honesty to extraordinary lengths. 'John was incapable of telling a lie. He just had to say what was in his mind – even if it hurt.'

And he soon discovered that the Irishman wanted to stay up all night chatting and drinking and yet would come down to breakfast next morning as fresh as a daisy. It puzzled him how he managed to do it. And while the lavish after-concert supper parties could be hugely enjoyable, Moore found that the singer simply loved an argument. 'I think John got some rare pleasure out of it, and would keep an argument blazing for hours. If he saw an opening he would delight in plunging his verbal rapier right in. The funny thing was that one evening he would argue as a most rabid Irishman and next you would swear he was the most imperialistic Britisher you ever met.'

As the provincial tour ended arrangements were made for McCormack's final farewell concert on 27 November at the Royal Albert Hall in London. He and his concert manager Frank Cooper drew up the special guest list that not only included the American Ambassador to Britain, Joseph Kennedy, but the endearing Mary Scott, the woman who helped to launch his career years before.

Not surprisingly the farewell concert aroused wide interest and the hall was almost full long before starting time. It was noticeable that two-thirds of the audience consisted of women of all ages – they had always loved his romantic and sentimental songs. Cyril McCormack came over to the box occupied by Mary Scott and her friends to tell her that his father was in great form and looking forward to the concert. Soon the tenor strode onto the platform, his small book of words in his hand, his accompanist Gerald Moore behind him, as the vast hall came to an expectant hush.

L.A.G. Strong hadn't heard him sing for two years and noticed that in the opening songs he sang carefully, and kept well within his powers until the last group when he once let himself go upon a fortissimo high note. Taking the recital as a whole, he had never heard him sing better. It was an astonishing performance. The encores alone would have exhausted most singers.

The audience were not prepared to go away. And not a few women were seen to weep as the tenor sang. As the evening finally came to a close, with McCormack thanking the audience for its tremendous reception, it marked the end of one of the most emotional occasions of his career. Lily described it as unforgettable.

'When we were leaving the Albert Hall, the last I saw of John the buttons were being torn off his coat by souvenir hunters, and the next thing I knew a husky policeman had grabbed me and lifted me over the heads of the milling throng into our car. If it hadn't been for him, I would have been a very late and crushed hostess at the cocktail party we were giving for Joseph Kennedy and his guests. John, who had sung twenty-seven songs at the recital, was exhausted; but after a hasty shower and change of clothes, he was soon the life and soul of the party.'

Next morning the *Daily Mail* critic, Edwin Evans, appeared to echo the feelings of the previous night's audience, when he stated: 'Listening to John McCormack it was difficult to discern any reason why he should think of retiring. His voice is as sound as ever. His enunciation is still an example to most singers and a reproof to the many whose words are unintelligible.'

McCormack crossed over to Dublin to give his farewell concert to an enthusiastic audience that refused to let him go until he had sung a dozen encores. Dr Douglas Hyde, President of Ireland, presented him with a gold cigarette case inscribed: 'To Ireland's ambassador of song.'

He told friends he was settling in the country and not as he had earlier intimated, in California. For a man who had bought and sold half a dozen houses in his time it was ironic that now with the approach of retirement he owned none. He was in a way the quintessential wandering minstrel. Or as Gerald Moore succinctly put it, 'This great minstrel will never be forgotten. He is enshrined in the hearts of the people, for his singing lifted them up and showed them beauty and romance.'

PART FOUR

Memories and Reflections

15

Gwen's Homecoming

W hen Gwen McCormack was born in Dublin in July 1909, John McCormack as a token of gratitude gave his wife Lily a diamond necklace which could be worn as a tiara. Two years earlier on the birth of their son Cyril, he had given Lily a diamond star which could be worn as a brooch or a hair ornament. McCormack, in fact, was so fond of buying expensive jewellery that Lily had to beg him more than once to be careful with his money, but as she admitted later, 'There was no stopping him. Any anniversary or birthday was a good enough excuse.'

When Gwen, his only daughter, was growing up he once asked her what she'd like for Christmas and she unhesitatingly replied that she'd love a brooch with her own initials inscribed in diamonds. Her father at first was puzzled by her request and enquired as to the reason and when she explained that she wanted to wear the brooch on her dress or hat, he agreed and went off and got it made for her.

'It's now my most treasured possession,' enthused Gwen when I met her early in 1995 at her picturesque bungalow home in Lisclogher, Co. Westmeath. Despite a hearing problem and the fact that she had not long recovered from a serious operation, she looked contented and in good spirits as we chatted in the sitting room where there are numerous photographic reminders of her famous father and the rest of the McCormack dynasty.

She had returned after a spell of over sixty years away from Ireland. She was married in September 1933 to a young British Army officer Teddy Pyke at Brompton Oratory, London, and on the occasion her father sang Panis Angelicus. Some weeks earlier when he suggested he'd wear his papal count's uniform at the wedding, Gwen protested. 'You'll do no such thing, Pop. This day is going to be my day and you're not stealing the limelight.'

She had always adored her father. Even now as she good-humouredly – and not without a hint of nostalgia – retraced those days her eyes lit up as she recalled touring with her parents in China and Japan and other parts of the world. 'My teachers at school never knew when I'd be off on tour with Pop and Mom and they'd get a little cross with me.'

'I think of Pop very often,' she said. 'I think of him when something happens in the McCormack or Pyke families. I'm inclined to say at such moments, '"Pop would love that," or "What would Pop think of that?" I always called him Pop. He was such a wonderful father to me and of course to my brother Cyril.'

Gwen's daughter Patricia arrived with a tray of tea and cakes, which was the cue for Gwen to tell me that when Patricia's eldest daughter was born they called her Johanna because it was on her great grandfather's birthday, 14 June.

Patricia is married to Frank Kelly and they farm about 300 acres of land. Just now it was the lambing season and outside could be heard the plaintive bleating of the sheep. The Kellys provided Gwen with her lovely home and are obviously delighted that she is happy and settled. They themselves live a short distance away in an attractive two-storey house reached by a long avenue from the road. Although she is now eighty-seven Gwen McCormack drives herself to the house and for relaxation may sit in the glass-covered patio and talk to the Kellys or one of their children.

She admits that she did not find it easy to leave her home in Lancashire and considers parts of that countryside as scenically beautiful as Ireland. For over forty years she had been happily married there and brought up her two children. Her husband Teddy Pyke died from a stroke in 1974. 'It was a terrible blow to me,' said Gwen. 'Teddy had been ill for a year before he died. I remember that when he served in the war I was left alone with the children for over three years, but like others we learned to carry on with our lives. Teddy was very fond of my parents and he used to enjoy listening to Pop's records.'

Gwen gave a short infectious laugh as she recalled the days in the 1920s when she was thinking of marriage. She dismissed the notion that her famous father discussed the kind of young men that he thought would be suitable for her. 'I agree that Pop was very protective of me his only daughter, but he never advised me about eligible young men; he wisely left that to myself. We are talking now of a very long time ago and in those days the word "relationship" was not mentioned. We preferred to call it romance and all that kind of thing. I had a few romantic affairs before I met Teddy but nothing very serious.'

Although her parents welcomed her independence, Gwen still asked their consent to become engaged to Teddy Pyke. In her family circle it was the custom. Already her brother Cyril had painted a very favourable picture to John and Lily McCormack about the dashing young English army officer who wanted to marry his sister Gwen. His father's reaction was good-humoured: 'Our Gwen wanting to get married, and to a man we don't even know!'

Eventually when Gwen got permission from her parents to marry, she said to her father, 'Pop, Teddy doesn't know what to call you and Mom – you both seem so young.' McCormack laughed. 'He can call me John, isn't that good enough?'

'I have such happy memories to draw on,' Gwen said, as she took down from the sitting-room wall the photograph of her wedding and reflected upon it. She said she had designed her own wedding gown of ivory satin with long sleeves and a cowl neck. Her veil of rare old Irish lace was from her mother's collection. She could say that where she was concerned her parents were determined to do things in style. Some years before her 'coming out' in New York they had arranged a ball in the Ritz Crystal Room which was wonderful fun.

Her mother Lily went further and gave a series of Sunday afternoon 'at homes' for her. Looking back, Gwen says that they were delightful days, uncomplicated and a most important part of her growing up. Friends regularly came to their apartment at 270 Park Avenue and it was there she first met Gloria Caruso, daughter of the great tenor, and sopranos Lucrezia Bori and Geraldine Farrar.

Now when I asked her if she had ever wanted to be an opera singer, she raised her head and said emphatically, 'Oh yes, it was one of my greatest ambitions. Pop knew this, so did Mom, although they both thought that Cyril would make his decision first because he had a lovely light baritone voice. I wasn't so sure, though, that it would be big enough to fill an opera house.'

Nor was her own soprano voice big, she said, but it was sweet and expressive and before long she was able to sing duets with her father. And she loved the glamour associated with opera at the Metropolitan and was brought there regularly. Once she went with her parents to hear Enrico Caruso in *I Pagliacci* and their seats were in the front row. 'I can recall Caruso looking down at Cyril and me,' she recalled, 'and making funny faces at us. I wasn't sure whether these gestures were part of his portrayal of the character Canio or not but at the time, attired in his long costume he appeared very funny to me.'

On other occasions she was allowed to meet the star singers after performances in their dressing-rooms and their success fired her imagination to be a singer. In her book Lily McCormack refers to Gwen's growing interest in opera. 'I noticed that she was spending a lot of time studying opera scores and I deduced from this she wanted to be a Geraldine Farrar or Lucrezia Bori. Singers used to encourage her and explain the amount of study and stamina needed. Lucrezia Bori was especially helpful in his respect.'

One day Gwen decided to face her father and ask him if he

thought she would make a success as an opera singer. First, she emphasised the fact that she didn't mind how hard she had to work. Realising that she meant what she said, he told her candidly, 'Darling, you'd never get beyond the first act. Your voice is too small.'

Despite her tender age, Gwen was philosophical. 'Well, in that case Pop I'm not going to bore my friends anymore.'

But Gwen says today that she continued to sing at parties and around the piano at their apartment and almost every week she attended an opera at the Met. She never had the pleasure of seeing her father on the operatic stage because she was too tiny when he was singing at the Manhattan Opera House.

Her schooling was divided between America and England. In the late 1920s she was attending Kensington Convent while Cyril was going to Downside. She makes no secret of the fact that her studies were interrupted by occasionally going on tour with her parents, sometimes on long voyages to Australia. 'Pop's philosophy was that it was no use having children if you couldn't see them and be with them, even if it meant taking us from school. But Cyril and myself learned a great deal of history and geography from these tours and I don't regret them.'

One of the most exciting phases of her life was going to Hollywood with her parents for the making of the movie *Song of My Heart*. She had, she said, always imagined it as a vast place, probably because of the Westerns she had seen but now it looked smaller, like a village with lots of film studios. She visited the studios and was intrigued when the Fox Company, who were making *Song of My Heart*, began to build a thatched cottage for the interior film shots.

And they built a special dressing-room for her father, the star of the movie. She was introduced to Will Rogers who was making a western, and to Frank Borzage, the director of *Song of My Heart* and was thrilled when he told her she had a small role. However, her best friend became Maureen O'Sullivan who was about her own age and

137

had a lively sense of humour. To Gwen, she had a lovely romantic part in the film and together they sometimes talked about it; on other occasions they played tennis or swam with friends. The beautiful Californian climate appealed to her and there was an air of excitement about the studios and talk about stars like Janet Gaynor who had started as an extra and went on to make her first feature, *The Johnstown Flood*.

With her mother, she had to take turns in the recording room so that they could tell her father how his voice was coming over. In her autobiography Lily McCormack recalled, 'In singing Blanche Seaver's little song, "Just for Today", in the church choir scene, John suddenly turned his back on the "mike" to give the effect of distance. The recording engineers objected strenuously, but John said, "Leave this to me. I have it all worked out in my mind and I'm expecting to get a fine result." He got it and I believe the same method is being used today.'

Gwen was genuinely sorry to leave Hollywood, yet she sometimes wondered if it was the place to live. From what she had seen it was best for stars. In summer she knew it was hard to surpass the sunshine and serenity of Moore Abbey where she said she enjoyed some wonderful times. 'Pop was truly happy there. After New York and his arduous concert tours I knew he looked forward to coming to the Abbey more than anything else. We played tennis together, Cyril rode horses around the fields and we usually had friends down from Dublin and from abroad.'

After her marriage in 1933 to Teddy Pyke she would not see America again for over twenty-four years, and with a young family coming along they would only make periodic visits to Ireland.

For those people who imagined McCormack as gregarious or as someone usually high-spirited it came as a surprise to me to hear Gwen McCormack say that the opposite was the case. 'I think my father was often misunderstood,' she said. 'I remember him as a quiet man, a shy man, although I agree that he had to be outgoing for

138

his career which is quite a different thing. He could read newspapers or a book for hours without a word, or listen to music in a reflective mood. When he was talking about singing or art or war he was usually serious. When something went wrong with the planning of a concert or his horse lost at the races he could become angry or annoyed. I seldom, though, experienced his darker moods.'

Being with him on a concert tour was a revelation, she said, as he wanted to learn about every new place they visited and was interested in everything, especially in people. For the first time in our conversation that afternoon she displayed a touch of irritability when she recalled that someone had once accused her father of being conceited. The writer at the time was referring to his Rolls-Royce and his opulent lifestyle and described it as ostentatious.

'This man was utterly wrong,' Gwen declared. 'Pop hadn't bought these cars to show them off but because he enjoyed them and to him it was fun driving them. Likewise, he bought some fine paintings because he liked having them round the house. Pop wasn't conceited at all. And he was a religious man but never preached religion. He was very human and certainly no snob.'

Gwen rose and perused the photographs on the walls in the sitting-room, as though hoping perhaps they would bring back more memories. More than once she used the word 'normal' in the context of having enjoyed a normal life and been fortunate to have done so. 'Mom was wonderful to Pop,' she mused, 'a great support. They were happy together during all their married life and I think this was because they understood one another so well. I don't think he would have got where he did without her.'

She still has many of the letters her father wrote to her when on tour in distant cities in America and in South Africa. 'Pop wrote wonderful letters, describing in detail how his concerts were received and the people he met. They are very personal, so I've kept them to myself. He used to write to Mom, too, and telephone her every day. I think he worried about us when away, but with Mom around there really was no need for him to do so.'

During the war she regretted she was unable to get to see her parents in Dublin. In June, however, of 1945 she received a letter from her mother telling her that she had asked John what he would like for his birthday and he said that more than anything else he wanted to see Gwen.

'I wrote back to Mom to tell her that I'd try to come over and seemingly she told Pop that I was coming. I did arrive in time for his birthday celebrations. It was like old times as a birthday cake with candles was wheeled into the dining-room on a trolley and he cut the cake. There was music and laughter despite the fact that he was ill and knew he was unwell. I could see his breathing wasn't good and that his voice was weak, but he tried to put on a brave front. I don't think he was afraid of death.'

A few months later he was dead. 'I've said a prayer ever since that I was able to come to Dublin to see him that June and talk about our life together. I have many of his records and his letters and such lovely memories, too.'

JOHANNA KELLY... McCormack's great grand-daughter with the 1984 centenary stamp issued to commemorate his birth. It was Johanna's 5th birthday.

THE TENOR... enjoying a moment of fun with his first grand-daughter Patricia Pyke, daughter of Gwen Pyke.

KATHLEEN RANSOME (assistant matron)... seated at the McCormack grand piano in the spacious reception room of Moore Abbey.

REV CANON EARLEY... Summerhill College President proudly holds the
McCormack gold chalice.

SIR JOHN MURRAY SCOTT... London patron of John McCormack.

TEDDY SCHNEIDER... the tenor's gifted accompanist.

FRANK RYAN... had an astonishing singing career.

JAMES JOHNSTON... blessed with a splendid tenor voice.

FRANK PATTERSON... popular in America

CAROL ANN McCORMACK... with her grandfather's gold medal won at the Feis Ceoil in 1903, and her grandmother's medal won in the previous year.

SYLVIA McCORMACK... pictured in Paint Mischief, her South Anne
Street shop in Dublin with examples of her own work.

Sylvia, busy in the shop's workshop, where she specialises in decorative
finishes. She is wife of Count John McCormack.

TISH TINNE... with her daughter Louise and her brother John ot Louise's
graduation day as a nurse.

LIAM BREEN... pictured in his private McCormack museum.

16

The Trust Fund

D ublin's Andrew Street is a veritable street of restaurants, with the QV.2 amongst the most popular with lunchtime and late night diners. When Count John McCormack, the grandson of the great tenor, bought it he decided on a new name. Since it was known originally as the Quo Vadis he reckoned that QV.2 ideally fitted the bill. The name has happily stuck, he says, and he has acquired a big and loyal clientele, particularly from the film and theatre worlds.

Few if any of them know, however, that the restaurant was purchased with money from the McCormack Trust Fund. The fund, Count John explained, was set up in the early 1930s and was made irrevocable so that his grandfather couldn't break it. 'The trouble was that he was such a big spender and kept spending money so freely something had to be done to safeguard it. I can recall my father Cyril telling me that on one occasion his father approached the family, saying that he wanted to break into the Trust Fund in order to buy a racehorse and they simply wouldn't allow him to have his wish.'

To Count John it was a wise decision for it secured the money for others in the trust. As far as he knew most of the $500,000 his grandfather got for his starring role in *Song of My Heart* went into the fund. Apart from that money, his grandfather, he said, made vast sums from sales of his records and receipts from the concerts that attracted hundreds of thousands of people all over America and elsewhere. It all added up to substantial wealth.

'The truth is that he did go through an awful lot of money in his time. Even today there are stories told of his betting on Irish racecourses and the bets he lost. Thanks to the trust fund, my grandmother Lily was looked after up to the time of her death in the early 1970s and afterwards my father and his sister Gwen became the beneficiaries. When Cyril died in 1990, the fund was split up and became the McCormack/Pyke Trust Fund. My sisters Carol Ann and Patricia, and myself, got a share of the money while my aunt Gwen continues to be a beneficiary.'

Patricia, who is affectionately called Tish, is a shareholder in the QV.2 restaurant and helps there at weekends. At other times she looks after the business side of the bakery project for the mentally handicapped at Athboy, Co. Meath.

While Count John McCormack agreed that his grandfather could be extravagant in ways, it was also true that the paintings he bought for their homes and the jewellery he presented to Lily were in themselves good investments. Today the royalties from his records were only a pittance, though they were now selling in CD and sales could pick up. His father Cyril, he said, was familiar with John's extravagance and told some amusing stories, especially about his involvement in racing.

Cyril had been quoted once as saying, 'Horse racing got a hold of my father like a drug, and he lost a fortune on it. When we lived in Moore Abbey he had over twenty horses in training in Ireland. For one animal alone, Cragadour, he paid £12,000 – and it never won a race. It went blind and had to be destroyed. Each horse cost £5 a week to keep, and there were the wages of the grooms and the trainers. On top of this there were the bets to be laid on his horses. It was a lot of money in those pre-war days. I think of all the horses and there were only two good ones, but the few races he won with them were a drop in the ocean compared with what he spent on them.'

Cyril was a fine raconteur and could always see the funny side of his father's racing activities, indeed the funny side of life as well. 'There must have been a jinx on father with the horses,' he said. 'At the end of one year he and I were working out the losses, and the only horse in the book showing a profit for the year was one he had given to me because he thought it wasn't much good! It was called Amonasro, from one of the operas, and I won a couple of small races with it.'

'Each year my father expressed the same wish, and that was to win the Derby. He was aware, though, of the expensive nature of his pastime and to placate my mother Lily he was fond of saying, "I'm getting rid of the racehorses any day now." In 1933 he sold them all except one horse, Franz Hals. It was supposed to be Ireland's hope for the Derby of that year, but again it failed to realise his dream. Looking back, I feel sure that my father's ambition must have cost him close on £100,000.'

Liam Breen admitted to me he was 'no racing man' but even he had heard colourful stories about the tenor's racing exploits. For one thing, he found that Lily McCormack always frowned on John's dabbling in horses and in their conversations she tended to avoid the subject. He wasn't surprised at that, for there had been talk in Dublin that her husband had been hoodwinked into purchasing some second-rate horses who never stood a chance of winning a major race, let alone the Derby.

It is easy to see that the word extravagance does not figure high in Count John McCormack's vocabulary. He is a busy restaurateur who puts in long hours at the QV.2 restaurant and bases his success on friendly staff relations and a price rate suited to most diners' pockets. In the 1960s his father Cyril managed the Old Conna Hotel near Bray for a consortium of Irish-American business men and in the halcyon days of filming at Ardmore Studios it was popular with stars such as Laurence Olivier, Alec Guinness, Laurence Harvey, Kim Novak and others.

'Cyril was more gregarious and outgoing than I am,' remarked

Count John. 'His personality was very suited to the hotel business and he was on equal terms with all his clientele. I think I am a bit more reserved and must get to know people before I become friendly with them. I do enjoy running the restaurant and while it's demanding work it's almost always interesting. We get in the QV.2 lots of theatre and film people and they can bring their own excitement to the place.'

Before he became a restaurateur he was in his own words, 'hovering round the theatre and film worlds.' He had originally written a comedy radio series in the late 1960s for RTE and it ran for six weeks, so that he began to visualise himself as a scriptwriter. 'Producer Tim Danaher plucked me one day out of obscurity in the Bailey restaurant. A few of us had been playing around with this comic idea and to his credit Tim went along with it. The series was eventually broadcast with actors Frank Kelly, John Keogh and humorist Eanna Brophy. I intended to follow it up but I'm afraid I was too lazy to capitalise on my brief hour of glory. I was attending Trinity College at the time and when I left there I sat down and wrote to all the television stations in Britain, telling them I was on my way but of course I'm still awaiting their replies.'

Entertaining was in the McCormack blood from his grandfather's side and at one time he thought of stage acting but he hadn't the confidence to see it through. He had no ambitions to be a singer, simply because he hadn't a voice. Movies interested him and he says he did work as 'a third or fourth' director on a film unit. 'My level was that of teaboy and I never really advanced beyond that.'

For a time, too, he worked in the production side of theatre, an experience he by no means regrets. One play was a success, the other a flop. Conor Cruise O'Brien's *Murderous Angels* came into the latter category and was panned by the critics. After that experience, Count John concluded that academics should tread cautiously in the theatre. 'I think they tend to be intellectual in a medium that's essentially an entertainment one, or at least that's the impression I got from people's reaction to the O'Brien play.'

By the early 1970s he had drifted into the restaurant business and underwent some initial training. He doesn't doubt it's a risky occupation, time consuming and for an owner like himself not without responsibility and worry. He was heartened by the modern trends among people of dining out more regularly, and they were also becoming more fastidious in their choice of food. Over the years he has become a connoisseur of wine, thus emulating his late father Cyril who once ran a wholesale wine business.

He was born in his grandfather's house "Glena", Booterstown, where he lived with his parents until the age of seven; after that the family moved to a house in Goatstown, Co. Dublin. From an early age he was conscious of the John McCormack legend, something that in one way perturbed him. Tour buses invariably stopped outside their house and passengers pointed at the building and seemed to exclaim, 'Look!....there it is!' As a boy he found this disquieting. 'I used to stick my tongue out at the passengers in the buses and I remember my mother ticking me off, though I suspected she wanted to laugh at me seeing me do it.'

It annoyed him when visitors came to the house and chucked him under the chin, and asked, 'Do you sing?' or 'Do you sing like your grandfather?' Soon he grew tired of their questions and told them, 'No, I don't sing,' or 'I can't sing like him.' After that, he found they lost interest in him because he showed no interest in them. On reflection, he says, 'It was hard to take at a time when I was trying to build up my own identity and confidence. Gradually the visitors were satisfied to know me for myself and as I grew up I developed my own personality and it didn't bother me any more.'

Years later his father Cyril was to tell a press man, 'Both my father and I greatly resented my being introduced as "John McCormack's son." He used to say, for God's sake, Cyril tell them who you are. This doesn't mean that I resented my father. We both hated it.'

Count John agreed that it was not uncommon for sons of famous fathers to be treated in this manner and naturally some of them came to resent it. 'My own father never made that mistake with me. I am intensely proud of my grandfather's achievements, but I do sympathise with children who may have to cope with these situations.'

Musically he has a genuine preference for his grandfather's operatic records, though he also derives pleasure from some of the classical songs and certain ballads. He admits he finds not a few of the ballads mawkish and has difficulty with them. The operatic arias, on the other hand, are first-class in his view, especially Mozart's "Il mio tesoro" and the Donizetti choices. He is quick to point out, however, that his grandfather was singing to his market and at the time this was undoubtedly the correct policy to adopt, just as Pavarotti, Domingo and Carreras are responding to their legions of fans with popular operatic airs on a mass television concert scale. No one complained, no one accused them of prostituting their vocal art.

'Therefore I cannot blame him if he sang the songs and ballads that his huge concert audiences wanted to hear; apparently this is what they demanded. They simply loved to hear him sing the songs of Ireland whether they were sentimental or otherwise. And as we all know songs like "I Hear You Calling Me" and "Macushla" are enjoyed even in modern times. Planning his concerts or recitals he was, it seems, meticulous about achieving a balance between Irish and classical songs and this was true whether he was singing in Paris, Prague or Dublin.'

When I reminded him that his aunt Gwen had described his grandfather as a shy man, he emitted initial surprise but thought what she meant was that he was reserved, though others tended to interpret it as aloofness, which was a different thing. He guessed he was the sort of individual who when the barriers were down could be gregarious and regard a person as his friend. 'I wouldn't be unlike that myself. I can be quite reserved until I get to know a person well and after that we're on a friendly wavelength.'

As we touched on the famous tenor's attractiveness to women, I remembered what Louis Browne had said to me a short time previously. 'Apparently in his young days women used to go crazy about him,' he said, 'and many of them went to his concerts not so much for his singing but more to see this incredibly handsome man.'

Handsome was a word that Lily McCormack had used on a few occasions to describe her husband early in his career and she must have known that women adored him. As in the case of most star singers, tenors in particular, rumours persisted over the years that at least two divas became infatuated with the boyish-looking John McCormack and at least one of them wrote a love letter or two to him which he tore up and tossed in the waste paper bin. He was supposed to have confided in Dr Vincent O'Brien about the 'infatuations' on their 1913 world tour together, but if the tenor, who was it must be remembered a bit of a practical joker, did tell O'Brien, his accompanist told only a few people about it. The truth remains that during his lifetime there was no serious scandal associated with McCormack, something unusual when related to today's more liberal trends in the operatic world.

Count John McCormack agreed that his grandfather's record in this respect appeared almost too good to be true, yet he had no reason to question it. 'I accept there was no whiff of scandal during his lengthy career as a singer, which I suppose is surprising in a musical sphere that sometimes feeds on gossip and the latest affairs. The truth is that my grandfather while very young met and fell in love with Lily Foley and henceforth entirely devoted his life to her and Lily to him, and consequently he had never any desire to have his ego boosted, so to speak. There were, I'm sure, still strong pressures on him because for some reason or other that kind of power and charisma and talent turns on people whether they are male or female and there are a host of people who will throw themselves at their feet – or their beds – simply because they are famous. As we know from his photographs, John in his youth was debonair and good-looking and must have attracted women and· he remained an attractive man all his life. He had a fine rounded face and twinkle in his eye and a sparkle to him that must have caught the fancy of a pretty woman or two in the bohemian world of opera singing.'

He recalled his father once telling him that on occasions in his bachelor days he would bring girlfriends back to Moore Park and they'd stay the weekend, but they'd spend some of the time listening to his father's stories and gazing into his eyes. 'I don't think it did Cyril any good in those days. My grandfather, it seems, was a charmer, so too was my father.'

He remembered his grandmother Lily fondly. In the years following John's death in 1945 he got to know her better and every summer she returned from New York to holiday with her relatives, often staying with the Kellys in Co. Westmeath. She continued to talk about 'her John' and whenever she had the time played his records. In New York she had a number of elegant old gentlemen friends and together they'd visit art galleries, the opera and theatre, and in the afternoon dine together. It was her scene, friendly and relaxed, but above all cosmopolitan.

Count John once went to a Broadway play, with his sister Carol Ann, Lily McCormack and one of her gentleman friends, in which Maureen O'Sullivan was the leading lady. 'I remember that after the show we all returned to the Oak Room in the Plaza Hotel where Maureen joined us an hour later. It was one of those delightful interludes that you conjure up about showbusiness life in that great city.'

He could see that John's death had left a vast void in his grandmother's life but she was coping as best she could with the support of her loyal coterie of friends. And in his view she had made the right decision to divide her life between America and Ireland, otherwise she might have become bored or lonely. She had told him how she looked forward to returning to Ireland for the summer months and meeting again her family and grandchildren. Once she was a judge at the Rose of Tralee Festival and that pleased her very much.

'Grandmother had a lot of poise and dignity but she was down to earth when she wanted to be. Her Irish humour stood out and she was absorbed in different aspects of life, artistic and otherwise. I regarded her as quick-witted and intelligent and above all very thoughtful where her grandchildren were concerned. My father used to say that he became exhausted reading Lily's letters, as they were full of interesting detail about the theatre and opera and the art world and included lots of names of the people she met in New York. I enjoyed her company enormously and listening to her talk about 'my John' I got new insights into my grandfather's life and career.'

The late Count Cyril McCormack was close to both his parents. 'Lily certainly helped John become what he became,' he once remarked. 'From the day they got married to the day he died you could say that they were still in love with one another. And after he died she always referred to him as "my John": never "my late husband" or any of that. And after she got over my father's passing, she blossomed. She became much more extrovert and began to make her own friends instead of concentrating on his. She was very smart and feminine in her dress. In fact, she loved clothes and used to get rather cross with me because I couldn't care less about dress.'

It was Cyril McCormack who during the hectic centenary celebrations in June 1984 to mark the tenor's birth, had acted as a kind of spokesman between the family and the media and various other organisations. For me, visiting his delightful home "Courtfoyle", nestling amid the greenery of Co. Wicklow, was a joy, and perched on a seat beneath the famous study of his father by William Orpen he belied his seventy-seven years. He answered my questions with an ease and frankness that instantly suggested he was happy to talk about his renowned father and his era.

'My father and I had a lot of fun together,' he began, sipping his claret. 'He remained young in himself mentally, and he was easy to get on with. Like myself, he loved conversation and people. We shared a lot of interests in sport, although he hated motor racing for fear I'd take it up, which I did later on.

'I am sometimes asked if I saw him much in opera. Actually, I only saw my father once, and that was in *La Boheme* in New York. I know there were people who said he wasn't the greatest actor in the world, yet I have heard other people say he was a better actor than he thought he was.'

The conversation came round to the recognition accorded his father in Ireland after his death. 'As you know the family agitated for quite a while, as did the John McCormack Society here,' Cyril said, 'that the National Concert Hall in Dublin be named after my father. But we didn't win that one. I have no doubt that he would have liked something permanent, like an opera house or a concert hall, called after him.'

When I raised the same question with Count John McCormack early in 1995, he said that his grandfather wasn't remembered as well as he might have been in Ireland. In his opinion, it took a long time for recognition to come to him, but then singers seemed to take second place to composers in this respect. In the National Concert Hall, for instance, there was a John Field Room and a Carolan Room but no McCormack room, although the foyer was now dedicated to him and has a neat gallery of McCormack photographs.

A trophy in the shape of the Ardagh Chalice stood on a sideboard in Cyril McCormack's sitting-room in "Courtfoyle". 'It's the only reminder we have that father was a racehorse owner,' he said, amused at the recollection. 'It's the Turf Club Cup, and you see here is the name of his horse, Mignonne, and the date of the Curragh, September 1930. His one regret was having spent so much money on racehorses.'

He remembered his father as a loving and generous man, disciplined and a perfectionist. He never drank or smoked before a performance but afterwards there would always be a bit of a party. He was always nervous, too, before going on stage. And he once remarked, 'The day I stop being nervous, I stop being good.' He had a quick temper, but it would as quickly subside and all would be forgotten. He was also a very loyal person who, in turn, received a lot of loyalty from friends and people who worked with him.'

Musically, Cyril said, his father could be misunderstood. He was never a music snob. At their parties at home there would be jazz, dance music, ballads and Lieder. Above all his father was a family man. As he said, 'Many people don't realise that he made a rule of setting aside three months every summer to spend with his family. He maintained, in fact, that it would be impossible to go on singing over a full twelve months, that it would kill him.'

To Count John McCormack, his grandfather always appeared to be a devoted husband and family man as best he could be in a demanding world that featured lengthy travel and countless concerts. 'It cannot have been that easy for him,' he said, 'but he managed it.'

The O'Brien Tradition

'Ialways think of Vincent O'Brien as a grey-haired Schubert. He is strikingly like Schubert might have been, had he lived longer: a mild, loveable, unassertive man; a fine musician who is doing notable things for Ireland's musical development, but who would blush deeply if you told him so.'

This intriguing description was penned by the English journalist and critic R. Stephen Williams in the 1930s prior to a charity concert in Liverpool at which Dr Vincent O'Brien's new hymn composition "Christ the King" would be sung by John McCormack.

If Schubert's mission was to create music, including his masterly art songs, to O'Brien music was a vocation that he obeyed for over half a century as church organist, piano and voice teacher, and choir master. Although Schubert, who died at the age of thirty-one, lived all his life in Vienna under the shadow of Beethoven – he never was his pupil, however – music lovers in Dublin, naturally regarded the McCormack/O'Brien scenario in a different light; indeed, the great tenor's attitude to his first voice teacher never changed and reading through their correspondence one is struck by the mutual respect and genuine friendship that existed between them.

Writing, for example, from Alton House, Hampstead, in the early part of the century, McCormack began one letter thus, 'My dear Vincent' and ended it 'Always your sincere friend, John.' This was the tone of all his letters, and in the case of O'Brien, who was incidentally a natural letter writer, the sincerity was also apparent. Furthermore, he had by now a host of musical friends such as Hamilton Harty, Edward Martyn, Teddy Schneider, W.B. Yeats, George Moore and the Scott sisters, Mary and Alicia and he was happy to correspond with them when the occasion arose.

And in another letter from Alton House in July 1914, the tenor at the outset seemed concerned about a concert engagement.

'My dearest Vincent – I wish you would have few artists at the concert; above all don't have them drawn out like the usual Dublin concerts. It is really immaterial to me who sings, you must decide that yourself, but I think a soprano, a baritone and instrumentalist are sufficient, don't you? You remember how well our concerts in Australia used to go.

'Another thing, do start to advertise as soon as you can, that is essential as people must be made interested. Little paragraphs in the paper and such like are an absolute *sine qua non* to the success of a concert in Dublin nowadays.

'Well, old friend, how are you? I suppose you are just as if you had never left Dublin. Do ask Edward Martyn to sign a copy of his play "The Heather Field" and send it to me. I would love to read it; you have spoken so much of it, also some of those sonnets you told me about.

'Well I have had the success of my life in Paris in *Boheme*, not bad for an Irishman, and my biggest Covent Garden success has been *Tosca*, so I feel I am a credit to my native soil, the most musical soil on earth. We are all well and send our united love whilst I am as always.

Your sincere friend
John.'

While the letter speaks for itself, it does show nonetheless how closely in touch McCormack was with music in Dublin and the interest he also took in the promotion of his concerts in the capital. And, of course, it demonstrates once again the trust he placed in his great mentor and closest friend.

In September, 1932, Teddy Schneider wrote to him from Moore Abbey, Monasterevin, where he was staying with the McCormacks: 'My dear Vincent – John was asking for a copy of your hymn that he is singing in Liverpool. Will you be so kind as to send it down to us, so I can make a copy of the words for his little book. We are planning to go over to Liverpool on the 17th. I suppose you will be taking the night boat from North Wall on the night of the 19th so as to have a look at the organ in the Philharmonic Hall. I am looking forward with much pleasure to seeing you again. With kindest regards in which John heartily joins me – Sincerely, "Teddy" Edwin Schneider.'

The Liverpool concert for the Metropolitan Cathedral was a resounding success, with more than 2,500 people present and many others unable to gain admission. McCormack sang two arias and four songs before the interval and Teddy Schneider played three piano solos. The culmination of this half of the programme was the first public performance of Vincent O'Brien's hymn during which the tenor was accompanied on the organ by the composer.

'It was one of my proudest moments,' O'Brien was to recall. 'Up to then my most thrilling moment was when I played for John when he sang "Panis Angelicus" at the Eucharistic Congress in Dublin in the previous June, and my fingers could hardly touch the notes because of the fullness of the emotion within me.'

As a singing teacher he kept in touch with London agents. In September 1911, he received a reply from the Quinlan International Musical Agency in London about one of his pupils. 'With regard to the lady you mention,' stated Henry Richards, 'I would like to hear her before giving any advice.'

Richards was coming to Dublin with Fritz Kreisler who was giving two recitals in October of that year, and he ended his letter with, 'By the way you might boom the Kreisler recitals for me amongst all your musical friends. I want two packed audiences in the Antient Concert Rooms, so make a note of it.'

And in early September 1945, he received a letter from Charles

Wagner, McCormack's first personal manager in America, stating, 'Dear Vincent – Here are two articles on John. I do not know Mrs McCormack's address; will you please pass these to her? This picture in *Newsweek* is the McCormack family I like to remember. It was taken in San Francisco on your arrival from Australia and the world tour of 1913. It is too bad, by the way, that John's exit in the United States was so badly bungled by McSweeney. He meant well but had antagonised too many local managers and musicians. I've often talked it over with one of John's best friends, Michael Francis Doyle, and we both feel that John should have had a grand farewell tour over here. My best wishes to you always. P.S. And still doing more business than ever, at the age of forty-seven!!!'

McCormack, to my knowledge, never made mention of McSweeney's role in any proposed coast-to-coast American farewell tour, so Wagner's assertion is entirely his own. It wasn't the first time that he wrote disparagingly about his former associate director, for he once tried to attribute to him the tenor's troubles on one of his Australian tours.

Count Cyril McCormack often thought that writers failed to highlight his father's wit and humour, and more often than not painted a dull picture. I feel this to be true. Once the tenor was asked to pay tribute to Dr Vincent O'Brien and revealed a light touch in his writing, as when he recalled: 'When Edward Martyn, the endower of the 'Palestrina Choir', heard me sing, he was not in favour of Vincent's engagement of me for the tenor line. He said my voice was too big and telling. Both Vincent and I smiled. Some years afterwards I told the story to a journalist in America who was writing a story of my beginnings. Martyn wrote a letter to the press contradicting the whole account, adding that he always thought my voice small and uninteresting.'

The second story was about Dr Vincent O'Brien and himself. 'We laughed over this the other day. According to the terms of the 'Palestrina Choir' gift, it was ordained – I understand – that any member of the choir who absented himself from choir practice or actual performance was fined a small sum which, however, was refunded when the absentee had severed his connection with the choir. I told Vincent the other day that the choir owed me about seven or eight pounds. Vincent roared with laughter.'

In his early sixties he was visited on one occasion by a Dublin newspaper columnist who was obviously fascinated by O'Brien's house in Parnell Square. 'The sun shone through the lace curtains of the large music room and made it look a quiet summer-house,' he wrote. 'And it shone on the soft silver of presentations, on the shining copper of old hearth – utensils long superseded by an electric stove, on the waxed lino, warm in worn pattern; it balanced patches of light on the walls, brought out photos, mementoes and memories.'

Dr O'Brien told his visitor that he had never changed anything in the room. As he said, 'This is the grand piano on which I taught John McCormack; and this is the room where James Joyce came for singing lessons, a lovely tenor, before turning to writing. Where I rehearsed operas with Margaret Burke Sheridan, a great singer and equally fine actress. May Devitt, another fine operatic soprano – ah, this room has so many happy memories and it has been such a lucky room.'

When he died in June 1948 many fine tributes were paid to him, but the lines which stick in my mind are, 'Though Dr Vincent's tastes were wide and his talents manifold, his heart was in the music of the Church. He was happiest and at his best when improvising a Prelude before High Mass or Vespers. On these occasions he poured out his musical soul and seemed at times to reach a state bordering on exaltation. His accompaniments to plain chant were always discreet and in good taste. He delighted in his bi-weekly visits to Clonliffe College, All Hallows and Carysfort which were a source of refreshment to him and a welcome relief from the daily round of teaching private pupils at his home in Parnell Square.'

Dr O'Brien was seventy-seven when he died. He conducted the first public performance of Our Lady's Choral Society in December

1945 and astonished Dublin by the vigour and intimacy of his treatment of the *Messiah*. He was the first Director of music in Radio Eireann, retiring in 1941 at the age of seventy. It is interesting to recall that it was he who established the R.E. Symphony Orchestra.

Oliver O'Brien not only kept up the outstanding music tradition in the family but virtually took over where his father Vincent left off. After his education at Belvedere College, he decided to take up music as a career and began to study for a music degree at University College Dublin under Professor John F. Larchet. Around this time his father was in failing health and Oliver would accompany him to the various seminaries where he taught music to the choirs and gradually he himself got into the swing of things.

'I counted myself a very fortunate young man because when Dad retired I stepped into his post at Carysfort College, Blackrock, and the same thing happened when he retired as Director of the Palestrina Choir at the Pro-Cathedral. Later on I succeeded him as music director of Our Lady's Choral Society and stayed with the choir for over thirty years.'

Growing up, he naturally became aware of the John McCormack legend as his father often talked about the tenor and followed his career closely. He first met him at about the age of thirteen at a concert in the Theatre Royal. 'I remember Dad saying to me, "Come round Oliver and I'll introduce you to the Count." I was in short trousers and as I walked into his dressing room he looked like a heavyweight boxer: big, robust and well-built. After John shook my hand, Dad said, "Oliver, sing your party piece for the Count." I started to sing and before long McCormack burst his sides laughing. I could see that he and Dad were great friends.'

On another occasion, his father took Oliver and his brother Colum to "Glena" in Booterstown, where they had been invited to dinner by John and Lily McCormack. After the meal they all retired to the sitting-room and began to listen to classical records. 'I remember John put on an orchestral piece with Toscanini conducting and at the end of the recording he said to me, "Well, Oliver, how do you like that recording?" I being very young and foolish in the ways of the world had the temerity to answer, "I enjoyed it, but I thought the brass played a little bit out of tune at one point." At that McCormack exploded into raucous laughter and said mockingly to me, "Ah, so you thought the brass played out of tune, did you, then? Well, that reminds me of the private soldier in the French army who said he thought Marshal Foch wasn't a good general." I felt cut down to size alright and made no remark when the next record was played, nor the next.'

McCormack could be generous, he knew. His father Vincent wrote the music for two songs which the tenor sang, "The Fairy Tree" and "Baby Aroon" and when the royalties came in for the latter he sent them to his brother Colum and himself.

The McCormack voice has always appealed to Oliver O'Brien, mainly because of its unique golden quality and because the tenor was able to make the most ordinary song sound worthy of his attention. Although he sang in German, Italian and French, his voice never lost its Irishness, something that brought to his recording of Irish ballads a poignant ring. In addition, his phrasing was always polished. 'I remember he once said that he was greatly influened in his singing by the phrasing of the great Austrian violinist Fritz Kreisler. Of course John also brought his own personality to his singing, though not to the extent that he would distort songs, and while he rarely stuck rigidly to each bar and quaver, he did nevertheless give a song his own little gloss. In a word I believe he injected simple songs with a pathos, humour and meaning that was special to him as an artist and singer.'

When the tenor moved with Lily into the Shelbourne Hotel for some months, Oliver O'Brien and his father sometimes visited him there for afternoon tea. To the young O'Brien, the singer loved a friendly argument, as though eager to raise the tempo of conversation. He remembered his father telling him once that he thought John could have made his mark in several different careers because of his fluency in languages as well as the brilliance of his mind. He also admired John's moral fibre when, as he said, he could so easily have been a philanderer.

'They remained loyal to one another over a lifetime because I believe they shared a lot in common, for apart from music they could see the humour in things or talk about a variety of subjects that included sport, chess, and history. John's great wealth didn't bother him nor did it affect their friendship in any way; he was happy with his own interests in Dublin and was totally fulfilled.'

Oliver O'Brien is now retired and lives with his charming wife Elizabeth in an attractive Georgian house in Upper Pembroke Street, Dublin. They met when Elizabeth was a pupil of his at Carysfort College; she is very musical and hopes some day to research the life of Vincent O'Brien.

Colum O'Brien lives in Milltown, Co. Dublin, and is four years older than Oliver. He has been organist at the Pro-Cathedral in Dublin for many years and happily still plays there every week. Like his father, he also gave private piano lessons.

He got to know McCormack reasonably well in the last decade of the singer's life; first, when he used to drive his father Vincent to Moore Abbey to meet John and his musical friends. 'I was studying music and in my spare time acted as chauffeur for my father who was Director of Music at Radio Eireann. I remember one rainy day driving him to Moore Abbey and the car was filthy from the muddy roads, so I deliberately on arrival parked it in an obscure corner at the side of the main building, away from the Rolls-Royces and Jaguars. After lunch, as I stood for a while with my father at the main door, I said to John, that if I lived in this beautiful place I don't think I'd ever want to stir outside it. With that, he looked at me and quipped, "If I had a muddy Vauxhall like you're driving, neither would I." He could be cutting when he wanted to. You had to know him to appreciate his sardonic humour. I was able to take it.'

'Occasionally at dinner when he was really enjoying himself, the tenor could be the best of company; and if something very funny was said he would laugh uproariously. Dinner was an informal affair but one could expect to meet anybody from a famed boxer to a sedate bishop. There was an engaging elegance about the place and Lily had an old-fashioned approach to things, which meant a good table and good conversation.

'The Countess did the hosting and her husband did the talking,' Colum said. 'John was fond of good anecdotes and he had a marvellous memory for detail about singers' names or the operatic performances that most appealed to him. He had a real presence at the table and there was an aura about him. After dinner, he liked a cigar and a glass of champagne.'

When the McCormacks later took a suite in the Shelbourne Hotel, he sometimes dropped in to have a chat with either John or Lily. If his father Vincent was free he might come along. Friends came and went during the day. Sometimes McCormack enquired of him how he was faring at his piano studies, and as if to encourage him he lent him music.

'One afternoon he gave me Rachmaninov's Piano Concerto No.4 that I hardly knew existed. I was already familiar with Nos. One, Two and Three. He told me to play it at home and learn it properly as it was a tone poem of himself in sound.'

On his visits to the hotel Colum O'Brien began to bring with him a long black box with a handle containing a cine camera; his intention was to make a short movie of the singer in retirement and as he was in the hotel suite. He had already filmed some other personalities in the music and entertainment world. Lily McCormack knew what was in the box but John did not. Lily said, 'One of these days, Colum, my husband out of sheer curiosity is going to ask you what's in the box. He's not going to satisfy you by asking you just now.'

Lily was correct. One afternoon as he was talking to John about music, John snapped, 'What the hell is that box doing over there?' Tentatively he told him it was a cine camera. 'I thought you might be

161

taking the cutlery home in it!'

When O'Brien told him it was a cine-camera and that he wanted to make a short movie, he looked across the room at him curiously. 'I see...you wouldn't be supposing that I'd do this for nothing, would you? Did I ever tell you what I got for *Song of My Heart*..? And here you are wanting to take me for nothing.'

O'Brien knew McCormack was having him on; it was typical of the man. Suddenly, he said with a smile. 'For old times' sake you can do the film on me.'

What McCormack disliked was the furniture being moved around the room so as to get the lighting right for shooting. Once he was ensconced in his armchair in his long dressing gown and scarf he didn't want to be disturbed. O'Brien angled him over towards the French windows and onto the balcony and began to roll the film. McCormack was in good spirits and did what he was told to do.

The outcome, however, wasn't satisfactory. Today Colum O'Brien says that the interior shots in the room itself did not work because of insufficient lighting, but he did get a few minutes of the balcony scene. It was the same with his previous films: he got his subjects only in flashes.

He sometimes suspected that the singer missed America and his many friends there. Sitting around in a hotel could not have been easy for him, though he threw occasional cocktail parties for old friends when they were in town from London or New York. Retirement could be a sad and even trying time for singers who now only had their concert and operatic memories to fall back on.

Soon the McCormacks moved to "Glena", Booterstown. Despite his weak heart, John was determined to celebrate his sixtieth birthday in style. He was delighted with the news that both the BBC and Radio Eireann were planning special programmes on his life and career. In that summer of 1944 he was able to sit at his grand piano and play his favourite tunes.

'His birthday celebrations were a tonic for him.' recalled Lily

McCormack. 'I was afraid that they might be too much for his heart but he obviously didn't feel the strain.'

Among the guests at the small dinner party was Dr Vincent O'Brien. After dinner, they all filed into the music room to listen to the radio tributes and the records that John had asked to be played for his birthday. 'The programmes were heart-warming, loving and beautifully done,' recalled Lily McCormack, 'and John was like a child in his happiness.'

Colum O'Brien accompanied his father to "Glena" occasionally and thought that McCormack was more his old self there than in the Shelbourne Hotel. 'He had more freedom to express himself, play the piano or his records, or while away the time with his grandchildren. He had kept up his interest in sport and talked about racing, hurling, football and cricket. He still consulted my father on personal matters or the development of music in Dublin. Once he and Dad talked with Hamilton Harty about a new concert hall for Dublin, but when the talk was over Harty turned and said, 'That's all very fine, but where are we going to get the money?''

To young O'Brien, who was completing his piano studies, the singer was fascinating to talk to as he reeled off stories about Melba, Rachmaninov, Kreisler and Paderewski. He was also well versed in the arts, politics and religion. He decided to be discreet about racehorses as rumours were rampant about the losses he had incurred. Once, during Horse Show Week at the RDS, Lily McCormack asked him to drive her husband to the Shelbourne Hotel, 'Whatever you do,' she warned, 'you go straight to the hotel and come back directly later. On no account stop at Ballsbridge.'

Colum O'Brien suppressed a smile. It struck him that Lily was afraid of the mention of horses, even show jumpers, but she could hardly be blamed for that if the rumours were true. He himself was always intrigued whenever the tenor recalled his singing days as he was adamant that 'outsiders' did not appreciate a singer's life and the attendant pressures.

'John told me once that he was often apprehensive about opening his mail because of the bundles of requests for money and for him to sing at charity events. In this respect, clergy here, there and everywhere either moaned that the roofs of their churches were falling down or that a new church was desperately needed. In another way, he found it amusing and used to joke, "I could spend the rest of my career building churches." Of course he did just that on numerous occasions.'

He could become annoyed when people talked about short cuts to success. He held firmly that there was no short circuit to the top deck, as he put it. He advised young singers and musicians to take the climb step by step and to be patient. He cited his own career and his time with Vincent O'Brien and Sabatini and the musical knowledge he garnered from working with great conductors.

In subsequent years Colum was sometimes asked about the chemistry between his father and John McCormack. In his view, it worked successfully because they were opposites in temperament though of the same mind musically. 'I remember my father as placid, unruffled, good-humoured and even-tempered. From my experience of John, he could explode, swear, and be outspoken. He hurt others, even though he didn't always realise it. My father was able for him and understood him. Their friendship was deep and lasting and went back a long way. I used to hear my father say that on tour it was Lily who kept the peace. You see, John was no diplomat. With my father he could share a laugh or a joke and at the same time talk about music seriously. It wasn't always his attitude with others.'

Colum O'Brien was to see the friendship at its richest when McCormack's health was deteriorating in September 1945. His father used to visit him at "Glena" and talk to him about the old days. Although he tried to be cheerful and joke about things, John knew he was ill and told Vincent he was not afraid to face death. Neither of them had lost a spark of that religious faith that had always characterised their lives.

Lily McCormack would regularly ring the O'Brien home in Parnell Square to say how John was doing. At other times either

Oliver or Colum O'Brien telephoned her enquiring about the lastest news. On the night of September 16 Oliver rang and was told by Lily, 'Unfortunately John died a few minutes ago.'

Oliver went upstairs to tell his father whose own health was beginning to fail. He was standing by the bedroom window and when he heard the news his head dropped and he began to cry like a child. He was absolutely overcome.

Meanwhile, Colum O'Brien was on holiday in Rockwell College, Co. Tipperary when early next morning one of the priests woke him and said, 'John McCormack is dead. I heard it on the radio news this morning. I'm sure they'll be looking for you at home.'

Shortly afterwards he received a message from home asking him to return immediately. By now his father had made out his tributes to McCormack for the newspapers and Radio Eireann. He looked terribly upset and said he couldn't possibly read out the radio tribute. Turning to Colum, he said, 'You do it for me, son.'

18

Teaching in New York

A t the age of eight, Carol Ann McCormack contracted scarlet fever and was removed to a Dublin hospital. Later, while recovering she sometimes passed the time in the ward playing with her jigsaw puzzle. One afternoon it accidentally fell on the floor beside her bed; picking it up for her a woman visitor remarked, 'Just because you're John McCormack's grand-daughter doesn't mean you can fling the jigsaw all over the floor.'

She had no idea what the woman meant and vowed that she must find out as soon as possible. The truth was that her father Count Cyril McCormack had not yet introduced her to the McCormack legend, preferring no doubt to leave that to another time. In hindsight she says there was good and bad in such an attitude, for in subsequent years she met people who knew more about her grandfather than she herself did, and it made her feel a little ashamed.

'We weren't brought up to think we were any better than anybody else, with the result that I've always counted among my friends people from different strata of society. I think that is why my father didn't emphasise the McCormack legend. He was also insistent that we weren't brought up to be snobs, but rather as normal children.'

We were lunching in the QV.2 restaurant and the conversation naturally revolved around the McCormack legend. She produced the two gold medals her grandparents had won years before at the Dublin Feis Ceoil; one was inscribed with the words *Tenor: 1903, John F. MacCormack*. The 'Mac' was mistakenly misspelt and should have read 'Mc'. The inscription on the second medal was: *Irish Solo Soprano, Lily Foley 1902*.

Like her brother John and her sister Patricia, Carol Ann was born in "Glena" in Booterstown. By the age of twenty she had trained as a Montessori teacher and decided to go to New York, the reason being that her grandmother Lily McCormack was living there and so in her own words she wouldn't be going there 'stone cold'. It was in the early 1960s and she got a post in the Holy Child School in Long Island.

At this time Lily resided in an 16th floor apartment in Fifth Avenue and though in her seventies was still vivacious and energetic. Sometimes Carol Ann stayed with her at weekends and described the apartment as lovely and functional, ideal for a woman of her age living alone. It was here she came face to face with the McCormack legend, with photographs of the great tenor on the sitting-room walls as well as the paintings he and Lily had once bought together.

'Gran talked about him as though he was in the next room,' she recalled. 'Her memory was spot on. She called him Johnny and in conversation would say, "Johnny would have liked it done this way or that way." I think she was disappointed that none of her children or grandchildren turned out to be operatic or concert singers. I think she would have loved to see that happen.'

Together she and Lily went to the opera at the Metropolitan and sat in one of her grandmother's friend's boxes. Once they went to a matinee which was being broadcast live and during the interval were invited into an adjacent room where a musical quiz was being held to fill in the time. Carol Ann was struck by her grandmother's deep interest in opera and at one performance she turned to her and said, 'Look at those microphones...we didn't have 'mikes' in your grandfather's day at the Met.'

She could see that Lily was never bored in New York. 'Gran

168

dressed elegantly and was always on to me to turn myself out nicely but I'm afraid I wasn't always able to do that as I had to consider the expense factor. For her age she was very with-it, fashion-wise, and possessed a fine wardrobe. And she liked to shop at Bloomingdales and once when I accompanied her she became incensed when she heard this woman remark in the ladies, "Wouldn't you think if she dyed her hair she'd dye her eyebrows as well." Like myself, she was naturally coloured but her eyebrows went grey. Anyway, she nearly bit the head off the woman, and turning to me remarked, "How dare she make such a rude remark."'

It was obvious to Carol Ann why she loved the city. Besides going to the opera and theatre, she dined out with old friends or went along to quiet dinner parties. She set her own pace, got on well with people and remained a good social organiser. In this respect, she had heard stories about her grandmother and how in John's days she knew the invitations to accept and the ones to turn down politely.

To Carol Ann, it was an important gift and she often wondered how her famous grandfather would have fared without an organising mind like Lily's behind him. She now concluded that they must have been an ideal combination: John, on the one hand, being idolised by his fans, Lily, on the other hand, working feverishly behind the scenes to ensure that he was being directed wisely.

'Lily was a very organised lady. For instance, she once went into her bathroom in her apartment and the door refused to open afterwards. Realising that her cleaner would be arriving in about four hours she decided to busy herself. She washed her hair and whatever clothes she had in there with her; then the entire room and sat around there quite happily until the cleaner came along. There was, it seems, no hint of panic, no undue anxiety.'

As she learned more about her grandmother and the McCormack legend, she was convinced that they were lucky people who had been born at exactly the right time and with exactly the right gifts. A lot of people in her view were either before or after their time but her grandparents were both absolutely of their time and age and were able to take advantage of whatever was going. Vocally, her grandfather was able to rest his voice as he sailed overseas to concerts, not like today's singers in the jet-age who were often expected to perform on the day of arrival.

In addition, he was able to capitalise on the advent of recording and the radio, most notably in America. Starting out his career in London he was also helped by individual patronage, something that scarcely existed nowadays. 'I regard my grandfather as a quintessential Irishman and musically there is proof of this, because he always included in his concert programmes Irish songs and ballads. Gran, for her part, was ever on to me about my accent. I can hear her say, "Carol, you mustn't lose your Irish accent." At the time in New York I was beginning to pick up Americanisms and she was afraid I'd lose whatever brogue I had. She had retained her Irish accent despite many years there; indeed, she had worked on it.'

To Carol Ann, her grandmother was living out her life in relaxed style. Below her Fifth Avenue apartment there was a restaurant and when she wanted the menu it was put into her letterbox, and after making a choice the dish was sent by lift to her floor. Furthermore, the view from the top window of her apartment was fascinating, as it took in the New York Zoo and the green expanse of Central Park. 'When I stayed with Gran I sometimes awoke to the roar of lions, and on St. Patrick's Day the playing of "The Wild Colonial Boy" went on for hours.'

In winter when the weather became bad she invited her grandmother to stay with her and she was as always great company. Sometimes she would recall the old days when she and John entertained Fritz Kreisler, Rachmaninov and others and music and good conversation was the order. 'I could see now what it all meant to Gran, yet she wasn't a woman to immerse herself in the past, in fact she was quite up with current happenings.'

When I asked her what six of her grandfather's records she would like to bring to a desert island with her, she plumped first for

"Il mio tesoro" and then "I Hear You Calling Me". There were others she liked to listen to at her home in Booterstown such as "The Fairy Tree", "I'll Walk Beside You", "Love Thee Dearest", "O del mio amato ben" and others, so she found it difficult to restrict the choice solely to six.

She thought that the celebrations in 1984 to mark the centenary of her grandfather's birth were memorable except for the poorly designed stamp to commemorate the occasion. 'I think they could have produced a better design, otherwise I enjoyed the fuss made about him and the excitement of the special concerts. I do think it's important to perpetuate his memory, if only to show the world that we Irish appreciate our talented people.

'In this respect, there's no fear that James Joyce will be allowed to slip into oblivion – I mean not while people such as David Norris are alive. But I can see no real successor to Liam Breen who has done such a wonderful job to keep the memory alive of my grandfather's achievements. I suppose in the years to come it will be up to the McCormack family to carry on Liam's unselfish and energetic work.'

In recent years Carol Ann has made it her business to make the presentation of the John McCormack Cup to the prize-winner at the Feis Ceoil and doing it, she says, makes her feel proud of what he had achieved singing all over the world.

Carol Ann's sister Patricia (Tish to her family and friends) was employed for six years during the 1960s as an Aer Lingus ground hostess and so had an opportunity to visit New York on a regular basis. Sometimes she stayed with her grandmother and came to know her better. 'Gran always gave me breakfast and in return I'd make tea for her in the afternoon.'

To Tish she was a great fun person and marvellous company to be with. Together they visited the Broadway theatre, ballet and the opera at the Met, and although her grandmother was getting on in years and was by now arthritic she was fond of shopping. In conversation she referred to her late husband as 'my beloved John' and liked to tell anecdotes about their happy days together.

'Gran enjoyed people,' Tish recalled, 'and she enjoyed life; she was gay in the best sense of that word. She could fit into any kind of society and still be a lady.'

When I joined Tish for dinner she was wearing a black opal brooch given to her by her grandmother. Good-humoured and vivacious, she said she was too young to remember much about her grandfather. 'I can vaguely recall sitting on his knee and punching the keys of the piano with my fists. At the time he appeared large and avuncular and because I was tiny he looked ever so tall. He wore striped trousers and I used to play with his waistcoat watch. Once, when we went to "Glena" for afternoon tea, he gave us a plate of strawberries and cream. I remember him as a big and kind man with a broad smile and hearty laugh.'

She would be about the age of thirteen before she became acquainted with the McCormack legend, simply because as children they were too busy growing up to dwell on the past. As the saga, however, began to unfold, especially when her father Cyril reminded them about their grandfather's astonishing popularity as a concert artist, it took on a new meaning for Tish. One evening in the old Met in New York where half way up the stairway there was a bust of John McCormack, an American friend turned and remarked to her excitedly, 'Gee, so you are his grand-daughter!'

Tish was never quite sure whether the Irish would greet her grandfather in such an ecstatic manner, although in 1984 – the centenary year of his birth – she was invited to take the salute in the St. Patrick's Day parade in Athlone and in her own words, felt very proud. She had also visited Liam Breen's private museum and thought he had done a wonderful job in collecting so much valuable McCormack memorabilia. She was also encouraged by the fact that many of his old records had now been issued as CDs. Her greatest favourite was "I Hear You Calling Me", though there were others like "Somewhere a Voice Is Calling" and "Macushla" that appealed to her.

172

Lily McCormack attended her wedding in University Church, Dublin, in 1969 when she married Englishman John Tinne – and she still has the photograph of herself, John and Lily together. Since she was obliged to quit Aer Lingus on getting married – a ridiculous rule, she reckoned at the time – she and her husband went into private catering. Later on her son Dirk and daughter Louise were born; today Dirk works with a chemical firm in Italy while Louise recently graduated as a nurse.

In the early eighties Tish took on a new challenge when she involved herself in the work of assisting the mentally handicapped. She started in Devlin, Co. Westmeath as a social therapist, preparing the young people for successful integration into society. She gradually became totally involved. However, she suffered her own private grief when her husband John became ill with cancer and died at the early age of forty-nine.

She now lives in Trim, Co. Meath and manages South Hill Enterprises – a co-op project based in a factory in Athboy, about seven miles from Devlin. Here a group of handicapped trainees produce a range of confectionery, including chocolates for sale in surrounding towns. What is important about this project, which is grant-aided by the EU, is that the disadvantaged are working near the open employment market.

'I really enjoy my work here,' Tish McCormack told me. 'And I derive a lot of personal satisfaction watching the workers getting more proficient every day. I'm also acquiring more business acumen.'

Helping in the QV.2 at weekends is, she assured me, a nice contrast and keeps her in touch with her family and Dublin friends. She and her sister-in-law Sylvia McCormack in fact painted the interior of the restaurant a striking yellow. 'Sylvia is very talented,' remarked Tish, 'and runs a unique shop and workshop in South Anne Street.'

The shop, I should add, is called Paint Mischief and specialises in decorative finishes as well as offering examples of Sylvia

173

McCormack's own work on terracotta pots, trays and candlesticks.

Inevitably, the conversation came round to singing. Had she a voice?

'Gran wanted me to have my voice trained,' Tish said, 'but I never did. All the McCormacks loved singing and I suppose we should have got vocal coaching. My brother John was a boy soprano in Downside where he went to school and once sang on a BBC programme. I think my father Cyril didn't want to be a singer because he feared that people would be forever comparing his voice to that of his father's. Gwen was of course eager to be an opera singer but seemingly her voice was too small.'

She thought that with the lack of opportunities here for singers, especially tenors, there was no great incentive for young people to consider a singing career. It was different, she thought, in John McCormack's day when there wasn't the same competition from rock and pop and television.

Tish, like most of the other members of the McCormack family, was upset recently when excluded from the guest list at the ceremony to mark the re-opening of the refurbished John McCormack Foyer in the National Concert Hall in early 1995. Needless to say, Count John McCormack could be excused for feeling peeved when his invitation was addressed to "Mr John McCormack" and with no mention of his wife Sylvia.

To Tish McCormack the gaffe was inexcusable, the more so since in the official speeches no reference was made to her grandfather. 'Can you imagine that kind of thing happening in America or Britain?' she said, more saddened than angry. Was it, I wondered, just another example of the kind of apathetic attitude one sometimes comes across here when we try to honour our great ones.

Both Carol Ann and her sister Tish had come to know Kevin Foley during his visits home from South Africa where he had worked in business. But it was Gwen Pyke who later told me that Kevin had died at his home in Johannesburg in 1993. Years before Gwen and Cyril McCormack had been particularly close to their adopted brother in New York and afterwards when he went to school at Downside in England.

Their mother Lily McCormack had always ensured that Kevin and his brothers and sisters remained close to the family. After she herself died at the age of eighty-four in 1971, her published will revealed that she had left an estate of between £100,000 and £200,000. She directed that her son Cyril and daughter Gwen, and Kevin Foley, should receive the bulk after bequests of £200 each to three grand-daughters, three grandsons, three nieces and a maid.

Lily further stipulated that Kevin Foley – or McCormack as stated in the will – should receive half of the remaining estate and the other half should be shared equally with her own daughter and son, who also received personal property and jewellery. In leaving half of her estate to her adopted son, Mrs McCormack said she was doing so because 'Cyril and Gwendolyn are well and amply provided for by the large trust created by their father.'

Gwen Pyke agreed that the adoption of Kevin Foley had brought great joy to her mother as well as her father and she was in no way surprised by her mother's generous gesture towards Kevin.

19

Back to Moore Abbey

Driving through the long avenue leading up to 17th Century Moore Abbey, you discover a strange new world compared with the days in the mid 1920s and '30s when John and Lily McCormack entertained their friends to the sound of music and laughter.

For as you approach the ancient Abbey, you are likely – as I did – to meet pedestrians strolling through the walled demesne of field and forest amid a scene of serenity. They are part of the 170 handicapped people being cared for there; and in the distance you can easily pick out the chalets and workshops where they fruitfully pass their time.

McCormack would undoubtedly have approved the transformation. As we have seen, he had a generous spirit and loved children and humanity as a whole. Lily McCormack used to call Moore Abbey her 'dream home' while her husband was fond of calling it his *only* Irish home. After the death of John, she sometimes visited the Abbey and on one occasion gave an inscribed photograph of him to the Rev Mother and today it rests on the McCormack grand piano in the large reception room on the ground floor.

And resting on a nearby table is the visitor's book with many names, including those of Liam Breen, Frank Patterson, Louis Browne, John McNally and Robert White. From time to time these singers gave individual concerts in the building, happy no doubt to be identified with the John McCormack links. Gone, however, is the air of grandeur that must have permeated the Abbey in past centuries; it has been replaced by a more pragmatic atmosphere and where the handicapped are concerned, one of real hope.

Gone also is the poplar tree on the river bank under which McCormack sang "A Fairy Story by the Fire" to a group of children in the film "Song of my Heart". It was levelled by a storm in 1957. For a long time the land was farmed under the direction of a steward at the Abbey but since the late 1960s onwards it has been leased out to local farmers.

Like many old Irish houses Moore Abbey has its ghosts, Sister Brighid Moloney will tell you in a soft voice. There is the red-haired monk for one, whose in corrupt body was disinterred in the last century and the headless horseman that rides on stormy nights, cloak flying, under the ancient yews in the Monks' Walk.

Since her arrival at the Abbey in 1973 Sr Brighid has explained to many an Irish and foreign visitor the history of the place and how the Sisters of Charity of Jesus and Mary came to buy it from Lord Drogheda, after John and Lily McCormack gave up the lease in the year 1937.

Incredibly, the house and the 300 acres on which it stands was sold to the Belgian order of nuns for £8,000. At the time, said Sr Moloney, neither Irish religious orders nor farmers showed any great interest in acquiring it, and with the Sisters of Charity of Jesus and Mary on the look-out for a suitable home in Ireland, Lord Drogheda agreed to sell to them. The Catholic Bishop of Kildare and Leighlin, the Right Rev. Thomas Keogh was not it seems enthusiastic about the nuns coming here, but in time came to accept that their arrival could be beneficial.

Many repairs had to be carried out to the building, but on the outbreak of war in 1939 all work came to a standstill. At last in Holy Week 1946 Mother Finbarr Broderick, Srs. Redempta McNamee, Carmel Walsh and Mary Rose Gleeson arrived at the Abbey. Cleaning, scrubbing and sewing went on non-stop while the interior was being prepared to receive girls whose handicap was epilepsy.

According to Sr Brighid, tragedy struck on 20 March 1947 when a fire broke out and gutted the entire Eastern wing. There was nothing else for it except to start all over again. In September 1948, however, it was officially opened by Dr Noel Browne, Minister for Health, in the presence of Bishop Keogh. In the mid-1950s when epilepsy was got under successful control, thanks partly to the care devoted to the victims in the special Moore Abbey medical units, the Order henceforth decided to take in mentally handicapped children and adults and extra units were provided to accommodate them. And in 1973 the extensive new buildings were ready for use as more were received.

Sr Brighid talked proudly about the provision of the two new indoor swimming pools, concert hall, physiotherapy department and the new chapel. 'The work for the handicapped here is arduous but rewarding,' she added. 'And we believe that God will provide, which was a favourite saying of our Congregation's founder, Rev Peter Joseph Triest. We look to the future as a challenge which we must meet.'

From an early age she said she was interested in the singing of John McCormack and collected his records. Inside the Abbey, in a hallway off the reception room, she showed me a small gallery of photographs of the tenor relating to some of the most memorable moments of his career. People still came to the Abbey just because of its McCormack associations and wanted to learn more about his life there.

During the 1984 celebrations to the mark the centenary of his birth in Athlone, Sr Brighid said that Count Cyril McCormack visited Moore Abbey with members of his family to renew acquaintance with the place that afforded him so many happy memories. He stayed for a few days and was happy to tell visitors some facts about his father's life. 'I like to show people over the walks which John McCormack used to take while he lived here,' she told me. 'I bring them into the library which is full of the most historic books on Irish and English literature and history and which were left here by Lord Drogheda, after he sold it to our Congregation. And although the McCormacks auctioned many of their own items on their departure from the Abbey in 1937, some valuables like these books remained as an integral part of the building.'

Before the McCormacks leased Moore Abbey from Lord Drogheda in 1925, they lived for a while in another large house in the village of Monasterevin, but the tenor was often restless where houses were concerned and decided to move to the bigger Moore Abbey which could accommodate more of his friends and had good fishing and hunting amenities.

Lily soon fell in love with the place. In her autobiography she gives a good idea of what the Abbey meant to her and the family. 'We always tried to get back to it for Christmas. John was never happier than when the house was filled with young people, and our own children always brought some school friends home for the holidays.'

Famous people from different walks of life signed the visitors' book, and these included conductor Hamilton Harty, boxer Gene Tunney and opera star Lucrezia Bori. Since McCormack loved parties it was not surprising that he should encourage the holding of an annual fancy dress ball. Lily McCormack remembered that at the first one in 1929 they had a real romance. Among the guests were a group of American naval officers from the flagship *Detroit* which had arrived in Dublin that week and she asked the Commander and his officers to the ball. The upshot was that a pretty female guest from Dublin danced 'half the night away' with one of the young American officers and in the subsequent weeks became romantically attached. 'They were married a year later,' Lily recalled.

During the months each year that the tenor spent in Moore Abbey he was never short of interests to occupy his time. The More O'Farrells continued to train his racehorses, one of which was named

Gwendolyn after his only daughter. Everyone knew that his avowed ambition was to win the English Derby and for five years he lived that dream. Sadly, it was a dream that was never to be realised, and although it cost him a great deal of money, he used to tell friends that it was well worth it.

He made no secret that his days at the Abbey were the most enjoyable of his life. The grandeur and size of the place seemed to match up to his gregarious and expansive personality; the role of the country squire suited him and he was, it was said, never self-conscious about his new status. There is a tendency in Ireland for people to criticise those who scale the heights and end up as one of the modern day gentry, as though they are not entitled to such elevation because of their humble origins. It is, of course, another example of begrudgery and something to be abhorred.

In McCormack's time some people complained of his lavish lifestyle, his remoteness from ordinary life and his outward show of wealth. As far as one can gather however, the upstairs, downstairs way of life was never very apparent in the McCormacks' time in Moore Abbey; indeed in describing one particular Christmas Eve scene Lily McCormack happily referred to the family, house staff and a few friends gathered in the chapel for Midnight Mass.

'We joined in the "Adeste Fideles", led by John.' Immediately after Mass, he proceeded to the piano in the truly "baronial" hall where there was a huge Christmas tree with presents for everyone, and we sang the "Adeste Fideles" again. I can see the great hall now, lighted by the candles on the tree and in the sconces, with John playing heavenly music. Christmas, and all that it means, was indeed with us and we were blessed.'

To illustrate once more that on these festive occasions there was little distinction drawn between staff and guests, gifts were distributed to all and sundry. And Lily recalled that they'd be given champagne and sandwiches and as the guests were leaving everyone would stand on the front steps and sing Christmas carols to wish them Godspeed.

Christmas day was another matter. By now the tenor's parents Andrew and Hannah were living in Greystones and he would arrange for them, as well as Lily's family in Dublin, to be conveyed by car to Moore Abbey so as to ensure a truly family gathering. The McCormacks' adopted son Kevin would be there and his brother Tommy, both of whose education at Downside College in England was being paid for by the tenor.

Gifts were distributed and before long McCormack would go to the piano and begin the singing in which everyone was soon expected to join. Afterwards they would all sit around the log fire in the open fireplace and chat and drink. Or as Lily McCormack remembered: 'Murphy, our devoted butler of many years, who was a host in himself on these occasions, invariably appeared at the right moment with a glass-laden tray of Christmas cheer. No matter how large the crowd, he'd say, "Ah, the more the merrier, Madam!"'

Ghost stories sometimes figured in the lively conversation. A headless warrior on horseback was, for instance, supposed to haunt the Monks' Walk near the house. Guests occasionally ventured down there to lie in wait for him, but even the brightest moonlit nights failed dismally to produce either the ghost or the sound of hoofs, which they were assured had been heard in the past. On other occasions Lily and her husband took the long, winding yew walk, which by now had become popular with guests refreshing themselves after a cordial lunch washed down with good wine. As Lily was to say, 'I have seen many lovely yew walks but none to equal the one at Moore Abbey. I hadn't known that yews could grow so tall and in their growing meet overhead in a Gothic arch. Entering the long walk, one felt a hush just as one does in going into a cathedral.'

McCormack never tired of entertaining. When his old friend Archbishop Curley of Baltimore joined him for dinner along with General Sean MacEoin and others, he'd occasionally start a friendly argument to ensure that everyone enjoyed themselves at the table. No one could be more provocative when he wanted. When his accompanist Teddy Schneider was the guest they usually talked about the music scene in America and elsewhere and the number of new songs that the tenor had received from Irish songwriters and those overseas.

When eventually he got rid of his racehorses and closed his stables at Moore Abbey his interest in country life began to wane. It was Lily who first noticed the change. 'After that, John never felt the same about the place. Perhaps this was because country life never had much appeal for him without excitement, even if he was a good shot and bagged a lot of pheasants.'

Would it have been any different if he had managed to win the Derby?

20

Patterson in America

At fifty-three, Frank Patterson has retained his soft Tipperary accent, personal charm, and zest for life. And there is a pattern to his life that bears comparison with that of John McCormack. He is also a product of an Irish town – Clonmel in his case – and while he has never sung at Covent Garden or the Metropolitan Opera House, his concert career blossomed when he went to America. Shades of McCormack in his halcyon days.

In settling with his wife Eily O'Grady and their son Eanan in the village of Bronxville, a 30 minute drive from Manhattan, he surprised not a few music lovers in Ireland in the early 1990s. For the tenor's television series, *For Your Pleasure* was enjoying top ratings and his records were selling widely, although on the concert circuit it was noticeable that it was getting harder to fill halls. The arrival of a vibrant new pop and rock culture was chiefly to blame and this proved irresistible to the young generation.

When I put it to him in the summer of 1995 that this was one of the reasons why he decided to go to America, he said it wasn't the chief reason. 'The main reason why we are now living there is because of our son Eanan,' he explained. 'He won a place at the Juilliard School where he is studying the violin and when time permits he joins Eily and myself on the concert stage. Although only seventeen, he's a formidable act, if I may say so. I was adamant that we should all be together, even if it meant pulling up our roots in Ireland.'

He admits he has found the entertainment scene in America refreshing. 'What I discovered there was my performing ability. Over there – or, indeed, outside of Ireland – people are not slow to tell you they admire your voice and this gives one encouragement and a new-found confidence. In Ireland there has been, to my mind, always a preference for the Italian tenor, even to the exclusion of the German or French tenor. All people seemed to want were rousing Italian operatic arias, little else. Of course there is much more to singing than that.

'I once went to hear Luciano Pavarotti at the Gaiety Theatre and found myself sitting beside two of his fans. When he opened his programme with a classical German song the applause in the theatre was lukewarm, in fact the fellows beside me never applauded at all. But the moment Luciano sang the big aria "O Paradiso" they almost jumped out of their seats with enthusiasm.'

He is a great admirer, though, of Pavarotti and says his voice has a lovely quality, but it is his magnetic stage personality that he finds so extraordinary. 'I've no doubt that he is the equal of some of the greatest tenors of the past.'

In any conversation on John McCormack the question inevitably arises about his phenomenal recording output and the tangible legacy he left in this respect. When I talked to Frank Patterson he had just recorded a new CD of Broadway songs, something he said, he had long wanted to do. It includes numbers from *Camelot*, the *Phantom of the Opera* and other popular shows. This brings to thirty-five the number of LPs and CDs he has recorded, featuring ballads, folk songs, operatic arias and classical songs in six languages.

His two dozen or more Polygram and Philips record albums – many gold and platinum – are available worldwide. He has worked with such distinguished conductors as Sir Colin Davis, Sir Charles Groves, Karl Richter and Paul Sacher. In America, however, it is concert work that keeps him on the road. In recent years he has been doing between one hundred and one hundred and twenty concerts across America and Canada, playing in city theatres to high school halls. He has discovered that Australia is a lucrative scene for him with audiences warm and responsive. When I reminded him that many years ago John McCormack had found the same thing to be true, he said that his name was still remembered there. In one big theatre there was a large photograph showing the tenor on stage with his accompanist Dr Vincent O'Brien.

Similarly in his concert tours in America, songs long associated with McCormack are requested. On occasions he is asked to sing "Macushla", "Kathleen Mavourneen" and "Maggie", and he usually includes in his programme "Il mio tesoro".

'I'm on the road constantly with Eily, who is my accompanist, sometimes staying over in California for four days to take in two or three cities at a time. It can be gruelling, particularly in the winter when you may arrive in a Canadian city where there's no-one to meet you at the airport and the weather is 40 degrees below zero. Now I know what it must have been like for McCormack doing coast to coast tours, which in his day meant lengthy rail travel; mostly I travel by plane or take the car if the venue is Boston or somewhere near.'

Another discovery he made in America was the improvement in his voice. 'I'm a better singer now I'd say, or at least a better singer than I was fifteen years ago. My voice has matured and the middle register in particular has strengthened. It's a great test of a man to be singing better in his fifties than in his twenties, as I feel is true in my case, so I must be doing something right. If your voice is looked after and if you're singing with the proper technique and within your own scope then I feel it will not be damaged.'

During his stay in Ireland this year during July and August he visited his throat specialist in Dublin. 'I've been going to Dr McAuliffe Curtin for many years just to ensure that everything is in order. He looked down my throat and did the usual tests and told me that the mechanism was in perfect shape. Needless to say, I found that most reassuring.' He also found time to make a brief appearance in the Neil Jordan film about General Michael Collins being shot on location in Dublin. In one important restaurant scene he sings "Macushla". Some years ago he made his screen debut in *The Dead*, which was based on a short story of the same name by James Joyce. Directed by the late John Huston, he played Joyce's classic tenor Bartell D'Arcy and in one scene is heard singing an old Irish folk song "The Lass of Aughrim" which stirs long suppressed memories in the character of Gretta Conroy (Anjelica Huston).

Frank Patterson made his first appearance as a boy soprano in his hometown of Clonmel in 1961 and as far back as he can remember, he says he wanted to be a singer. After leaving school at the age of fourteen, he was apprenticed to the printing trade for the next four and half years. At nineteen he decided to come to Dublin to pursue a singing career. He had already written to music colleges and individuals and was disappointed to receive no replies.

'For a while in Dublin I felt despondent,' he said. 'I wondered if I could possibly succeed. But gradually things fell into place. I began my vocal studies with the famed Dr Hans Waldermar Rosen while at the same time attending a course of acting at the National Academy of Theatre and Allied Arts. When I began to win major awards at the Feis Ceoil I believed in myself and what people I respected were saying about my voice.'

Meeting Eily O'Grady, he agrees, was also a turning point in his life. He joined her on an American tour with a group of singers and their romance blossomed and inside a few years they were married. Frank had become part of one of the most musical families in Ireland, as Eily's three sisters, including Geraldine, were all gifted musicians. Unlike John McCormack, who took the road to London and was lucky to find a patron, he and Eily went to Paris and stayed there for four years.

He began to study with the famous soprano Janine Micheau and on his own admission acquired a mature vocal technique. Since she had sung with some renowned tenors in her time, he found her approach exceedingly good. 'I got my top notes from her and also how to achieve a balance between the different voice registers. At the time I was singing a lot of baroque music and more or less specialising in the classical field. But by the time I returned to Dublin I had a good knowledge of the true art of singing.'

He was in demand in oratorio in Ireland and Britain and was also a guest soloist with the Royal Philharmonic, the Orchestre de Paris, the Academy of St. Martin in the Fields and the Liverpool Philharmonic Orchestra. As a recording artist, he was kept extremely busy with new releases once or twice a year. And he made regular appearances on television. He says the highlight of his career came in 1979 when he was invited to be the soloist at the Papal Mass in Phoenix Park, during Pope John Paul's visit to Ireland. Over one million people were in attendance.

As time went on his career was inviting greater comparison with John McCormack's, except that he was not attracted to opera. He was honoured by the Vatican when Pope John Paul II conferred on him the Knighthood of St. Gregory the Great in 1984. And anyone looking for a whiff of scandal in his life and career will not find it, or at least nothing of the sort has come to my notice. His wife Eily is very supportive and I imagine acts as his honorary private secretary when she is not accompanying him in concert.

After about nine years of married life, their son Eanan was born and his arrival gave a new impetus to their lives. As Frank recalled, 'Up to then we had done everything we wanted to do in music in Ireland, we were happy and secure, but now there was someone else to think about. I think Eanan's coming gave me an urge to try something new.'

Eventually it led to his and Eily's decision to go to America. For sometime they had been back and forward doing concerts, so settling there seemed almost the natural thing to do. The music scene had, of course, changed dramatically since McCormack's time; a whole generation or two of Irish had passed on and with them the audiences who enjoyed ballads such as "The Irish Emigrant", "Green Isle of

Erin" and "Believe Me". The big names now were Paddy Reilly, of "The Fields of Athenry" fame, Clannad, Makem & Clancy, Phil Coulter, the Chieftains and a host of other popular entertainers. Competition was razor-keen and it seemed Americans and Irish-Americans were only prepared to pay for the very best vocal acts.

With his networking flair, good connections and ability to sing in six languages, Frank Patterson soon made his mark. He proved his versatility by combining in his concert programmes Phil Coulter's "The Town I Love so Well" with Mozart's "Il mio tesoro" and Schubert's "Serenade" with "Danny Boy". Because he sang to different ethnic groups, he even learned some Jewish songs on one occasion to go along with Italian, French and Irish songs.

'The new generation of Irish in America want all kinds of music and songs,' he says, 'and these include good new songs. I'm always on the lookout for them but they're not easy to find.'

When I talked to him in Dublin he had three hundred songs in his music bag and admitted that he had a huge repertoire to draw upon. He is fortunate: he can learn a song very quickly.

For the past six years he has managed to pack New York's Radio City Music Hall to its capacity of 6,000 people and attributes the success of the show partly to producer Fred O'Donovan. 'It's a big spectacular with Irish traditional dancers and folk groups and Fred makes the whole thing gel extraordinarily well. He is an imaginative director and understands the Irish scene in America and the kind of material they enjoy.'

With more and more of our singers and entertainers going abroad to eke out a living, I asked him if it was possible for a tenor to make a decent living in Ireland. 'I don't think you can,' Frank replied thoughtfully. 'It's just too small. I mean, you might last a couple of years and then your audience would diminish and you'd be forced to look elsewhere for work. The truth is the world must be your oyster; you have to get out there on the road, live in hotels, travel all over the place, ignore the hardship travel entails. To put it another way,

Ireland is a lovely little market, a great little place, but you can't have a career here. I used to think you could. I cannot say that anymore. I suppose I'm fortunate that I've got Eily with me on the road, it makes it easier for me.'

When I told him that tenors were nowadays in short supply in Ireland, he said he had been impressed by Ronan Tynan's voice; he had also heard about Finbar Wright. He hoped to live in America for another ten years, or at least until their son Eanan's education was complete – he was planning to be a surgeon.

'Eventually I would like to come back here and do some voice coaching. Having travelled the road myself, I think I could be helpful to aspiring tenors. I could identify problems and offer good advice; a lot of people tend to write off a singer because he may not have the top notes at a given time. I think I've the patience to be a teacher and to explain things just as Janine Micheau in Paris used to describe to me what the sensation should be hitting a particular note.'

Like McCormack, who was a friend of American Presidents, among them Roosevelt, Frank Patterson has also graced the White House and sung for more modern presidents such as Reagan and Clinton. And he counts among his friends Robert Merrill, who is a golfing colleague. It will be remembered that Merrill was one of the great American baritones of his time, a firm Metropolitan favourite.

'Robert still sings at clubhouse functions and his voice is as powerful and well-projected as ever,' Frank says. 'For a small man I don't know where all that power comes from.'

Despite changing tastes, he is optimistic about the future for the concert artist. He argues that everywhere you go there are people who love to hear a good song well sung. They differ from opera buffs and symphony concert audiences; for these people it is the song and the singer and they will sit back and listen and feel relaxed. Many years ago, he said, thousands of people came out in America to hear "their man" who happened to be John McCormack, and they idolised him. There were still people who followed their favourite

191

tenor. 'I have people coming to listen to me about a dozen times in the year; they follow me round.'

After a lifetime in singing, had he any regrets?

'Not really,' he said. 'I suppose I'd like to have done more opera, apart from that I think I've achieved most of the things I wanted.'

And like McCormack, he loves to return to Ireland, to meet the plain people of the country, to sing for them, and to project on stage the kind of amiability that is the hallmark of his personality.

Personality is after all, he says, essential to a singer's success.

CHAPTER
21

Cheapening his Art?

Why is it when operatic or Lieder singers feature in their repertoire or recorded music folk songs, ballads or pop they are accused of cheapening their art or pandering to the sentimental even sometimes vulgar tastes of the public? When José Carreras, for example, recorded two of America's most famous musicals, *South Pacific* and *West Side Story* he was criticised in certain quarters but he was quick to reply that both musicals were of exceptional appeal and charm.

'My reasons for singing the so-called popular music are several,' he explained in his recent autobiography, *Singing from the Soul*. 'First, I enjoy it, as do millions of other fans. I also find it relaxing to sing. But deep down I confess to an ulterior motive: I sing popular tunes because I believe that this is the way to capture new fans for the opera. My hope is that record buyers who listen to *South Pacific* and *West Side Story* may develop an interest in Carreras the vocalist and then discover through him a whole new world of beauty and fascination – the opera.'

There is, I believe, some logic in Carreras's philosophy, just as there is in the claim that singers like Gigli, Schipa and more recently Giuseppe di Stefano won new friends for bel canto by recording Neapolitan songs. Carreras calls it 'abandoning the grand manner' for the sake of the tune. It doesn't always follow, of course that those who love to hear "Nessun dorma" would buy a ticket for *Turandot*.

And in his autobiography, *My First Forty Years*, Placido Domingo, perhaps the greatest singer/actor on the current operatic circuit, talks candidly of his excursion into popular music and how he came to make the album "Perhaps Love" with John Denver. It sold over a million and a half copies in its first year and a half on the market.

Like his friend José Carreras, he finds it gratifying that he can be appreciated by people who do not enjoy opera, and claims that through non-operatic recordings he is actually helping to stimulate interest in opera.

For example, in England people had written to him to say that until his recording of "Perhaps Love" with John Denver they hadn't heard of him but it had aroused their curiosity and led them to buy tickets to hear him in the *Tales of Hoffmann* at Covent Garden. Now opera, they said, had become their great love.

Domingo, nevertheless, admitted that he also recorded popular music for 'selfish motives' – meaning royalties, no doubt – but reading his book one gets the impression that he enjoys worthwhile popular music. Perhaps it relaxes him after singing performances of Verdi's *Otello* and Wagner's *Lohengrin*.

Early on in his career John McCormack was also aware of the criticism being levelled against him for singing songs such as "The Croppy Boy," "The Foggy Dew", "The Boys of Wexford" and a host of others. But like the modern day Carreras, the Irish tenor was quick to answer his critics. 'The first duty of any artist is to his public,' he asserted. 'He may cultivate them, if he can, but he must do so wisely, so that the people may not be made aware that they are being educated. To them this is distasteful.'

He emphasised that he had 'different tastes to respect' and as his audiences were invariably of great size, he had a particular responsibility to satisfy those tastes. As he elaborated: 'After years of endeavour I have succeeded gradually in incorporating into a programme from six to eight song compositions of genuine musical substance, so have managed to hold the attention of each audience during the interpretation of these "better" songs.'

He was wary of what he described as 'intellectual' tastes. 'I am conscious that some so-called "highbrows" charge me with singing "popular stuff". So I do, and I am proud to be able to sing it, so that it performs its mission: a mission that banishes sadness from darkened hearts, that turns the thoughts in the way they should go, that lifts and encourages – or sends a tear into the eye. If a song that appeals to our better nature happens to have a sentimental touch which is simple enough to reach the simplest heart, is it any less a song for having a purpose than some song more finely made musically, which touches only the few? From the aesthetic standpoint I concede the connoisseur's objection, but two varieties of tastes require my consideration, and I must heed them.'

When he began to sing on a regular basis in concerts in the United States from the year 1912 onwards, his object was, he recalled, to please his audiences. 'I felt then that I could develop a following only by giving people what they wanted to hear and this proved right at the time. My success as a singer of songs has fortunately never been in doubt; indeed, so many people had told me my singing gave them pleasure that I finally concluded that perhaps my mission was to extend my repertoire of songs and my concert tours to ensure that as many people as possible could share in that pleasure. Subsequently my audiences grew in size and in appreciation until eventually I decided to concentrate almost entirely on giving what my audience wanted.'

Careful to avoid misunderstanding by what he meant by a 'simple song', McCormack said he did not mean trashy songs of the order that many Americans knew as 'popular'. What he had in mind were the songs of Stephen Foster which could be described as simple and often beautiful and he had no doubt they would endure because they aroused people's sincere emotions. For his own part, he could say he derived the same enjoyment singing the songs of Bach, Schumann and Schubert as he did singing the simple songs of Ireland or America.

He made a few exceptions. 'Personally I do not care for the music of Debussy, because I miss the note of sincerity in his work. Yet I would feel guilty if I were to find fault with what he has achieved in other respects musically. Ravel, I do admire immensely, and Strauss – there is a master. But when I get to talking about the subject I never fail to think of what George Bernard Shaw once said, replying to the question, "Who is the greatest musician?" I remember Shaw's reply was, "Beethoven, but Mozart was the only master."'

In conversation McCormack while drawing a distinction between those people who appreciated simple songs as opposed to the classical song cycles, would add, 'If a man or woman does not happen to understand a Bach fugue it does not follow that they have no perception of musical beauty. The music potentially may be there without having been cultivated. What I mean is, give it food and light and air in the form of understandable songs sung in a language that the hearer knows and he or she will come to appreciate and, in due course, begin to acquire musical intelligence.'

When Henry Pleasants' *The Great Singers* was published in the middle 1960s McCormack's name figured along with Pasta, Malibran, Lind, Flagstad, Caruso, Tamagno, Zenatello and the de Reszkes. The author sang as a baritone in America and later became a music critic for a Philadelphia newspaper. When he settled in London he was appointed music correspondent for the *New York Times* in central Europe from 1945-55.

The majority of the singers highlighted in the book won fame on the operatic stage and while McCormack comes into this category, Pleasants states he included him because of his versatility as an artist: a singer who was on the one hand capable of exciting connoisseurs of opera and Lieder and, on the other, delighting lovers of folk songs and ballads. The tenor was remembered today, he argued, mainly as a singer of songs like "Kathleen Mavoureen", "Macushla" and "The Rose of Tralee". However, the records he made early in his career such as "Il mio tesoro", "Where'er you

Walk" and "O Sleep, why dost thou leave me" are held by some collectors to have remained unsurpassed in the perfection of their style and vocalism.

Inevitably, Pleasants revived the controversy about McCormack 'lowering his vocal sights' by singing inferior songs and ballads. As he wrote: 'Throughout his long career, he was plagued by critics who, while acknowledging the beauty of his voice and the elegance of his singing, deplored his taste and judgement in the selection of what he sang. His response was always that to sing nothing but the best music was a form of snobbery. "It isn't everyone," he used to say, "who appreciated the more artistic music. The world is full of men and women with humble thoughts and simple sentiments, and who shall despise them – for are they not men and women?" His reward for this democracy was an earned income of about a million dollars a year.'

To Pleasants, the McCormack repertoire was remarkable and must have confounded even his own contemporaries and at the same time caused a certain envy. 'The critics were encouraged in their view of his self-debasement, paradoxically, not only by the inclusion in his programmes of what he felt to be bad, but also what they knew to be good. For example, two groups were always devoted to such composers as Bach, Handel, Haydn, Mozart, Schubert, Schumann and Wolf. The critics were thus reminded continually of how well – and how tastefully – he could sing the best music. It only aggravated their scorn for the sentimental Irish ballads and songs that came at the end – and attracted the masses; and the scorn was not moderated by the fact that he sang this music beautifully, too. Such singing of such stuff, they insisted, was prostitution.

'One might argue – and some did – that McCormack, like Fritz Kreisler, possessed the art of turning lesser metals into gold; there was, certainly, never the trace of condescension toward anything he sang. The same attention of line, tone, phrase, diction and intonation was expended upon the plainest Irish or other popular ditty as upon a Handel or Mozart aria. McCormack's art as musician and vocalist was always admirable, whatever he sang, and as such a source of aesthetic pleasure. But he was hurt by the criticism, and he was always touchy on the subject of repertoire. "I suppose you think," he remarked in 1923 to Sir Compton MacKenzie, editor of *The Gramophone*, "that I sing nothing but muck!"'

In discussing the tenor's wide repertoire, the fact must not be forgotten that as a concert artist he created a powerful impact at big and small venues. A burly figure, he commanded the stage from first to last. He always carried his tiny book of words for fear of 'drying up' in a song, but audiences got used to it, just as Pavarotti's concert audiences today do not question the white handkerchief he holds in one hand. Luciano admits it looks silly in some ways, reminiscent perhaps of the old divas who carried a fichu. He uses the handkerchief, he says, to make himself look less silly. By holding it in his hand he manages to keep himself more in one spot and it also relaxes him. 'It is my security blanket while on the concert stage.'

The same no doubt could be said about McCormack's little notebook containing words of songs. Without it he once confessed he would feel apprehension. That fine Scottish tenor Canon Sydney MacEwan, who probably sounds the closest of all tenors to McCormack, while lauding his voice recalled that 'it was hard for those who never attended a McCormack concert to realise the tremendous excitement that prevailed – the ovation, the love extended to him when he appeared. The perfection of his singing, the limpid velvet of the voice, the musicianship, the warmth, the clarity of diction – his generosity with encores and our reluctance to let him go.'

He was to hear McCormack many times and was never disappointed by any performance. His diction was remarkable. Once while a student at the Royal Academy in London he sat in the cheapest seats of the Royal Albert Hall, high 'in the gods'. He looked so far away and tiny and yet he heard distinctly every word and this was in the pre-microphone age. 'I have so many memories of his glorious concerts in those far-off days and for me this was the only style of singing I wanted.'

It was obvious that audiences, especially in America and Australia, expected McCormack to sing the nostalgic songs of his homeland and they were rarely disappointed. Declan McCormack, a past pupil of the Marist brothers in Athlone, though no relation of the tenor, made the point that his later popularity rested largely, although not exclusively, on the extent to which he became the sad-sweet voice of the Irish diaspora (particularly in America). He expressed the heartache of exile through songs like "Come Back to Erin" and "Kathleen Mavourneen".

'Perhaps some of the poignancy and sincerity with which he sang these songs of personal and ethnic loss came from his witnessing as a growing boy the heartrending emigration scenes which were regular occurrences on the platform of Athlone's Great Southern Railway Station. For it was there that many emigrants from the West of Ireland took their leave (often forever) from their loved ones amidst shrieks of anguish which resembled keening.'

Declan McCormack added that even if McCormack himself was a voluntary emigrant to America, he knew from first-hand experience that for many emigration was a form of 'death-in-life' with 'the bereaved' left at home bemoaning their lost ones and the living 'corpses' floating out to sea in order to be 'buried' in America.

While music lovers could be forgiven for thinking that McCormack sang mostly in coast-to-coast concerts in America, the records reveal that he was revered also in Paris, Berlin and other Continental cities. Writing about his appearance at the Theatre des Champs-Elysees in May 1923, the Paris correspondent of the *New York Herald* stated, 'McCormack is no stranger to Paris. He has sung here many times, both in opera and in song recital. His first appearance here in 1912 at a special performance of *La Boheme* with Madame Melba, was a benefit for the old artists of the Opera-Comique. Some years later he appeared at a benefit concert for the aged professors of the Conservatoire. It was an undoubted triumph.'

And in that same month of May the tenor gave a concert in the Philharmonic Hall, Berlin and attracted not only Berliners but a contingent of Americans in the city, notably from the U.S. Embassy. There was an unanimous demand from members of the audience for the ever popular "Mother Machree" as well as other well-known Irish songs. It was during this successful visit that McCormack was introduced for the first time to Richard Tauber, the popular Austrian-born tenor who made his name both in grand opera and operetta. He and Tauber became good friends and occasionally renewed acquaintances in London, New York and Paris.

In *The Great Singers*, author Henry Pleasants examines the career of Tauber and draws a parallel with that of McCormack, emphasising that both singers achieved legendary fame in different kinds of music, with Tauber remembered best for musical comedy songs like "Dein ist mein ganzes Herz" from Lehar's *Das Land Des Lackelns* ("You are my Heart's Delight" from *The Land of Smiles*). And like McCormack he made an exemplary record of "Il mio tesoro". If the two tenors were to be judged solely on their singing of this single aria, contended Pleasants, the Irish tenor would have the edge, thanks to his Italian schooling. Furthermore, he felt Tauber's voice was less beautiful, and hardly as large. 'One cannot imagine Jan Kubelik, the violinist, saying of Tauber, as he once said of McCormack, "The man must have a Stradivarius in his throat."'

To Pleasants, McCormack was an extremely intelligent singer. Hardly another singer had combined so successfully an immaculate enunciation with a perfect melodic line, and this was one of the secrets of his art, particularly in music of an inferior order, where the melody, however compellingly voiced, was not sufficiently communicative to stand alone. Where the great Chaliapin had 'acted' a ballad, McCormack 'told' it. Chaliapin's art was the lyrical extension of the actor's sustained speech and declamation, assisted by facial expression and gesture; McCormack's was rather an Italianate extension and refinement of the Irish minstrel's storytelling.

His Successors

Bring up McCormack's name in any discussion on Irish tenors and almost inevitably you'll find the question being asked: Who is his real successor? It is on the face of it an unfair question – like asking who are the rightful successors to Caruso or Gigli. Any of us with knowledge of the Italian operatic scene could probably name a dozen or more contenders but that would not necessarily mean there would be agreement among opera buffs. Similarly, in the case of McCormack, the list is a long one, though the qualifications of a number of the candidates falls far short of vocal requirements.

'There's only one McCormack,' Fermoy-born tenor Frank Ryan was reputed to have said when he was asked once in his butcher's shop in Tallow, Co. Waterford whether he considered himself the 'real successor.' It was shortly after he had won the Fr Mathew Cup at the Dublin Feis Ceoil at the age of thirty-five, and the adjudicator had likened his voice to McCormack's. A Dublin evening newspaper headlined the story, THE NEW McCORMACK, but the amiable Frank while chuffed, never thought of billing himself as McCormack's successor.

While his reply to the newspaperman was a wise one, it does not end the debate, so one is left with the problem of the approach to take in naming a list of tenors in the reckoning. Is one talking about the best voice since McCormack's or the best *singer* in terms of musicianship, vocal technique and style? Or perhaps a combination of the two?

The combination of talents seems the more logical approach. Before we proceed with names, it is well to point out here that there are Irish tenors who resent being compared with McCormack, preferring instead to be judged on their own merits and achievements. That is both reasonable and understandable; there are some others, however, who do not mind the great tenor's name being mentioned in their company. Louis Browne, for example, will discuss his records and his approach to singing without any hint of envy.

Finbar Wright is happy to sing at a McCormack commemorative concert, and veteran tenor Hubert Valentine has never shown reluctance to recall personal memories of the tenor. It is a different matter, though, when the question of McCormack imitators arises and tenors are accused of aping him. It can become a controversial subject and I've seen resentment aroused.

I am reminded of the first occasion that the late Michael O'Higgins, the accomplished Dublin vocal tutor, first heard Dermot Troy sing for him at the Royal Irish Academy of Music and made the comment that while other Irish tenors aped John McCormack young Troy did not do so. 'It is a voice that is universal in tone and quality,' Higgins said, and he had no hesitation in offering young Troy a free scholarship to study at the Academy.

The fact remains, however, that Irish tenors could scarcely escape being influenced by the genius of McCormack, just as young Italian lyric tenors have always used Tito Schipa as their model. Nonetheless, there are tenors in Ireland who refuse to sing songs that are closely identified with McCormack such as "I Hear You Calling Me", "The Snowy-Breasted Pearl" and "Molly Bawn". In this unwise? I believe so, for with new musical arrangements quite a number of the McCormack songs could be sung or recorded successfully by contemporary tenors.

In choosing my twelve best candidates for the McCormack

crown I am conscious of the fact that a new generation of music lovers may not be familiar with all of the names, so some background information is being supplied. The names of the twelve are as follows:

1. James Johnston
2. Dermot Troy
3. Josef Locke
4. Frank Ryan
5. Frank Patterson
6. Louis Browne
7. Hubert Valentine
8. Christopher Lynch
9. Michael O'Duffy
10. John Carolan
11. Finbar Wright
12. Charles Kennedy.

The following tenors are also worthy of mention: Patrick O'Hagan, Terence Molloy, Ull Deane, Frank Egerton, Brendan O'Dowda, Sean Ryan, Joseph McNally, Thomas Fletcher, Laurence (Jack) O'Brien, Edmund Browne, Liam Devally, Edwin Fitzgibbon, John Feeney, John Bennett, Brendan Kavanagh, Desmond Jennings, Paul O'Leary, Peter Tomelty, John Thornley, Leo McCaffrey, Bryan Hoey and Ronan Tynan.

Finding the No. 1 successor to McCormack posed, I must admit, no real problem. Belfast-born James Johnston had some of McCormack's finest attributes, namely, superb diction, musicianship, vocal range, easy technique, breath control, a versatility that enabled him to excel in opera, oratorio and in concert work, and he possessed the gift of communicating with an audience.

It is a pity that audiences in Southern Ireland got so few opportunities to hear Johnston as a concert artist as I'm told that in his own Northern Ireland setting they loved his wit and robust personality. He became identified with songs like "Star of the County Down" and "Ireland, Mother Ireland", but would also include in his programme other popular songs such as "The Dark-eyed Sailor" and "Bonny labouring boy".

Like McCormack, he could be blunt and had a propensity to speak his mind – a trait that did not always go down well with opera house managements when he felt they were acting unreasonably. James Shaw, a Belfast colleague and lifelong friend, said of him, 'When you asked Jimmy for his opinion that was precisely what you got – and it wasn't always what you wanted to hear.'

Although his recordings of the *Messiah* and *Elijah* are exemplary, it was as an opera singer that he won fame, first at Sadler's Wells in the late 1940s and later at Covent Garden. Dame Joan Sutherland, with whom he sang in numerous operas, made the point recently that Johnston sang most of his roles in English and this was a deterrent to his being invited abroad to perform. She also felt his operatic career started somewhat late, as he was over forty when he came to the forefront at Sadler's Wells.

He was born in Belfast on 11 August 1903 and started his life as a butcher in the family business. He gained his early music training in church choirs, but when a benefactor offered to pay his way for voice-training in Italy his Methodist father angrily rejected it. 'No son of mine is going on the stage; it's the sure way to hell!'

The singer's chance arrived, however, when he was performing in Edward German's *Merrie England* in Derry. Bill O'Kelly, chairman of the Dublin Grand Opera Society, was on the look-out for tenors and after the performance visited Johnston in his dressing-room and invited him to sing the role of Faust with the DGOS later that season. Back in Belfast, the tenor's voice tutor John Vine advised caution. Eventually, Johnston wrote to O'Kelly and offered to sing the Duke in *Rigoletto*.

His offer was accepted. He made a fine impression as a Verdi singer and the *Irish Independent* stated: 'At least we have got a tenor who can sing Verdi.' During the following season he sang Alfredo in *La Traviata*, Don José in *Carmen* and Manrico in *Il Trovatore*. It was inevitable that London managements would hear about his achievements, therefore it was no surprise when Sir Tyrone Guthrie and Joan Cross offered him a contract to sing principal roles at Sadler's Wells.

There is a story that when Guthrie told him they could not pay him more than £30 a performance, Johnston stared up at the towering figure before him and replied, 'I could earn that kind of money in my wee butcher's shop any day of the week. I tell you what, I'll go over for six months and if I don't like it, and if Sadler's Wells doesn't like me, I'll come home again to Belfast.'

He stayed in London until 1958. His greatest success at Sadler's Wells was achieved in the role of Gabriele Adorno in the British premiere of Verdi's *Simon Boccanegra*, when the critic of the *Evening News* was prompted to say, 'It was the noblest singing I have ever heard in this theatre. He sang with a declamatory power and dazzling brilliance of tone that rose to international levels.'

His first appearance at Covent Garden was on 2 January 1949 in *La Traviata*, and although he did not possess the innate stage elegance for roles like Alfredo or the Duke of Mantua, his splendid singing and ringing top notes fully compensated. And he sang with stars such as Elisabeth Schwarzkopf, Ebi Stignani, Ljuba Welitsch and Victoria de los Angeles, who made her British *Madama Butterfly* debut with him in 1951. He sang with Maria Callas in *Il Trovatore*, also at Covent Garden, in the early 1950s, after a brush with the diva at rehearsals.

When he returned to his native Belfast in the late fifties, his voice was still in excellent shape. He retained his love of singing until his death at home on 17 October 1991 at the grand old age of eighty-eight.

It was always one of McCormack's abiding regrets that he never got the opportunity to sing Don Ottavio at the Metropolitan Opera

House New York, the more so because he had been acclaimed earlier in this role at Covent Garden. At the time, however, the Met had no plans to present the Mozart opera. Likewise, Dermot Troy years later longed to sing Tamino in *The Magic Flute* at Covent Garden and probably would have done so were it not for his untimely death in the early 1960s.

Born in Tinahely, Co. Wicklow on 31 July 1927, Troy's career blossomed when he was offered a contract to sing in Mannheim in Germany. With his flair for languages, he quickly mastered German, so well in fact that some people believed he was a native. After a year at the opera house, he was being described as the perfect Ottavio and a singer wonderfully suited to Mozart. In his second year he began to guest in other leading German houses, including the Hamburg State Opera where he was to be engaged as leading lyric tenor under unusual circumstances. He had sung in a performance of *Il Seraglio*, stepping straight onto the stage without any rehearsals. At the first interval the General Manager Rolf Liebermann offered him a contract for three years.

At this point his name was being mentioned in the same breath as that of the renowned Fritz Wunderlich, one of Germany's most revered Mozartian exponents. Dermot Troy never envied Wunderlich his popularity; indeed, he once remarked to his wife Eithne, 'Dear, there's room for Fritz and me in Germany.' To Eithne there was a humility about her husband that was matched by his charm and sensitivity and she never once heard him say he was famous.

Joining the Hamburg State Opera meant a tremendous lot to him; it was as though he had reached some kind of summit in his career. However, just as he was about to take up his contract in Hamburg, he suffered an unexpected heart attack in June 1961. It was a shattering blow. He and Eithne and the children returned to Dublin where he was ordered to rest by his doctor. He stopped smoking and obeyed his doctor and put a brave face on his illness. And he managed to laugh with his old musical friends when everyone realised it wasn't easy for him. He had responsibilities, he wanted to sing, and deep down he hated not working – what singer doesn't?

Feeling much improved, and with a clear bill of health from his doctor, Dermot Troy returned to Hamburg in April 1962. He was able to resume his career and scored a notable success as Lensky in *Eugene Onegin*. Eithne and the children joined him and for a while he seemed his old self. There were times, however, during the following months when his face looked drawn and after rehearsals he appeared very tired.

In late August 1962 he decided to have a medical check-up and insisted on seeing his doctor alone. It was around the time that Eithne's father died and she returned to Dublin to attend the funeral. It was during her absence that Dermot suffered a fatal heart attack. He died on 6 September 1962 at the age of thirty-five.

The operatic world was stunned by the news of his death. Michael O'Higgins summed up: 'The death of Dermot Troy at the peak of his career is tragic for those who love him; it is equally tragic for Irish music. He was the first tenor to break through to the world outside since John McCormack, and in doing so, he reflected credit on our musical standards and good taste.'

It has often struck me that if McCormack had arrived on the operatic scene in the early 1960s instead of fifty years before, he too would probably have followed the trail to Germany, for his was the kind of polished Mozartian voice the Germans would have appreciated. When he sang his German Lieder repertoire in Berlin in the 1920s it was said that it was superior to most of the German artists singing in this sphere at the time.

It is a pity, though, that Dermot Troy did not make more recordings. In this respect, it is a small legacy that he left to his many admirers.

In giving the No. 3 spot to Josef Locke, I am swayed by his voice rather than his musicianship. 'Joe, you've a better voice than mine,' James Johnston once told Locke, and he was sincere in what he said.

When he arrived in Dublin in the early 1940s under his own

name of Joseph McLoughlin, he cut a striking figure. He was tall, handsome and blessed with a voice that could charm audiences in the Theatre Royal or Gaiety Theatre. It was a light, high-pitched tenor ideally suited to musical comedy or romantic Irish ballads and soon he acquired a big following.

With the war raging in Europe and overseas operatic singers unable to come to Dublin, Bill O'Kelly decided that Joseph McLoughlin could be groomed as a grand opera singer for the DGOS. When approached, McLoughlin was astounded – he had never even seen an opera, never mind sing in one. 'Please Bill, I can't do it,' he pleaded with the tough, single-minded O'Kelly.

As in the case of James Johnston, O'Kelly had his way and soon the young Derry-born tenor was learning the role of the American naval officer Pinkerton in *Madama Butterfly*, being assisted by Julia Grey, DGOS's repetiteur, and by his Cio-Cio-San, May Devitt. The tenor and Ms Devitt were inseparable and their romance was the talk of musical circles. Sometimes they were seen happily together in a horse-driven carriage in O'Connell Street, with May Devitt going over the Puccini's music with her lover.

'We hammered the role of Pinkerton into Joe McLoughlin,' recalled Col. Jim Doyle, the well-known conductor, when I talked to him in the early 1990s at his Dublin suburban home. 'I can say he worked very hard to get it right, and although he lacked musicianship and had some difficulty with the text, he sang it well enough and got a good press.'

'The DGOS would have to go a long way to find a better combination then May Devitt and Joseph McLoughlin,' summed up the *Irish Times* critic. He praised them for the Act One love duet and added that Ms Devitt's "One Fine Day" was beautifully sung.

Bill O'Kelly decided the tenor had done well enough to be cast as Rodolfo in *La Boheme* and the opera would again be sung in English. McLoughlin found it hard to say no to O'Kelly and even harder still to refuse to sing opposite May Devitt's Mimi. As expected, she dominated the newspaper reviews for her tender portrayal of the Puccini heroine, though at least one Dublin critic praised the tenor's ringing top notes in the Act 1 love duet.

If McLoughlin was winning new friends in Dublin as an opera singer, privately he was worried about the financial rewards. 'I was being paid £10 a performance,' he recalled. 'I told May I was mad and would be better off singing Irish ballads up and down the country. She wouldn't listen. She said I had it in me to become an opera star.'

When he sang the role of Enzo in *La Gioconda* the young tenor got his chance to meet McCormack who was a first night guest of the DGOS at the Gaiety Theatre. After the final curtain McCormack was accompanied on stage by chairman Bill O'Kelly to meet the principals and chorus and immediately shook the hands of May Devitt and mezzo-soprano Patricia Black. When he walked further along the line to where McLoughlin was standing he looked at him and was supposed to have said, 'As for you McLoughlin, grand opera is not your forte.'

Today, Josef Locke is insistent that McCormack uttered these words. Col. Jim Doyle, on the other hand, says from his spot on the conductor's podium he didn't catch the exact words. 'I knew at the time that McCormack could be blunt and outspoken when he wanted to be,' he added, 'but I don't believe he would deliberately insult a fellow artist. He might have said to Joe in a whisper to confine himself in future to operetta, ballads and popular songs. I would probably have said the same thing. I felt at the time that Joe would make an excellent interpreter of the musicals of Lehar, Sullivan, Offenbach and Johann Strauss.'

With the war over, the Blackpool lights twinkling again, and the Palladium opening its doors to singing stars, Joseph McLoughlin soon departed the Dublin operatic scene in search of fame and fortune in the variety scene in Britain. Before long, under the name of Josef Locke, he was to become a popular star, packing halls all over the country, topping bills in Blackpool and other resorts, earning in one night more money than he earned singing in four grand operas in Dublin.

He is now happy in retirement with his charming wife Carmel in a neat bungalow in the village of Clane, Co. Kildare. A few years ago he was immortalised in the movie *Hear My Song* and his CDs continue to sell extremely well in Ireland and abroad, ensuring that the Locke legend lives on. I am left wondering what would have happened if the young Joseph McLoughlin had won a scholarship to study operetta in Vienna. Imagine his impact in *The Gipsy Baron* and in *The Merry Widow!*

Judged by his early background Frank Ryan gave little indication that he would in time sing the title role in Verdi's *Ernani* or Tamino in *The Magic Flute*. Yet how he came to sing these and other leading parts is surely one of the most fascinating stories in Irish musical history. Born in Fermoy, Co. Cork in 1901, he was only four years of age when his father died. His mother moved to Tallow, Co. Waterford where she opened a butcher's shop in which he soon began to work after school hours.

Later on he joined the Tallow church choir where he acquired his first interest in music. In addition, he played the trumpet in the local band and also found time to train as a volunteer in the Irish Republican Army and during the Troubles went on the run. Afterwards, he moved to Dublin and was married in the Pro-Cathedral in 1923, and inside a few years had qualified as a butcher. It was around this time that friends encouraged him to have his voice trained and like other tenors before him, he went along to Dr Vincent O'Brien.

'Dr O'Brien told me I had a natural tenor voice and urged me to think about a full-time career in singing,' Frank Ryan later said. 'Being newly married and anxious to do well in my business I was cautious, so with my wife Josephine we returned in due course to live in Tallow.'

He was an outdoor person and apart from working in his butcher's shop he had an interest in dogs and hunting and was also fond of horses. He occasionally sang at parties and found it relaxing. A friend of his heard that the Fermoy Choral Society was on the look-out for a tenor for its annual show and recommended him. 'I knew nothing about acting, and little enough about music,' he recalled, 'but after one audition I was asked to sing the principal role of Nanki Poo in *The Mikado.*'

Before a week was out the people of Tallow and many a cattle-buyer at the fairs he attended had, he said, good reason to regret the society's decision. For in every spare moment he had the rumpled old operetta score in his hand. And his acting was tried out in the privacy of the slaughter-house. But he was launched as a promising musical comedy singer and went on to perform more leading roles. He found it great fun. 'One night during the performance of *The Gondoliers* I whispered to one of the chorus that I felt hungry. He nodded and when we left the stage for a three-minute break he caught my hand and took me out of the hall and up a little side-street. At the shop he brushed past a waiting queue shouting in a rich baritone, "Make way, make way, and give us two pen'orth o'chips for the King of Barataria." There was a heavy vinegary smell on the stage for the rest of the night. It came from the front right leg of my throne, behind which was hidden my fine bag of chips.'

After he had won the Fr Mathew Cup in the Dublin Feis Ceoil, he thought it unfair for the newspapers to describe him as 'Another John McCormack', for he was aware of his own limitations. 'At the time my phrasing, tone and diction showed complete lack of professional training' he confessed.

With good tenors as scarce as diamonds, the Dublin Grand Opera Society stepped in and offered him his first grand opera role – Lionel in *Martha*. In spite of his wooden acting, he was a revelation. The highlight of the evening was his impassioned singing of the aria "M'Appari"; here his effortless top notes and intense feeling for the music roused the packed audience. So impressed was the Society, that in subsequent seasons he was engaged for *La Boheme, Faust, The Magic Flute, Ernani* and *The Lily of Killarney.*

211

Harold White, the distinguished music critic of the time, writing in the *Irish Independent* about the *Boheme*, stated: 'I was tremendously impressed with the singing of Frank Ryan, who though an almost bashful Rodolfo, sang his music, particularly "Che gelida manina", with superb tone and without the least physical exertion.'

If John McCormack's inadequate stage acting had been the bane of his operatic career, Frank Ryan was faring no better in the realms of grand opera. When he sang Turridu in *Cavalleria Rusticana* for the DGOS one morning newspaper critic noted: 'Frank Ryan's robust tenor voice found the music of Turridu quite grateful, but his stage deportment is not yet all the part calls for: he is too fond of that one gesture with both hands to express all emotions.'

Off-stage, Frank Ryan was a big, jovial man with the gift for the blarney which he readily deployed in his butcher's shop in West Street, Tallow. There was a smile and a little good-natured gossip with each purchase. By the 1940s he was a farmer as well as a butcher, having purchased two farms in the county. He was secure, he didn't smoke or drink, he had no reason to sing for his supper, yet he had come to love opera and concert work, even if he discovered that unlike amateur musicals, grand opera in Dublin was serious business.

As a concert artist, he visited America fairly regularly and his appearances at Carnegie Hall afforded him tremendous pleasure. His programme was not unlike McCormack's and included Handel's "Wher'er You Walk", Balfe's "When Other Lips" and traditional songs, "Love Thee Dearest", "The Ministrel Boy" and "Macushla". And he sang in most of the big British centres, often being accompanied by his daughter Myra whose repertoire featured "The Last Rose of Summer", "On Wings of Song" and "The Fairy Tree".

Although Frank Ryan never sang continuously as a semi-professional – as this was the way his wife and family wanted it – his stamina had, nevertheless, to be admired, if not wondered at. Sometimes during the war years he'd work by day in the butcher's shop or on the farm and after tea get into his dress suit and set out for a concert miles away, returning afterwards on his bicycle so as to be ready for work the next morning. Once he sang the tenor lead in *The Lily of Killarney* in Cobh and cycled the twenty-eight miles home every night.

His last public appearance was at a festival concert in the Palace Theatre, Fermoy on 29 June 1965, when a capacity audience heard him sing his special favourites, "I Hear You Calling Me", "Angels Guard Thee" and Bizet's "Agnus Dei". He was joined by members of the Choral Society in selections from musical comedies, which must have recalled happy memories since he had begun his operetta career in the town. For a singer of sixty-four he displayed unusual energy and before the evening was over responded to calls for "M'Appari".

Within a month he was struck down by a heart attack and died only after a week's illness at his home at Grange, Curraglass, Tallow. His death would be mourned especially by those societies who were able to call upon him to sing the leads in *Maritana, The Lily of Killarney* and his beloved *Martha*. With his death a truly fine voice was stilled, but it is good to know that his recorded voice can still be enjoyed on a recent CD.

Frank Patterson divides his time between Ireland and America, although increasingly in the 1990s he has shown greater commitment to the States where he is offered regular engagements. He continues to be a popular recording artist and his CDs are among the best-sellers around. His sweet tenor voice allied to admirable artistry and musicianship are his hallmarks, and as a concert artist he projects a warm personality on stage; he is versatile, too, with a programme that features modern new Irish songs, operatic arias and ballads more easily identified with McCormack. With his fine feeling for Mozart's music, it is a pity that he did not get the opportunity to sing operatic roles like Tamino, Ottavio and Ferrando in *Cosi fan tutte*.

Louis Browne will tell you that as far back as he can remember he wanted to be a singer. Listening to John McCormack's records was the spur and today he includes a number of the great tenor's songs in his concert programmes. It was in opera, however, that he was to make his name, singing leading lyric roles with English National Opera, among his most outstanding portrayals being Almaviva in *The Barber of Seville*, Ernesto in *Don Pasquale* and Giannetto in *The Thieving Magpie*.

Because he is Athlone-born, Louis is invariably asked about McCormack. 'Of course he was unique. The feeling he brought to a song has never been surpassed and that is why you hear his records played regularly.' Louis and his wife Therese settled in Dublin where the popular tenor still sings at the National Concert Hall or on tour in Britain and America. Few Irish singers have displayed such durability.

Hubert Valentine is the real veteran of my list of McCormack successors. He has been living in America since the late 1930s and in the last few decades has included many Irish voices in his popular classical radio programme. After a short stint in opera in the 1940s, he decided to concentrate solely on concert and oratorio work and went on to make a very good living. Like John McCormack, he was trained by Dr Vincent O'Brien and has recorded "Macushla" for HMV. His first appearance at the London Palladium was a big success and led to a concert tour of British cities. It is not a big tenor voice but projects well and Valentine has always used it with care. Although in his late seventies, he can still sing the "Panis Angelicus" with power and sensitivity. He visits his native Dublin at least once a year.

Christopher Lynch had a typical Irish tenor voice: light, warm-toned and musical. A native of Co. Limerick, he became a friend of John McCormack's and had voice lessons from him in the early 1940s. Like Hubert Valentine before him, Lynch decided to settle in America where he soon became known on the "Voice of Firestone" shows on radio and television. He had been chosen to succeed no less a tenor than Richard Crooks on the programme, which is some indication of the merit of his voice. He stayed with the show until 1954.

Lynch often toured the United States, appearing with orchestras including the Philadelphia Orchestra under Eugene Ormandy; he also sang the songs for the film *The Hills of Ireland* and recorded for RCA and Columbia. Fred Manning, who knew the tenor, wrote recently to me: 'When I first heard Christopher Lynch in three of the Firestone shows I was bowled over by the beauty of the voice, by a technically sound delivery and by his matinee-idol presence. At once, it struck me that John McCormack had made no mistake about the talent and its potential.'

Lynch subsequently left America for England and settled in Worcestershire, where he died in April 1994 at the age of seventy-three.

Michael O'Duffy's is a voice that has always recorded exceptionally well. It is refined and musical in tone, ideal for songs like "My Lagan Love" and "The Meeting of the Waters". It is by no means an operatic voice and as far as I could gather, O'Duffy did not interest himself in opera, wisely preferring to sing the songs that best suited him. He is now living in England but from time to time RTE radio music presenters play his records and they seldom fail to give pleasure.

John Carolan is retired and teaching in the Cork School of Music. In Ireland he is best known as an operatic artist of merit. I first heard him as Edgardo in *Lucia di Lammermoor* and was greatly taken by his feeling for the bel canto style and his smooth vocal line. He sang lyric roles with success at English National Opera and here his Faust is remembered as one of his best portrayals. He guested with numerous operatic societies and was a most dependable artist. As far as I know, there is no CD available featuring him either as an operatic or concert artist. What a great pity.

Finbar Wright represents the modern school of Irish tenors. He has a fresh voice and clear timbre and a personality that exudes charm. Although the voice has enough range and power to cope with lyrical operatic roles, he has concentrated on the concert stage and is evidently making a good living. In recent years he has presented his own tribute to John McCormack and his appealing programmes included such favourites as "Believe Me", "I'll Walk Beside You" and "Panis Angelicus".

That musical stage tribute is now available on CD. In an introductory note, he stated: 'John McCormack was born with a rare and beautiful talent. With determination he disciplined and honed his gift and consequently his artistry and music enchanted and uplifted not only his own nation but listeners in every corner of the world. His recordings have a special place in the cultural treasure-chest of Ireland. His life and career is an inspiration to all Irish musicians and it is with pride and fondness that I pay him this tribute.'

One day perhaps as his voice matures Finbar Wright may well make a convincing Rodolfo, thus emulating McCormack in one of his greatest operatic roles. The decision is his.

I chose Charles Kennedy as my No. 12 because of his delicate vocal artistry and expressiveness. He never forced his light tenor voice and he always appeared to me an intelligent singer who knew what he was singing about. He sang a number of songs associated with John McCormack and invested them with his own interpretation and imagination. In his day he was quite frequently heard on RTE radio programmes.

For years Ireland produced a crop of tenors who were a mixture of the good, bad and indifferent. The problem today is that we are producing very few tenors at all of any note; indeed the same can be said of baritones. There is no doubt we have a surplus of sopranos and mezzo-sopranos. The stage, radio and television opportunities for tenors are unfortunately deplorable in the modern entertainment scene with the result that the most talented must seek work in the United States, Australia and to a lesser extent Britain. RTE television has, for example, no show featuring a tenor, despite the fact that Finbar Wright and Frank Patterson would, I have no doubt, welcome the opportunity to star in such a programme. And surely there are enough viewers to make the whole thing worthwhile.

23

McCormack Society Revived

Early in 1995 Count John McCormack, Donal McNally, Liam Breen and a few friends dined together in the QV.2 restaurant in Andrew Street. Their sole purpose was to revive the defunct John McCormack Society which was founded exactly thirty-five years earlier to foster a love of the art of the renowned tenor.

'I was eventually talked into becoming its Life President,' said Liam Breen, 'and it was decided to hold a number of recitals this year to mark the golden jubilee of McCormack's death.'

The enthusiasm among former members for the revival soon became apparent – they had clearly missed the recitals and the bonhomie that had become part of them. Dermot McDevitt was appointed hon. secretary and Joe Clarke the treasurer. Subsequently a series of gramophone recitals were held in the spacious downstairs room in the QV.2 and attracted fine attendances.

Needless to say, Liam Breen's recital, devoted solely to John McCormack, was the highlight of the season, with the genial Co. Wexford man playing what he called some of the 'unpublished' records by the tenor, or those that weren't released publicly. He punctuated his recital with amusing anecdotes about John and Lily McCormack and also played a few of his own McCormack favourites, including the appealing Handel aria "O Sleep, why dost Thou Leave Me."

Unfortunately Liam became ill later in the year and was unable to join members on their outing on Sunday 25 June to Avondale, Co. Wicklow, where in the glorious sunshine everyone enjoyed a few leisurely hours of relaxation before being conveyed by coach to nearby Avoca for an evening meal. Feis Ceoil prize-winner Dermot McDevitt did not let the occasion pass without singing Thomas Moore's "The Meeting of the Waters".

In retrospect, the first President of the John McCormack Society was Lily McCormack and Liam Breen remembers her giving an enjoyable gramophone recital to members. 'Lily's Dublin accent was pronounced and before she'd play a record by John she'd say a few brief words about it. She always referred to him as "her John". Count Cyril McCormack became our first patron and his sister Gwen also took a keen interest in our affairs. Cyril was somewhat shy of publicity and preferred to keep out of the limelight, but the society could always depend on his support. We were determined to keep his father's memory alive and at the same time put strong pressure on record companies to re-issue John's finest recordings. In time, we achieved our objective, so that today you can purchase the best of his singing on CD.'

Count John McCormack attended all the gramophone recitals during 1995 and was obviously delighted that the revival had stimulated such interest. He thought that the society's past achievements could not be measured in words. 'Keeping the name of any great artist or singer alive for future generations takes time, energy and lots of enthusiasm. Liam Breen, I know, has given of his time generously to promote renewed interest in my grandfather's career, giving recitals and talks in many parts of the country. And, of course, his private museum deserves to be housed in the National Museum as both an attraction and treasure. Personally I am very grateful to him for what he has done so unselfishly and on a voluntary basis.'

When I talked to Gwen McCormack at her home in Co. Westmeath in late June, she was emphatic in her tribute. 'My brother

Cyril used to say that Liam Breen helped enormously to keep my father's name before the public and at a time when pop was all the rage. The family is eternally grateful to him; indeed, I don't know what would have happened if the John McCormack Society had not taken up his cause. So many famous singers are forgotten these days because no-one goes to the trouble of keeping their memory alive or playing their records.'

The society really came into its own in 1984, the centenary year of the tenor's birth. Liam Breen recalled that they began planning late in the year 1983 and decided to book the National Concert Hall. 'We took a risk in booking the hall for a full week's events but we felt that the centenary should be celebrated in style. I remember going to London to meet agents and engaged tenors Dennis O'Neill and Stuart Burrowes. Robert White agreed to come from America for one of our concerts. Not only was the week a great success but it helped to clear the society's debts. We had packed attendances almost every night and managed to put the name of John McCormack firmly in the news again.'

Magazines and newspapers carried special features, one of the most comprehensive being in the June issue of Bord Fáilte's *Ireland of the Welcomes* under the headline: IN MEMORY OF JOHN McCORMACK. James Maguire, a young singer of note, contributed a revealing article in which he made the point: 'If McCormack enhanced the image of Ireland as a musical nation by sole virtue of his Irishness, his most significant achievement for the country must be the manner in which he promoted its songs and ballads. His sweetness of tone and above all the perfection of his style bestowed upon such widely popular favourites as "Maggie" and "I'll Take you Home Again, Kathleen" an honest artistry that is far removed from the sentimental which they all too often meet with.

'Although Ireland has not yet produced a performer to rival McCormack, it can boast that now there are more Irish musicians successfully engaged in international careers than ever before. This is largely due to the huge expansion that has taken place in the country's musical activity over the past decade.'

Maguire argued that new generations of Irish people would find it difficult to identify with the McCormack era simply because the present age is essentially anti-romantic and anti-nostalgia. As he stated, 'These things are legitimate so long as they remain as a kind of sophistication on the fringe, but have little place in the mainstream of popular culture. The unfortunate fact, that people are switched off McCormack by much of the music he sang, sadly means that even some of the most genuinely interested young people never come to understand his greatness. I have never seen this reason as being the quality of his voice. Rather, I would see it as being the inspired manner in which he used it.'

What was written by James Maguire more than a decade ago is still accurate today, perhaps even more so. For since the advent of U2 and other pop and rock groups hundreds of thousands of the younger generation have not only rejected the McCormack era but current operatic and symphonic music as well, with the result that the National Concert Hall for the most part caters for the over-thirties.

The 1984 centenary celebrations did, however, prove an important milestone, especially in the fresh assessment made of the tenor's worth and what a new generation of Irish singers could learn from his achievements, and it did keep his legend alive. Wearing the gold medal her grandfather won in the Feis Ceoil of 1903, Ms Carol Ann McCormack in that jubilee year presented the cup that honours her famous grandfather to the Feis Ceoil winner.

Carol Ann, in a brief address, said she could only recall her grandfather rather dimly: 'I really only remember his pinstriped trousers, because that is only how high you can see as a child. But I remember he used to sit us on his knees and feed us with strawberries out of the jam, which horrified the grown-ups.'

Which invites the more general question as to how people like to remember McCormack. During my research for this book I raised the question with many people in Ireland and abroad and everyone had their own idea. One artist was reminded of the tenor every time he cast his eye on Sir William Orpen's portrait which is generally held as one of the finest ever executed of him, although Lily McCormack thought it didn't 'bring out John's spiritual side.' I found there is much admiration for Sir John Lavery's family portrait painted in Esher Place in Surrey, a house the McCormacks had rented and whose ornate music room caught Lavery's eye. And the Leo Whelan portrait of the tenor in the National Concert Hall was also mentioned to me.

There are others who have only to put on a McCormack record like "I Hear You Calling Me" or "Silver Threads Among the Gold" to be with the tenor in spirit. I can count myself among that group, for no other singer I know evokes his own era more movingly than McCormack. His voice has an extraordinary pathos and poignancy and one can easily appreciate why in his time exiles bought his records in thousands. Someone has surmised that this poignancy which he injected into these songs of personal and ethnic loss came from his witnessing as a growing boy the heart-rending emigration scenes on the platform of Athlone's Great Southern Railway Station. I can well believe it.

Some old-timers in Dublin like to remember the tenor as they saw him at the Eucharistic Congress in Dublin in the summer of 1932, when attired in papal uniform, he sang "Panis Angelicus" with a choir of five hundred men and boys in the Phoenix Park before a congregation of half a million people. The choir was conducted by Dr Vincent O'Brien who was seen in the singer's company a good deal during the week's ceremonies. For McCormack the Congress was a memorable occasion and whenever he was asked about the highlights of his career he invariably included the event and recalled how delighted he was to be asked to sing at the Pontifical High Mass in the Park.

In musical and literary circles there are people I have encountered who liked to recall the friendship between McCormack and James Joyce and regarded it as an important part of his life.

Brenda Maddox alludes to it in her biography of Nora Joyce, the wife of the novelist, and tells how all the Joyce family attended a concert given in 1920 by McCormack in Paris. 'Nora no doubt reminded her children as she did everybody that their father had once shared a platform with him and that next day he wrote the tenor a fan letter.'

That event took place on 27 August, 1904 in the Antient Concert Rooms as part of the Irish Revival Industries Show and the singers were McCormack, Joyce and J.C. Doyle. There was a capacity audience present. The *Freeman's Journal's* critic referred to Joyce's 'sweet tenor voice' and stated he sang most charmingly "The Salley Gardens" but gave 'a pathetic rendering' of "The Croppy Boy". It went on to add that McCormack was the hero of the evening.

In the course of his 'fan letter' to McCormack, Joyce was to write: 'In the general confusion the other afternoon I had not an opportunity to tell you how delighted we were by your singing, especially the aria from *Don Giovanni*. I have lived in Italy practically ever since we last met but no Italian lyrical tenor that I know (Bonci possibly excepting) could do such a feat of breathing and phrasing – to say nothing of the beauty of tone in which I am glad to see, Roscommon can leave the peninsula a fair distance behind. We are all going to hear you again next Tuesday and I am sure you will have another big success.'

Their friendship began when McCormack and his friend Richard Best encouraged Joyce to enter for the Dublin Feis Ceoil in 1904. This took place on 16 May, exactly one month before the first Bloomsday. The adjudicator, Professor Luigi Denza, intended, it seems, to award the gold medal to Joyce, but when Joyce was asked to sing a third piece at sight, he refused, and strode off the platform much to Denza's dismay. As a result he was awarded the bronze medal which, according to Gogarty, he tossed into the Liffey as he was unable to pawn it. Denza was, nevertheless, highly impressed by Joyce's voice and urged him to think about a professional career. But the young tenor lost interest and had already decided to leave Ireland.

Joyce's interest, though, in singing and singers never waned. He was very friendly with Co. Cork-born tenor John O'Sullivan and as in the case of McCormack, urged his Parisian friends to purchase tickets for the operas in which he was performing. The story is told that he insisted that his large party should sit in various parts of the opera house so that the applause for O'Sullivan should come, not only from one group, but from all over the theatre.

To Louis Browne, the tenor is an institution whose legend will never fade as long as his records are played. A few years ago he was travelling on a train to Galway and his carriage included some Dublin traders on their way to the races, when someone turned on a radio. 'Next we heard Kenneth McKeller singing an Irish ballad,' he recalled, 'and instantly one of the old ladies with the basket of apples and oranges sighed, "Ah, John McCormack, the Lord be good to him." Her words reminded me of the reverence in which McCormack was held, even though it was someone else singing his song.'

On another occasion Louis was in Hyde Park Corner on a September Sunday morning when an unemployed Dubliner got up to speak and in an unmistakeable Liffeyside accent addressed the crowd:

'I'll tell yous why I came over here...When England wanted a great playwright we sent yous over Sean O'Casey...When England wanted a great poet we sent yous over William Butler Yeats... When England wanted a great Shavian we gave yous George Bernard Shaw...and when yous were looking for a great singer we sent yous over John McCormack.'

With that the speaker took off his hat and bowed his head and acknowledged the ripple of applause. Wherever Louis Browne goes, whether it is to Britain or America or Canada, he is asked about McCormack because he hails from the same town. 'I had the pleasure once while on tour of meeting Lily McCormack in Hollywood and seeing the house that they once owned. Again the conversation came around to my aunt Molly, and Archbishop Curley and John's visits to my aunt's house. Suddenly I was back home again playing his records and listening to his voice that has stayed with me for years.'

Since the tenor's death fifty years ago, the music scene in Ireland has changed dramatically. 'My dream,' he once said, 'is to found a first-class symphony orchestra in Dublin and to agitate for a Ministry of Arts to encourage love of music and poetry in Ireland. There is the nucleus of such an orchestra in Dublin now, and I shall appeal to Irish people in America to help.'

It was the dream of a visionary. For in subsequent years it would be implemented by the government of the time so that today we have not only the National Symphony Orchestra but the RTE Concert Orchestra, the Irish Chamber Orchestra – which is based in Limerick – and the National Youth Orchestra. We have also the National Concert Hall as well as the Limerick University Hall, both venues of exceptional merit.

The new post of Minister for the Arts was created in recent years and is currently filled by Michael D. Higgins, a politician and poet. In addition, the Irish Arts Council has the unenviable task of funding the various Arts bodies and unsurprisingly not everyone by any means is pleased with the grant aid coming their way. Theatre, with its long and noble tradition, seems to fare best of all; classical music, on the other hand, cannot be said to be treated generously. Dublin Grand Opera Society is struggling to present twenty nights of opera in the entire year. The society's chairman Frank O'Rourke says they need at least £1 million in grant aid annually to do the kind of programme that is needed, but at the present time less than half that amount is given to the society.

Over the past decade Cork impresario Barra O Tuama has presented a series of first-rate operatic concerts at leading Irish venues, featuring a galaxy of outstanding home and overseas singers such as Suzanne Murphy, Patricia Bardon, Marzio Giossi, Dennis O'Neill, Tito Beltran and the unforgettable Dimitry Hvorostovsky. O

Tuama has been fortunate to attract consistent sponsorship for his concerts. 'I could not stage them without it,' he says. In a country starved of grand opera these concerts undoubtedly fill a musical void.

McCormack would, I have no doubt, be disappointed that Ireland's capital city has still no opera house of its own to cater for the many talented operatic singers the country is now producing and who unfortunately have in the majority of cases to seek their living abroad. Veronica Dunne is hoping that one day a small opera house can be provided so that music lovers will get continuity of performance. Opera Theatre Company, directed by James Conway, is providing occasional employment for young Irish singers and in this respect its record is good, and its repertory is also imaginative, if sometimes experimental, and it has discovered in Gerry Stembridge a satirist who can write witty and telling operatic texts.

The jewel in Ireland's operatic crown is undoubtedly the Wexford Festival founded in the early 1950s by Dr Tom Walsh, a visionary of rare distinction. Today it is thriving, achieving 99 per cent seat occupancy in the Theatre Royal, a figure that is considerably higher than, for instance, the Glyndebourne Festival's. Its new Artistic Director is Luigi Ferrari, an amiable Italian, who is already planning three years ahead. It is truly a festival of the people with the townspeople providing tremendous voluntary support. On the commercial side, its guiding lights are chairman John O'Connor and managing director Jerome Hynes, who lays enormous emphasis on global marketing, with the result that many of today's festival-goers come from Britain, France, Italy, America and even Australia.

'We cannot rest on our laurels for one moment,' Hynes says. 'When you are presenting operas new for the most part to the public you have got to be able to sell them, and also sell the musical and social advantages of coming to Wexford.'

Any conversation on the vocal achievements of McCormack tends to be dominated by his songs and ballads as though his operatic recordings and classical songs did not count for much. It is a fallacy.

I have listened for hours to his operatic output and have found it stimulating. His recording, for example, of the arias "Fra poco a me ricovero" and "Tu, che a Dio spiegasti l'ali" from *Lucia di Lammermoor* is a lesson in *bel canto* singing. And I consider his duet with Sammarco from *La Boheme*, "Ah Mimi, tu piu" one of the most eloquent of its kind. There is also much to admire in his singing of *Salve dimora* from Gounod's *Faust*.

Music lovers will have their personal favourites; here are my own twelve:

1. *Il mio tesoro* (Mozart's *Don Giovanni*)
2. *Fra poco a me* (Donizetti's *Lucia di Lammermoor*)
3. *Per viver vicino* (Donizetti's *The Daughter of Regiment*)
4. *Elle ne croyait* (Thomas's *Mignon*)
5. *Then You'll Remember Me* (Balfe's *The Bohemian Girl*)
6. *Ah Mimi, tu piu with Sammarco* (Puccini's *La Boheme*)
7. *Spirto Gentil* (Donzetti's *La Favorita*)
8. *O Soave fanciulla with Lucrezia Bori* (Puccini's *La Boheme*)
9. *Where'er You Walk* (Handel's *Semele*)
10. *Salve dimora* (Gounod's *Faust*)
11. *Tu, che a Dio spiegasti* (Donizetti's *Lucia di Lammermoor*)
12. *O Sleep, Why Dost Thou Leave Me?* (Handel's *Semele*)

The twelve classical songs that have most appealed to me and which illustrate McCormack's delicate vocal technique, intense feeling and interpretative insights, are:

1. *Panis Angelicus* (Franck)
2. *Serenade* (violin obbligato by Kreisler (Schubert))
3. *None but the Weary Heart* (Tchaikovsky)
4. *Caro amore* (Handel)
5. *Who is Sylvia?* (Schubert)
6. *Is She Not passing Fair* (Elgar)
7. *When Night Descends* (Rachmaninoff)

8. *Now Sleeps the Crimson Petal* (Quilter)
9. *O del mio amato ben* (Donaudy)
10. *Automne* (Faure)
11. *Wo find 'ich Trost* (Wolf)
12. *In Waldeseinsamkeit* (Brahms)

The tenor has made in all over 700 recordings, the majority of them Irish songs and ballads, so the task of choosing a mere twelve reduces one's choice considerably. Among the collection which have provided me with most pleasure are:

1. *I Hear You Calling Me*
2. *The Meeting of the Waters*
3. *Molly Bawn*
4. *Eileen Alannah*
5. *When My Ship Comes Sailing Home*
6. *The Rose of Tralee*
7. *Macushla*
8. *God Keep You Is My Prayer*
9. *The Fairy Tree*
10. *Somewhere a Voice is Calling*
11. *Come Back to Erin*
12. *The Garden Where the Praties Grow*

Count Cyril McCormack had been close to his father, and being unusually perceptive, was aware of his different qualities that he said ranged between child-like to mature and worldly. He experienced the heady days in the early 1920s and onwards, toured with him, and one of the few occasions in which they differed was when his father wanted him to become a singer. Cyril would have none of it. Singing around a piano for fun or at a party was to him quite sufficient.

He was with him in his days of retirement and illness and eventually at his bedside when he died peacefully. There was one record of his father's which never failed to move him deeply. 'The man lives again for me whenever I hear it,' he recalled. 'It is "The Old House" and John sang it at his farewell concert in the Royal Albert Hall in 1938. The lyrics are like this:

Why stand I here
Like a ghost or a shadow
'Tis time I was moving on
Tis time I passed on.

24

The Final Tributes

M any tributes were paid to McCormack after his death. A few of them are worthy of inclusion here because they came from distinguished musicians who were more interested in truth than in sentiment. Teddy Schneider, his brilliant accompanist, felt that if the tenor had been able to perform at the concert planned for the Salzburg Festival of 1914 it would perhaps have changed his career as a concert artist. It will be remembered that war intervened and he lost also the opportunity of singing with a star-studded cast in Mozart's *Don Giovanni*.

Schneider's was an interesting observation. Tasting Salzburg's unique Mozartian atmosphere for the first time might well have prompted McCormack to concentrate more in future on the classical side of his art: more perhaps on Handel, Wolf, Schubert, Schumann and Rachmaninoff. Did Schneider, in fact, want him to become accepted as the supreme exponent of Lieder in Europe?

Judging by McCormack's concert programmes at the time it was doubtful whether he wanted to specialise. His fans, for one thing, wouldn't have tolerated it, nor for that matter the record companies. In recording terms he was by now an industry in himself, highly productive and a money spinner. I believe he would have welcomed appearances in Mozart operas at the festival or concerts where he chose his own programme. But not solely as a Lieder singer.

Teddy Schneider went on to state:

> It was Fritz Kreisler who had often said to John, 'You owe it to your art to sing in all the countries of Europe,' but it was not until 1923 that he gave his first and only recital in Berlin. I have never seen John so nervous before nor since.

> In the early days of our long association, I had the pleasure of seeing John's development as a musician. When I first mentioned Brahms to him, he laughingly said, 'I thought it was the name of a tooth wash.' I remember his old friend, Sergei Rachmaninoff, showing his new composition for tenor, chorus and orchestra. John started reading the tenor solo part at sight when Rachmaninoff exclaimed, 'What, a tenor who can read!'

> On tour, we spent hours at a time going through most of the German Lieder, not only songs suitable for tenor voice, but many essentially for soprano, alto, baritone and bass. Whenever our engagements took us to cities that supported a symphony orchestra, we never missed a concert, so that John soon learned to appreciate the highest form of musical expression.

> Arturo Toscanini was his favourite conductor. I can still see John standing before his big Capehart gramophone going through the motions of conducting *à la* Toscanini. Had he an early theoretical training in music, he might easily have become a great conductor.

> John never had a piano lesson in his life, yet he could sit down at the piano and play some of his favourite operas from beginning to end, playing and singing all the roles

as well as the chorus numbers from memory. He often remarked, 'If my left hand were as good as my right, I'd be a concert pianist.'

Michael O'Higgins was of the opinion that those who had not heard him sing at the peak of his powers could form a true estimate of the tenor's greatness as a singer. He himself was fortunate in this respect.

It was at the Albert Hall I first heard him. The excitement of the occasion plus the anticipation made me wonder whether perhaps I should be disappointed. His first notes had such spiritual intensity that it produced a paralysing tenseness in the vast auditorium. Indeed it was hard to relax and listen with the ease one would like.

In that programme he included a song I have always associated with him since, "La Procession" by Cesar Franck. In Dublin, too, I heard him sing this song and while I have heard many singers render it since, I have never experienced since the thrill of John's rendering.

Charles Lynch was the most distinguished concert pianist of his generation in Ireland. In 1921 he went to London to study at the Royal Academy of Music and there, in his own words, was whirled into a perfect torrent of music of every description – orchestral, choral, operatic and ensemble. And he also began to attend concerts as part of his musical education. On one occasion he went along to hear McCormack at the Queen's Hall and was overwhelmed by the experience.

I still remember the peculiar feeling of tense excitement which emanated from the crowded house. Then John

233

McCormack nodded to his accompanist, who began to play the opening symphony of a Handel aria. When McCormack's voice entered I realised that I was listening to the most perfect voice I had yet heard, taken as an example of sheer vocal sound. The performance of this Handel aria was well nigh flawless from start to finish. During the course of the evening many songs were sung, but the performance of three others remains fixed in my memory. These were Schubert's little masterpiece "Der Jungling an der Quelle", Frank Bridge's "Go Not Happy Day" and "Next Market Day" by Herbert Hughes.

The thrill I felt when I heard Toscanini conduct the New York Symphony Orchestra in the Albert Hall, and Sir Thomas Beecham conduct the Delius Festival Concerts in 1929 was equalled by the thrill which John McCormack's performance of these songs gave me. It was not merely the perfect vocal sound. That was something one took for granted. Rather was it the consummate art which lay behind this, and which turned the mood of each song into a real, living world, in which each person and image in the poems seemed to become endowed with a life of its own. The voice literally floated through the hall, with the words seemingly floating on top of it. This had the effect of making the words seem separate from and, at the same time, emotionally one with the vocal line. Consequently the simultaneous perfection of both vocal and verbal articulation was truly memorable.

In the course of his tribute the accomplished accompanist Gerald Moore observed:

Those who want to hear McCormack at his best should hear his record of "Il mio tesoro" from Mozart's *Don Giovanni*, the quality and flexibility of voice, the legato line and the purity of his Italian are to be marvelled at. Of course the man in the street went in his millions to hear him sing "I Hear You Calling Me", "Mother Machree" and "The Rose of Tralee", and John would have been a very hard-hearted man if he had not catered for this overwhelming demand. Yet, in none of his programmes did he ever neglect to give the more serious music lover a treat; there would be something from the old Italian classics, from Handel, Schubert and Wolf. Indeed the secret of his hold on the vast public was his sincerity. If he could not sing a song with conviction he would throw it away. Every song had to have some special message for John. This great minstrel will never be forgotten. He is enshrined in the hearts of the people, for his singing lifted them up and showed them beauty and romance.

Low as the singer lies in the field of heather, Songs of his fashion bring the swains together.

Ernest Newman, one of the outstanding music critics of his day stated:

Of the millions who enjoyed the singing of John McCormack, few realised how great an artist he was, and why. To the multitude he was the unrivalled singer of simple things expressed in a simple musical way, with a special gift for clear enunciation and clean-cut melodic line drawing. But these gifts, admirable as they were in themselves and in his use of them, were only part of a much larger whole. He was so perfect in small things because he was steeped in greater ones, was subtly intimate with them, and had attained complete mastery of the expression of them.

What he did was to carry over into his performances of simple songs an art based on, and subtilised by, the one intensive study of the masterpieces of song from Handel, Mozart to Hugo Wolf. Of Wolf he was a passionate admirer and unremitting student, though for obvious reasons he could not include much of him in his programmes. If the music lover wants to get an idea of what rare qualities of musical understanding, of poetic feeling, of style, of phrasing, of nuance McCormack was capable in music of the finest kind they should study his record of Wolf's great "Ganymed" in one of the albums of the Hugo Wolf Society.

It is fitting that the final tribute should come from Dr. Vincent O'Brien, his life-long friend, mentor, accompanist and occasional touring companion.

Many a time the comical thought occurred to me that if John McCormack hadn't been the great artist he was he would have made a fortune as a mimic. A great treat it was when he would 'choose a cast' for an opera: Melba, Caruso, all the great ones, and then he would sit down at the piano, and give us them all, a little of each, perfect imitation; he would go up into the high register of the soprano; and he would conduct it all. And the conductor would always be Toscanini. Toscanini was his idol.

I remember once Toscanini was conducting *Aida* at the Metropolitan Opera House in New York. Caruso was the tenor. Pasquale Amato was the baritone (and I

236

remember, too, that Amato 'stole the opera', as they say. A wonderful artist). John bought three seats, right behind the conductor. He put me in the middle, Lily and himself sat on either side of me. John was entranced: he was intent on the conductor and wanted me to note every movement for myself.

Author's Acknowledgements

It is eighteen years since the publication of the last book on the life and times of Count John McCormack, so a fresh assessment of his achievements was overdue, particularly as viewed in the context of today's changing musical scene in Ireland. And of course this new publication was specifically planned to mark the 50th anniversary of the great tenor's death, a milestone in itself.

In the preparation of *John McCormack: A Voice to Remember*, I wish to express my sincere indebtedness to the McCormack family: to Gwen Pyke, the singer's only daughter whose lifetime reminiscences of her father proved invaluable, and Gwen's daughter Patricia (Kelly) of Lisclogher, Co. Westmeath, for some rare photographs from the McCormack picture album; Count John McCormack, the singer's grandson, whose memories of his grandmother Lily McCormack, and indeed those of his father Count Cyril McCormack, were most useful for my research purposes; and Count John's sisters, Carol Ann and Tish Tinne.

My thanks to Liam Breen, President of the John McCormack Society, without whose generous assistance and inspiration I could not have written this book. At all times he made available to me his library of rare publications and pamphlets on the life of the tenor and added his own fascinating commentary.

I must not forget the inimitable O'Briens, Oliver and his brother Colum, whose recollections of their father Dr Vincent O'Brien, as well as Count John McCormack, were crucial to my research. Oliver's wife Elizabeth is also due my thanks for her assistance with photographs, magazine and press cuttings.

There are others: Louis Browne (Dublin), Canon Kevin Earley (Summerhill College, Sligo), Mary O'Rourke (Athlone), Sr Brighid Moloney & Assistant Matron Kathleen Ransome (Moore Abbey), Frank Ryan (Tallow, Co. Waterford), Rev Fr Michael Dunning, P.P. (Clover Hill, Co. Roscommon), Frank Patterson and photographer Eamon Gilligan.

Agencies who lent useful assistance include: Covent Garden

Archives, the Metropolitan Opera House, New York, *Irish Times* Library, Irish National Library, Trinity College Library; and the editors of the following newspapers for their permission to quote from reviews of opera and special features: *The Times* of London, the *Daily Telegraph*, the *Daily Express*, The *New York Times*, The *Melbourne Herald*, *Irish Independent*, *Cork Examiner*, *Sunday Tribune*, *Westmeath Independent*.

I also wish to acknowledge the following authors and their publications: *I Hear You Calling Me* by Lily McCormack (W.H.Allen), *John McCormack* by L.A.G. Strong (Methuen & Co. Ltd.), *Melodies & Memories*, the autobiography by Nellie Melba introduced by John Cargher (Hamish Hamilton), *The King of Song* by Ruth and Paul Hume (Hawthorn Books, Inc. New York), *John McCormack*, a comprehensive Discography compiled by Paul W. North and Jim Cartwright (Greenwood Press), *Monte Carlo Opera*, 1910-1951 by T.J. Walsh (Boethius Press), *Bravo* by Helena Matheopoulos (Weidenfeld & Nichlson Ltd.) *Opera at Covent Garden* by Harold Rosenthal (Victor Gollancz Ltd.) *John McCormack: His Own Life Story*, transcribed by Pierre V.R. Key (Small, Maybard & Co., Boston), *Seeing Stars* by Charles L. Wagner (G.P. Putnam's Sons, New York), *Nora: The Real Life of Molly Bloom* by Brendan Maddox (Houghton Mifflin Co., Boston), *The Great Irish Tenor* by Gordon T. Ledbetter (Duckworth), *José Carreras: Singing from the Soul* (YCP Publications, Seattle), *Great Singers on Great Singers* by Jerome Hynes (Victor Gollancz Ltd), *La Sheridan, adorable Diva* by Anne Chambers (Wolfhound Press), *The Great Singers* by Henry Pleasants (Victor Gollancz), *Irish Stars of the Opera* by Gus Smith (Madison Publishers Ltd.), *Hans Hotter: Man and Artist* by Penelope Turing (John Calder, London), *Enrico Caruso, his Life and Death* by Dorothy Caruso (Laurie, Simon & Shuster), *My Mad World of Opera* by Harold Rosenthal (Weidenfeld & Nicolson), *London Music*, 1888-89 by Bernard Shaw (Constable), *My Life of Song* by Madame (Luisa) Tetrazzini (Cassell, London), *Am I Too Loud?* by Gerald Moore (Hamish Hamilton), *Prima Donna* by Rupert Christiansen (Penguin Books Ltd.).